Creative Financial Accounting

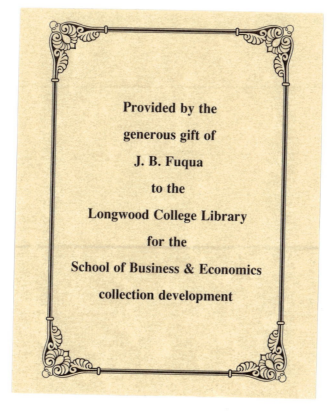

Creative Financial Accounting

Its nature and use

Kamal H. M. Naser

Cardiff Business School

Prentice Hall

New York   London   Toronto   Tokyo   Sydney   Singapore

First published 1993 by
Prentice Hall International (UK) Limited
Campus 400, Maylands Avenue
Hemel Hempstead
Hertfordshire, HP2 7EZ
A division of
Simon & Schuster International Group

Typeset in $11\frac{1}{2}$/13 pt Bembo
by Vision Typesetting, Manchester

Printed and bound in Great Britain by
Redwood Books, Trowbridge, Wiltshire

Library of Congress Cataloging-in-Publication Data

Naser, Kamal H. M.
    Creative financial accounting: its nature and use / Kamal H. M. Naser.
      p.   cm.
    Includes bibliographical references and index.
    ISBN 0-13-061763-6
    1. Accounting.   I. Title.
    HF5635.N24   1993
    657 – dc20   93–4009   CIP

British Library Cataloguing in Publication Data

A catalogue record for this book is available from the British Library

ISBN 0-13-061763-6

1 2 3 4 5 97 96 95 94 93

To my wife Rana and my daughter Dina

Contents

Preface

This book presents a comprehensive analysis of the issue of creative accounting. It assumes previous knowledge in accounting. Care has been taken to make a balanced explanation of the procedures used in accounting and the concepts upon which they are based. Justifications have been given to explain different choices in accounting measurement and disclosure and how if these are used they may result in creative accounting. This book seeks to discuss various financial accounting topics which in recent times have become subject to creative accounting. Each chapter contains a group of review questions related to the text material to make this book more useful in the classroom.

This book has also been written to cater for the needs of accountants, financial analysts, bankers, businessmen and all those individuals who require to know a little or even a lot about creative accounting.

ORGANIZATION

Chapter 1 provides information on the structure of the book. The issue of regulation is discussed in Chapter 2. The topics covered include the case for and against regulation and who should enforce accounting regulation. Chapter 3 covers the cash flow accounting system. It provides early examples of creative accounting, the history of cash flow accounting and the argument for and against the use of cash flow accounting.

The accounting profession's response to the issue of creative accounting is considered in Chapter 4. The chapter defines creative accounting, and discusses the causes and the potential consequences of the continued use of creative accounting.

Chapters 5 to 10 illustrate schemes of creative accounting associated with accounting for short-term investment, accounting for stock, accounting for tangible fixed assets, accounting for intangibles, accounting for long-term liabilities and accounting for shareholders' contributed capital (equity).

Further examples of creative accounting investigated in Chapter 11 include non-subsidiary dependent companies, the abuse of acquisition accounting, foreign currency transaction, extraordinary items, interest rate swaps, project financing arrangements, captive finance companies, and options.

In Chapter 12, different aspects of creative accounting are empirically investigated. For example whether or not the use of creative accounting is explained by the status of the company, or the industry in which the company operates? Which creative accounting techniques are most frequently used in practice? Whether the use of creative accounting is perceived by respondents as a legitimate business tool? Whether creative accounting is perceived by respondents as a serious problem? Whether it is solvable? What motives are behind it? What are the consequences of its continued use or the measures that may be taken to minimize its use.

ACKNOWLEDGEMENTS

I wish to thank the many people who have contributed to this book. Special thanks go to my colleagues at Cardiff Business School, Professor Maurice Pendlebury, Professor Edward French, Dr Segun Wallace, Mr Michael John Jones and Mr Yusuf Karbhari who took time and trouble to read, comment and criticize the book. Without their valuable comments this book would not have been presented in its present form.

Appreciation is extended to the three anonymous reviewers for their generous and helpful comments.

Heather Rowlands and Nona Pritchard have my special appreciation for their cheerful and skilful typing and related help.

I wish also to thank Cathy Peck and the editorial board of Prentice Hall.

Finally, my family needs special mention. Rana has assisted me in so many ways giving me the time, space and encouragement to finish this book. My daughter Dina also gave me a great deal, creating much needed diversion to my writing and constantly reminding me that there is more to life than writing a textbook.

CHAPTER 1

Introduction

Accounting provides interested parties with quantitative financial information that helps them to make decisions about deployment and the use of resources in all organizations. In the last sixty years or so, economic entities have increased so much in number and diversity that the responsibility placed on the accounting profession is greater today than ever before. Financial statements are one of the principal means through which information is communicated to those outside the entity.

Accounting, like other social science disciplines and human activities, is largely a product of its environment. The environment of accounting consists of social–economic–political–legal conditions, restraints and influences that vary over time. Accounting is not important because it is a product of its environment, but rather because it reshapes its environment and plays a significant role in the conduct of economic, social, political, legal and organizational decisions and actions. It provides information for the re-evaluation of social, political and economic objectives as well as the relative costs and, more specifically, publicly reported accounting numbers influence the distribution of scarce resources. Resources are channelled, where needed, at returns commensurate with the perceived risk. Accounting information is both by nature and design useful in assessing the perceived risk and return associated with the investments.

The economic effects of reported accounting numbers directly affect the transfer of resources among entities and individuals. Thus, it is expected to see organizations adopting accounting procedures that minimize any unfavourable economic effects and enhance the favourable ones. This phenomenon may be attributed to the flexibility provided by the present day accounting system, which gives the opportunity to choose among alternative accounting pro-cedures. The accounting system in Anglo-Saxon countries has been designed to be flexible enough to accommodate a variety of situations and present them fairly in the accounts.

The freedom of choice provided by the Anglo-Saxon accounting system could be abused, however, but the role of the regulatory process is to minimize the abuse of this freedom. However, to the extent that choice is still abused then creative accounting exists. Apart from the issue of many available accounting options, there is also the case of hiding the abuse of the system; there are more direct methods of hiding the true picture. In other words, flexibility and freedom of choice sometimes are not enough; they are usually supported by clever disclosure or non-disclosure methods. Thus, creative accounting can range from those techniques which are openly displayed (window dressing) to those which are so sophisticated that may not be detected by even the most qualified auditor (off-balance sheet financing). Creative accounting is the transformation of financial accounting figures from what they actually are to what preparers desire by taking advantage of the existing rules and/or ignoring some or all of them.

The ICAEW (1986) defined, in TR 603, window dressing as: '... to arrange affairs so that the financial statements of concern give a misleading or unrepresentative impression of its financial position.' The release also alluded to an aspect of creative accounting when describing the schemes of off-balance sheet financing as: 'the funding or refunding of a company's operations in such a way that, under legal requirements and existing accounting conventions, some or all of the finance may not be shown on its balance sheet.'

The use of specific accounting approaches by management might be explained by the nature of the principal–agent relation between shareholders and managers. Agency theory assumes a conflict of interest between managers and shareholders. The manager might not act in the best interest of the shareholders. To minimize this conflict, shareholders may offer incentive schemes (i.e. profit sharing, share option plans) or try to monitor management's behaviour. Monitoring costs tend to be high. Since the manager determines these costs, he finds ways of convincing the shareholders that he will take optimal action. These incentives lead to the development of institutional arrangements such as the use of accounting numbers in contracts and a willingness to agree to an independent audit. However, the demand for monitoring is not restricted to the manager/shareholder relationship; debt contracts also produce such a demand.

Since the early 1980s, when the truth and fairness of the reported financial statements came under attack, the removal of avenues for creative accounting has come to the forefront of the agenda of regulators of accounting information, and in particular to the accounting profession. The main purpose of this book is to undertake a comprehensive examination of the issue of creative accounting.

CHAPTER 2

Regulating Financial Information

INTRODUCTION

It can be said that accounting is an essentially practical artifice, designed to serve the needs of its users, through a series of workable rules and principles. Indeed, accounting, as currently understood, has developed in order to meet the needs of an expanding economy which has become commercially more complex over the years. A far reaching development, which did much to establish the overall system of accounting was the formation of the Joint Stock Companies Act 1844. Subsequently, ownership became more widespread and consequently owners (*principals*) were divorced from managers (*agents*).

Once the divorce between ownership and control in the business enterprise took place, there was a need to control the actions and decisions of management by the owners of capital in terms of how their funds had been utilized. This meant that accounting procedures were needed to meet the requirement of the stewardship functions. *Stewardship accounting* came into existence to guarantee both the physical safety of assets and prove that those who administrated them had done their job properly.

This produces what was called agency theory (Jensen and Meckling 1976; Watts and Zimmerman, 1978; Leftwich, 1983), where shareholders represent the principal, and managements represent the agent. The principal–agent relation seems to generate a contract which identifies the rights and duties of the involved parties.

Under this contract, the principal provides the agent with instructions on what actions are expected of him and the required power to maintain these actions. Gray *et al.* (1987) demonstrated that the principal places two responsibilities upon the agent: namely, responsibility for action and responsibility to account for those actions (accountability). They summarized the principal–agent accountability contract as shown in figure 2.1.

Figure 2.1 explains the agent–principal relationship and the need for accountability from managers to their principals (for example shareholders). It could be pointed out, as Gray *et al.* (1987) contend, that in modern times accountability is applicable to a wider group than simply shareholders. In other

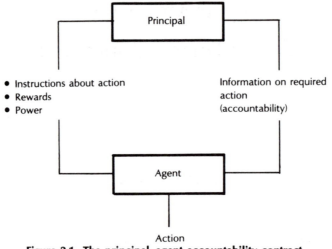

Figure 2.1. The principal–agent accountability contract.

words, the principal should be thought of as shareholders, employees, lenders, society and other stakeholders. Hence, the agent's accountability involves a degree of social responsibility.

The divorce of ownership from management leads to the need for accountability. An important aspect of accountability is financial accounting and auditing. The accountability cycle (as shown in Figure 2.1), would be unattainable unless the end user of financial reports can use them to assess the business performance and can compare their underlying accounting methods with those *bench mark* methods or approaches (standards) chosen and established by the authorities responsible for setting accounting standards. Thus, a regulatory framework is suggested as a means of reporting by corporations in order to streamline and formalize the manager's accountability to shareholders and/or society.

The rest of this chapter discusses the demand for and the supply of financial information, the necessity or otherwise of regulating financial information, and who should enforce accounting regulations.

THE DEMAND FOR FINANCIAL INFORMATION

Accounting provides interested parties with quantitative financial information which assists them to make decisions about deployment and the use of resources in business and non-business entities in the economy. The identification of users' needs might be achieved by asking them what they want. However, this approach is difficult to achieve. An alternative approach would be to identify decisions users might make and to provide information which will help to make these decisions as rational as possible (normative approach).

According to Foster (1986) the demand for financial statements arises from a diverse set of parties, including shareholders, employees, creditors, customers and government agencies. These parties need financial information to help them in decision making; facilitate the overseeing of management; or to shed light upon agreements and contracts that include articles based on such information (covenants, contracts, bonus schemes).

Hendriksen (1982), Glautier and Underdown (1976), Foster (1986), Arnold *et al.* (1985), and Harvey and Keer (1983), among others, reported why and how diverse parties demand financial information.

Decisions taken by *investors* typically have either an investment focus or a stewardship focus. In the former case, investors concentrate on selecting a portfolio of securities that is consistent with their risk, return, dividends and liquidity preferences. Thus, financial information aids the shareholders and new investors to decide what shares to buy, retain or to sell. On the other hand, decisions concerning stewardship functions concentrate on monitoring management behaviour and attempt to affect this behaviour appropriately. In fact, management has substantial choices to make concerning the use and the abuse of a firm's resources. It can make decisions that divert these resources from existing shareholders, leaving them with only a corporate shell. The existence of this potential conflict has created a desire for information to be presented by management and other parties that disclose how management has used the resources under its control. Thus, when predicting the timing, amount and uncertainties of future cash flows of the firm, the track record of management in relation to the resources under its control can be a critical value.

The demand by *employees* for financial information arises from the fact that employees are interested in the security of their jobs and consequently their firms' profitability and survival. Employees can use financial information to monitor the validity of their pension plans and to determine whether or not to remain with their existing employer. Furthermore, employees need financial information to make decisions concerning bargaining procedures with the existing employer; for instance, regarding claims for wage increases and other conditions of employment.

Management is perhaps the major user of an enterprise's financial information. As managers they have complete and immediate access to financial information within their firms, and they do not need to wait for, nor are they limited by, the information contained in the published accounts. Nevertheless, management knows that published financial statements will provide information on its ability to manage as these statements indicate to other user-groups how successful the organization has been. Thus, although for these day-to-day decision-making and operational control purposes management will be using information about revenue and expenditures immediately after the information is generated, they would still want to keep an eye on the potential reactions of other user groups to the published accounts and reports of their organization.

Financial information is extremely important for *creditors*. One of the main concerns of all creditors is likely to be whether or not the business enterprise will be able to meet its financial obligations. Thus, they are interested in the profitability of the business as it affects its ability to pay its debts. Also, creditors are likely to be very concerned with the firm's liquidity. If there is any doubt that the firm may not be able to pay, they may well press for a specific arrangement regarding the management of the debtor's company and may possibly drive it into bankruptcy, though the firm's prospects may not necessarily be bad in the long term. Therefore, creditors are mainly interested in financial accounting information provided by their debtors to determine their solvency, liquidity, changes on their assets and claims against them, and profitability, that is, with obtaining reports which will describe the firm's financial position.

Customers need financial information to, in a competitive environment, ensure the continuity of supply. For example, they may purchase items which require after sale services in the form of maintenance and repairs, and they may want to know whether they would be able to obtain that. Industrial consumers might want to know about the continuation of sources of supply of raw materials and components. Consumers might also want to know whether a monopoly situation exists and if so whether they are likely to be exploited.

The government and its agencies demand accounting information for taxation purposes as well as for economic planning. In the case of governments formulating their economic plans, they would require information concerning such things as the enterprises' intention about their investment and activity plans which would be more helpful.

Although the demand for financial statements arizes from a diverse set of needs of different parties, many of these needs are common. Most of the parties demand information on the profitability and financial position of the organization (for more details see 'Framework for the Preparation and Presentation of Financial Statements' published by IASC, July 1989). Even so, it must also be recognized that each of the above parties has its own set of particular needs and, according to Foster (1986), any action taken by one party, or more, may result in wealth redistribution among them. For example, when a firm makes a large acquisition at an excessive price, shareholders' wealth may decrease, while managers' compensation may increase, because the larger combined organization which results often pays higher salaries to management. On the other hand, shareholders' wealth may increase as a result of large dividend payments. Both decrease the assets available as security for creditors of the firm. These are just two examples of areas where the interest of the parties may be in conflict. Moreover, the economic rationality argument suggests that in specific cases there will be conflicts in which the requirement of one user-group is resisted by another. Bacharach (1976) in his theory of games (coalition theory) assumed that individuals seek their own objectives in a rational way. If this is considered in the context of the use of accounting measurements and disclosures to monitor the action of the companies, then it should mean that all participants are willing to accept any accounting reforms which improve the lots of one person without harming the welfare of others (Pareto distribution). In this respect, Jenson and Smith (1985) pointed out two important factors connected with the demand for financial statement information:

1. Each party tends to value the disclosure and timing of information differently. An individual party would typically resist the disclosure of information if it may negatively affect his/her own interest.

2. Financial statements have a crucial role to play in the mechanism used to monitor wealth redistribution among parties. Hence, those whose wealth may be affected by the actions of a company and its management had to be interested in financial statements.

Thus, the demand for financial statements comes from many potentially conflicting sources. Hence, when considering the information required by individual parties, the self-interest of each party is an important factor. In these circumstances, accounting standards may play a profound role. The necessity or otherwise of regulating financial information is discussed in the following section.

THE NECESSITY OR OTHERWISE OF REGULATING FINANCIAL INFORMATION

The early stage of accounting (the nineteenth century) was characterized by the voluntary measurement and disclosure of financial information. Each firm had great freedom to develop whatever accounting methods and principles suited its particular needs. The accounting profession lacked any influence and according to Fitzpatrick (1939) accounting behaviour was a response to the objectives of the individual managers. Industrial firms, typically, had no capital account, made no distinction between capital expenditures and revenue expenditures, and failed to determine total income or return on investment. This resulted in inconsistency and diversity in the reported information.

The next stage was characterized by widespread share ownerships through big corporations (divorce between ownership and control is discussed below). Accounting procedures became important to meet the ownership requirements of monitoring managers' actions. The following stage was characterized by the use of stewardship statements for decision making (i.e. lending/or share trading) which had implications for capital market resource allocation and this led to calls for regulations. In terms of stewardship/accountability, the desire to reduce monitoring costs meant (according to the positivists) that external regulation was not necessary because there was an incentive to adopt the best practice. However, the next stage aimed at regulating financial reporting measurement and disclosure. Regulation permits flexibility in both disclosure and measurement. Allowable alternative treatments makes the broad principles of accounting appear to be less effective and this might give birth to creative accounting. Underlying the notion of creativity is the belief that there are acceptable, preferred or benchmark accounting practices and the attempt to make unacceptable accounting practices look acceptable is what may be described as creative accounting. So implicit in creative accounting is the regulation or definition of accounting principles and practices, – or regulation in short. Thus, creative accounting is likely to occur with or without regulation. Consequently, accounting researchers have employed extensive efforts to answer the question *why regulate financial accounting?*

In the USA, the FASB's (1974) justification for regulation is that financial information is used to make decisions and therefore assumes that mandated disclosure of such information will procure the best allocation of resources. Hopwood and Page (1987) argued that, in dealing with financial measurement and disclosure problems, accounting standards are brought into existence without introducing any theoretical framework that would identify the objectives of financial reporting, or the contribution which the standards were supposed to make nor was any sustained body of research and inquiry undertaken. However, despite the controversy surrounding the activities of the FASB and ASC, Hopwood and Page (1987) believed that they achieved some success in providing standards which temporarily ought to reduce the difference in accounting practice and disclosure.

The question *why regulate financial accounting?* is considered to be the most controversial issue among accounting researchers. They are divided into those who are against and those who are for regulation.

The Case Against Regulation

The case against regulation is discussed below under the following headings: the stage before regulations was adequate; the historical accident interpretation; standardization is a political process; limited concern of economic efficiency and social responsibility; agency theory; positive accounting theory; direct and indirect cost of regulations.

The Stage Before Regulations Was Adequate

Previous researchers (Benston, 1969, 1973; Dillon, 1977) claimed that financial reporting in the decade preceding the passage of Security Acts was adequate. Dubis and Neimark (1982) also stated that the voluntary disclosure prior to 1933–1934 provided evidence that the existing mechanisms were sufficient to ensure production at an optimal level of disclosure to investors. Philips and Zecher (1981, p. 51) stated that: 'from the public interest view point, the economic case for our current mandatory disclosure system is extremely weak.'

On the other hand, as Flynn (1934) suggested, the report of the Study and Investigations of the Protective and Reorganization Committee (U.S, SEC, 1937) and the Bethlehem Steel investigations provided examples of manipulated reporting practice during 1920. For example, large companies concealed extensive bonuses in cost of sales and recorded stock dividends of controlled affiliates as sales revenue or as other income at the market value of stock. Observers like Kohler (1926), Ripley (1926), Couchman (1928) and Far (1933) were highly critical of reporting practices in the period. Chatfield (1977) showed that many companies failed to disclose depreciation methods, failed to establish separately reserves against receivables, inventories and marketable securities, and failed to disclose the methods employed in inventory valuation or the nature of goods included in the inventories. Some companies classified common stock and preferred stock as current assets, including dividends on those stocks, and generally utilized consolidated statements in ways to conceal, rather than reveal, the truth. Edwards (1976) looked at the accounting profession and disclosure in published reports between 1925 and 1935 and found that published financial information at that stage was limited in quality to the extent that it might mislead the users rather than benefit them. Edwards (1976) quoted Sidney Pears as saying:

> under the old 1908 Act, as far as I am aware, there was no obligation in law to compel the director of a company to separate the assets or to separate the liabilities, and they were within their legal rights in showing capital, creditors and the balance of profit and loss on one side, and sundry fixed assets, debt, etc. on the other side. Now although such a statement may possibly come within the letter of the law, I think you will agree it would not be of much interest to the shareholders.

In the period 1925–1935 companies relied on secret reserves to smooth their profit, by making undisclosed transfers between the profit and loss account to the secret reserve account. Hence, the secret reserve was a policy of great advantage to most companies. The use of secret reserves has been criticized on the ground that it gives scope for distorting the actual behaviour of income from one accounting period to another. Thus, the argument for non-regulation would seem to lack support if the passage preceding the Securities Acts is considered.

The Historical Accident Interpretation

Another argument used against regulation is what is known as 'historical accident interpretation'. This argument suggests that the American Security Acts were established in the era of depression and financial crisis. Hence, without the occurrence of the crises accounting regulations would not exist. However, the weakness of the historical accident explanation is that all free market countries are similar in disclosing financial information. Lev (1988) emphasizes the inconsistencies in the historical accident argument, that is, that historical accidents are usually country and period specific, making it difficult to argue that they explain persistent world-wide phenomena. Yet, unless one can argue that the world-wide regulation is contemporaneous while no depression and financial crises could be noticed in non-US countries, one may be ignoring the potency of the historical accident explanation that is posited on the belief that many other countries follow the countries they perceive as the leader. If indeed the United States was the first to experience depression and financial crises of the 1929–1933 magnitude, other countries may copy the United States' rules in the belief that such rules are necessary to correct the effects of future depression and financial crisis.

Standardization Is A Political Process

Those who oppose financial regulation argue that regulations are not concerned with economic efficiency or with the equity concept. The main objective of regulation is to meet the demand of the organized interest groups, to expand the scope of their power and operation or to avoid public rumours. As Hopwood and Page (1987) contend, standard setting in the United Kingdom is influenced by the view of the preparers of the accounts and the views of others are increasingly being unheard. At the same time, a growing number of minority companies are playing around accounting standards taking advantage of their weak points. Hopwood and Page (1987) warned that the lack of compliance will call into question the ability of the profession to regulate itself. Horngren (1972) and Gerboth (1973) demonstrated that the standard setting is political in most meanings of the word. Gerboth argued that: 'the politicisation of accounting rule making is not only inevitable, but just ... when a decision process depends on public confidence the critical issues are not technical, they are political.'
Horngren (1973) said that:

the setting of accounting standards is as much a product of political action as of flawless logic or empirical findings. Why?, because the setting of the standard is a social decision. Hence, standards place restrictions on behaviour, therefore they must be accepted by the affected parties. Acceptance may be forced or voluntarily or both. In a democratic society, getting acceptance is an exceedingly complicated process that requires skilful working in the political arena.

Likewize, Solomons (1978) stated that: 'to judge from current discussion of the standard setting process, accounting no longer can be thought of as nonpolitical. The process by which the accounting rules are made is said to be political.' May and Sundem (1976) took the same position when they stated that:

'in practice as well as in theory, the social welfare impact of accounting reports apparently is recognized. Therefore it is not surprising that the [Financial Accounting Standard Board] is a political body and, consequently, that the process of selecting an acceptable accounting alternative is a political one. If the social welfare impact of accounting policy decision were ignored, the basis for the existence of a regulatory body would disappear. Therefore, the FASB must consider explicit political (i.e. social welfare) aspects as well as accounting theory and research in its decisions.

The political process, according to Watts and Zimmerman (1986), seeks to transfer wealth among interest groups. The interest group argument (captive theory) proposes that regulations are set to benefit specific groups of market participants. The argument of Schwert (1977) and Kalt and Zapan (1984) could be used to suggest that the accounting context does not support the captive argument. On the contrary, the economic rational theory proposes that individuals look to their own objectives in a rational way. Individuals are willing to accept any accounting reforms that have no prospects of affecting the welfare of others. Such a reform is said to bring about a Pareto improvement (at least one person is better off without making any one worse off). Bromwich (1985) argued that no studies have been undertaken to investigate whether any of the reforms considered by the standard setters are of the type to generate Pareto improvement. Most accounting reforms may impose costs on some parties without maintaining equivalent benefit.

Limited Concern of Economic Efficiency and Social Responsibility
An integral part of any public policy is the impact it has on society. To assess the effectiveness of regulation, it is important to predict all the consequences of regulations and compare them with the situation before regulation. However, the consequences of accounting regulations on society can be assessed through: (a) allocation and redistribution effect; (b) corporate governance and responsibility; (c) market reaction tests; (d) information asymmetry.

(a) *Allocation and redistribution effect*. The proponents for information regulation argue that market failure suggests that social welfare can be improved by government regulations. In other words, market failure exists because the output of the information in accounting reports in the absence of regulation is non-optimal in a Pareto sense. Burton (1974) demonstrated that accounting market failure exists because the resource allocation resulting from the market for financial information is inequitable; that is, unfair to some group of individuals. Watts and Zimmerman (1986) contended that this type of market failure has not been pursued by market researchers who employ economic theories because it is difficult, if not impossible, to set a criterion of fairness to be accepted by everyone.

In fact, it can be argued that the economic consequences of accounting regulations can be detected through the allocation and redistribution of individuals' wealth and income. Hence, the debate on standard setting, which is regarded as a political exercise, gives reasons for doubting that redistribution effects can be ignored even when primary resource allocation decisions are being made. This suggests that an empirical exercise should be mounted to gauge whether the proposed standard is likely to have significant distribution effects. However, it is difficult to set a criterion for a useful standard which maintains optimal economic and social consequences. What is considered to be useful for one specific group of society might not be useful for another, and what is useful for this specific group within the present circumstances might not be useful if the circumstances are changed.

Bromwich (1985) stated that standard setters should not mount the highly complicated studies necessary to discern all the major economic consequences of all proposed standards. It is suggested, rather, that studies should be initiated at an early stage in drafting the standard when it is believed that major economic consequences of a fairly direct kind can be expected. Neglecting a major effect of this type may lead to criticism of the standard setters and other organizations seeking to fill the gap left by accounting policy makers. The government is the most obvious candidate, especially where a reasonable majority in parliament allows it to tackle any economic consequences without any necessity for debate or study.

In reality, accounting standards are not neutral and thus will have various effects on different sectors of the society. Solomons' (1978) view is that standard setters should evaluate accounting rules in terms of their representational accuracy of underlying physical reality, leaving any economic consequences to fall where they may. However, standards can improve efficiency on the face of redistribution effects on the assumption that government will cope with any adverse redistribution.

(b) *Corporate governance and responsibility.* Benston (1983) examined the usefulness of accounting standards through two specific concerns: corporate governance and social responsibility. He found that accounting standards are not likely to play a beneficial role for corporate governance or social responsibility because the measurement required for useful standard cannot be made. However, the difficulty in identifying the measurement does not mean that the standard is not useful. On the other hand, Benston showed that accounting standards might be useful in respect of corporate governance, particularly in reporting misuses of shareholders' assets by corporate managers. Even in this respect, the cost of accounting standards may exceed its benefits to shareholders. Benston concluded that the rules of accounting standards to enhance manager's concern of their shareholders, and/or society, is not likely to be beneficial. His conclusion is based on the fact that it is difficult to achieve the required measurement for a useful standard. This inherent limitation is absolute with respect to social responsibility concern.

Tinker, Merino and Neimark's (1982) socio-historical approach leads them to conclude that the Securities Acts were designed to maintain the ideological, social and economic status quo while restoring confidence in the existing system and its institutions. They suggested that broadening the scope of disclosures requirements beyond their present financial orientation is needed to address better these issues of corporate accountability. However, in May 1991 a committee on the financial aspects of corporate governance (the Cadbury Committee) was set up by the Financial Reporting Council (FRC), the London Stock Exchange and the accounting profession and according to the *Certified Accountant* (July 1992) the committee's draft report contains 'A Code for Best Practice'.

(c) *Market reaction test.* In general, the stock market has been used to monitor the impact of regulatory accounting policy. Lev (1988) argued that to evaluate the impact of regulation setting the following factors should be considered:

1. Bid-ask spreads and volume effects;

2. changes in price informativeness;

3. inside information.

Empirical studies made by Benston (1973), Morse and Ushmar (1983), and Venkatesh and Chiang (1986) emphasized the relationship between information asymmetry and bid-ask spread. If the objective of disclosure regulation is to increase capital market equity, then this could be evaluated by identifying the impact of changes in accounting regulations average bid-ask spread and trade volume of the affected securities. Beaver (1968); Morse (1981); Ohlson (1979); and Bamber (1986) took the trade volume as an indicator of social desirability. They were aimed at inferring the information content of specific releases, such as earnings from volume changes at the disclosure date. They found that both the magnitude of unexpected earnings and the firm's size were associated with the information content of annual earnings announcements. Lev (1988) suggested the examination of long-term changes in average volumes before and after specific regulation changes. However, the stock market reaction is not enough to assess the impact of regulation on the society.

(d) *Information asymmetric.* The impact of regulations on the society can also be evaluated by determining whether a particular regulation has decreased information asymmetry. In 1970, SEC asked multiproduct firms to disclose revenues and expenses on each product line. Collins (1975) investigated whether reporting information on each product will affect the return. He found that the 1967–1970 product line data was useful as an input to specific trading rules for investing in securities; it yielded statistically significant excess returns from the year 1968–1969. Thus, investors who had information on product line prior to 1970 could have earned abnormal returns relative to informed investors. From the equity point of view, SEC product line disclosure requirements seem desirable in decreasing information asymmetric.

Thus, the anti-regulation body argument is that the stage before regulation was adequate and regulation is a product of depression and financial crises. They also believe that standardization is a political process and does not pay attention to the economic efficiency and social responsibility.

Actually, the above discussion illustrates that, of all of the points raised by opponents to regulation, only the politicization argument is acceptable.

Agency Theory

The basic assumption underlying agency theory is that individuals are trying to maximize their own expected utilities and are sufficiently skilful and innovative to do so. Thus, the disclosure issue raised by the agency theory is that an individual expects to benefit from a particular course of action. According to Taylor and Turley (1986) and others, an agency is defined as the relationship between a manager and a shareholder as a consent between two parties, while one party (agent, manager) agrees to act on the behalf of other parties (stockholder, principal) (see Figure 2.1). By the same token, the relation between managers and auditors, and between stockholders and auditors is an agency relation.

The theory assumes that there is a conflict of interest between the shareholders and the managers. The conflict of interest arises from the belief that managers are trying to maximize their utility and shareholders are trying to maximize their wealth. The conflict of interest is likely to occur when decisions made by managers to maximize their utility do not maximize shareholders' wealth. The conclusion drawn from the agency theory is that multiple methods of accounting for similar circumstances have been developed from the decision of various individuals, such as managers, shareholders and bondholders, to minimize agency costs (agency cost according to Watts (1977) is the cost of measuring and monitoring the agent's behaviour and cost of establishing compensation policies, etc.).

Opponents of regulation argue that both suppliers and users of accounting information experience sufficiently strong motives to ensure that a trade for accounting information will take place in the absence of regulation. On the supply side, management has strong motive to provide adequate and reliable information in order to attract and keep resources and to ensure a positive influence on economic indicators such as share prices, while on the demand side the users look for information which is relevant to their decisions. Taylor and Turley (1986) distinguished between two related motivations for voluntarily trading financial information. Users of information are interested in obtaining information to help them in making decisions about trading in the market and therefore to realize profit. To ensure the reliability and adequacy of the information, the user prefers to see the reported information examined by an independent auditor. The other motivation for trading information lies in the relationship between managers and shareholders. The relationship is an agency one and is associated with agency costs. To reduce the agency costs, contracts between shareholders and managements are signed to restrict management's action, therefore reducing agency costs. From the management side, they try to prove that they are working according to the contract by reporting good information which results in a reduction of agency costs.

Jensen and Meckling (1976), Watts and Zimmerman (1978), and Leftwich (1983) applied the agency theory on this relationship. The agency theory affirmed that a mutual benefit is perceived by shareholders and management from the disclosure of audited financial information. Under the agency theory, agents (managements) present information concerning the business enterprise and the principal (shareholders) tries to observe management behaviour. This inequality of information creates what is called a 'moral hazard' problem (moral hazard refers to the pursuit by management of activities which are not in the best interest of the principal). To cope with this problem, the principal offers incentive schemes such as stock option and profit sharing schemes. Indeed, the principal may collect information to control the agent's behaviour. However, the collection of information is an expensive exercise and according to Watts and Zimmerman (1978) the agent has the incentive to reduce the cost of the principal of monitoring the agent. Under the efficient market hypothesis the shareholder is a price taker. He pays the price associated with the change in the owner–manager behaviour. The market expects the owner–manager to equal his marginal rate of substitution between wealth and non-pecuniary benefit and prices the shares appropriately. Thus, because the shareholder is price protected, the owner–manager will bear the full cost of the changed behaviour. Watts and Zimmerman (1986) demonstrated that agency costs cause managers to write contracts with shareholders to restrict their action, thereby reducing the agency costs. They also wish to provide information in order to minimize the principal's reliance on incentive schemes which may involve the agent in undesirable risk taking. For similar reasons Watts (1977) pointed out that the agent will favour an external independent audit. The audit helps the principal in assessing the agent services. Benston (1976, 1979), Ross (1979), and Grossman and Hart (1980) all argued that regulations are redundant since managers have enough incentives to report financial information voluntarily and that the present regulations are unproductive in carrying out socially desired goals. Watts and Zimmerman (1986) showed that by providing additional information managers can convince the market that they will be involved in less insider trading, and they can increase the firm's market value, given that the manager's compensation depends on the market value, and their own welfare. Consequently, the manager has incentives to disclose information and will continue to do so as long as the cost of disclosure is less than the effect of the disclosure of the value of the firm. In this respect, Watts and Zimmerman (1986) discussed the agency theory rational of the firms and the contracts with which management binds itself, particularly debt contracts and management compensation contracts. The general view advanced is that political costs create an incentive to choose accounting methods which diminish reported earnings. The larger the firm, the more likely it is to choose accounting procedures decreasing current earnings. Watts and Zimmerman (1986) ran a series of empirical tests to explain the choice of accounting methods by contract related variables and the effect on the stock price of choices in accounting methods. They examined the hypothesis that mandatory restrictions on accounting choices reduce stock prices. The studies found significant stock price changes associated with the announcement of mandated changes (accounting standards). However, the associations are inconsistent across the studies. Hence, Whittington (1987) demonstrated that Watts and Zimmerman's principal evidence for most parts are weak and inconclusive. Watts and Zimmerman, themselves, pointed out that their theories and tests are at present crude. In truth, the advocates of agency theory believe that it helps to explain financial statements in the absence of a comprehensive accounting theory. On the other hand, the main assumption which underlies the agency theory is that every one tries to maximize his expected utility, and suppliers and customers of accounting information have strong incentives to trade in information to make sure that trading will take place in the absence of regulations. According to Whittington (1987) this makes the theory unacceptable, both politically and socially.

Actually, the agency theory is not without its weaknesses. The opponents to the theory argue that some managers may publish information to the extent that shareholder interests are enhanced, and some may not. Even those managers who are concerned with shareholders' interests may not disclose information or fabricate information if they feel that this information will affect their own interest. In this case, accounting regulation provides a generally accepted and understandable measurement of the event of concern. Moreover, regulation may reduce the amount of manipulation in numbers which may be likely to occur in the absence of the regulation.

The agency theory attributes the superiority of normative theories of accounting to the impact on the political process. When a crisis occurs officials defend their position on the basis of a 'public interest' argument. These positions are grounded in the reason that the problem is a product of an insufficiency in the market and can only be solved by government involvement. Officials will justify their position in the form of normative procedures to be used to increase the information available to decision makers or to make the market efficient. Adams (1988) pointed out that the relation between the conflicting parties is a prosecution–defence one. The prosecutor (ASB) demands increased disclosure, greater standardization of accounting practice and heightened ethical and moral accountability from the preparers of financial information. The defence (the corporate management) will reject any action which limits its freedom. If a company perceives the standard as contrary to its best interest it may resort to creative accounting to mitigate the adverse economic effect of the standard. According to Adams, research has shown that there is evidence to support the hypothesis that management is likely to oppose any standard which is perceived as having a negative economic impact, either for itself or for its organization. This evidence is clear in the case of oil and gas exploration costs, research and development expenditures, price levels adjusted financial statements and off-balance sheet financing.

In spite of this, the standard may provide covers for managers to hide their actual performance especially if the standard is subject to manipulation. It should be remembered that the flexibility in accounting measurement and disclosure rules have always permitted creativity.

Positive Accounting Theory

The so-called 'Rochester School' of accounting (Watts and Zimmerman) emphasized that the objective of accounting theory is to explain and predict accounting practice. The thrust of the positive theory is that it explains and predicts behaviour, in contrast to the 1960s normative theory, which is prescriptive. Watts and Zimmerman (1986) emphasized the explanation of accounting practice across firms and industries, not accounting rules, in providing valuation information. They built up their theory on a discussion of rational disclosure regulation. Their main theme is to discredit the public interest view of regulation, which argues that regulation is intended to increase social welfare, in favour of the view that politicians and regulators are not different from any one else, that is, they act in their own self-interest. It is suggested that a manager's choice of accounting methods may be determined by its consequences for political process (utility rate regulation) and also by its implications for various contracts which use accounting data (as debt contracts). Jensen (1976) called for the development of a positive accounting theory which explains why accounting is what it is, why accountants do what they do, and what consequences these events have on people and resource utilization. Jensen went on to say: 'without such a positive theory neither academics nor professionals will make significant progress in obtaining answers to the normative question they continue to ask.'

Watts and Zimmerman's (1986) proposal of positive accounting theory is to explain and predict accounting practices and to exclude theories which tell how accounting should be done. However, the 'Rochester School's' proposal was subject to strong criticism. Whittington (1987) stressed that the advocacy of the methodology of positive theory is the most controversial aspect of their work in general and their book in particular.

In all events, the positive theory is not free from value judgement or prescriptive implications. Moreover, Whittington (1987) demonstrated that it would be incorrect to assume that all theories which are not positive, in the sense of leading to an empirically testable proposition, are normative in the sense of leading to prescriptions. Christenson (1983) made a fundamental criticism of Watts and Zimmerman's approach and considered it as a sociology of accounting rather than an accounting theory, since it is concerned with describing and predicting the behaviour of accountants and managers and not that of accounting entities.

Whittington (1987) questioned Watts and Zimmerman's discussion of the theory of accounting choice and stated that if some of the empirical evidence suggests that accounting standards which restrict accounting choices reduce firm value why, in the world of efficient markets, does this occur?

Interestingly, the proposal of the 'Rochester School' raises a number of methodological issues that are addressed by Christenson (1983). He argued that: 'the Rochester school criticism of traditional accounting theory is off the mark because of the failure to distinguish between two different levels of phenomenon.' According to Christenson the idea of the positive theory is based on the misconception (derived from nineteenth-century positivism) that empirical science deals with actual events, 'what it is'. Finally, it is argued that the standards advocated by the 'Rochester School' for the appraisal of their own theories are so weak that those theories fail to specify Popper's (1959) proposal for demarcating science from metaphysics.

Zimmerman (1980) claimed that positive theory seeks to develop a theory that can explain observed phenomena. According to Blaug (1980) the methodology of science is rational for accepting or resisting its theories or hypotheses. Thus, methodology is normative and for that reason it would presumably be called unscientific by Jensen and Watts. For all that, no science can exist without making a methodological commitment. In the same manner, Hayek (1952) affirmed that science as a whole is normative: 'Its concern is not what men think about the world and how they consequently believe, but what they ought to think.'

Friedman (1953) argued that the social sciences need to be self-conscious about their methodology. Popper (1972) pointed out that the problem of understanding the behaviour of the problem solver is at a higher level than the problems which concern the problem solver.

Lowe *et al.* (1983) demonstrated that policy making is complex. It might be possible to make a general statement concerning a policy that attempts to make these statements deterministic and universal to gain legislation through claims of productive power can only be doomed to failure. They believe that Watts and Zimmerman's use of an economic framework is unjustified and hence casts doubt upon the rest of deductive process. The only possible justification of the positive proposal is explained by the work of Friedman in The Methodology of Positive Economics (1953), where it is still open to dispute. The framework by Watts and Zimmerman is similar to that of the natural sciences and its validity is doubtful in the content of social science.

Direct and Indirect Cost of Regulations

The costs associated with regulating the disclosure of financial accounting information are classified into direct and indirect costs. The direct cost represents the cost of resources consumed by the regulatory body in developing releases and enforcing compliance. The indirect cost can be seen in the impact of regulations on investment, financing and production decisions. (The indirect cost might be much higher than the direct cost.) According to Watts and Zimmerman (1986) the appropriations for the SEC were $3 million in 1936, $9.5 million in 1961, $23.6 million in 1971 and $72.3 million in 1981. It is apparent that there is a high rate of growth in resources used to regulate the disclosure of financial information. However, the SEC is not the only regulatory body which consumes resources. The FASB also consumed $4.13 million in 1975. Besides the costs consumed by the SEC and FASB, there are costs consumed on monitoring, compliance, lobbying and expected increase in losses from lawsuits against accounting and corporations as a result of rules that change disclosure. In addition, companies' contracts might be based on accounting figures (lending agreements and management compensation contracts); when standards change, the accounting figures will be changed and this will affect the contracts.

Other examples of the indirect cost of regulation derive from the fact that standards might affect corporate decisions concerning investment, financing and production. Managers will make decisions to minimize the costs likely to be imposed on their firms by a new standard. For instance, to avoid the adoption of SSAP 20 (1983) *Accounting for Foreign Currency Translation*, a company may engage in hedging contracts.

Overall, those who oppose regulations argue, that although the regulatory process involves high costs, there is no evidence that the benefits of improved social welfare match these costs.

The Case For Accounting Regulation

The proponents of market regulation argued that unregulated markets raise problems in two respects: first, markets may fail to meet conditions necessary for the achievement of Pareto efficient allocation and therefore the market fails. Second, if an unregulated market for accounting succeeded in maintaining efficient allocation of resources which meets the Pareto efficiency, a problem of choosing between alternatives on distribution grounds arises, that is, exercising the social choice on issues affecting equity and distribution.

Market Failure

According to Taylor and Turley (1986) markets may fail to produce efficient allocation of resources for the following reasons: (a) lack of rules governing the market behaviour; (b) asymmetric information in markets; (c) market distortion; (d) externalities and public goods; (e) merit and demerit goods.

(a) *Lack of rules governing the market behaviour*. One of the reasons given for the inability of the capital market to distinguish between efficient and less efficient firms is the lack of uniformity of procedures which is generally connected with the naive investor criticism. The market can only function under a set of clearly identified rules which governs market transactions. The UK government provides a framework in which the market operates and UK Company Law regulates the relationship between the management of a company and its shareholders. Company Law also identifies the requirements for accounting statements to be audited.

(b) *Asymmetric information in markets*. The rationale for corporate disclosure regulation is that investors and the stock market would not otherwise be able to distinguish between efficient and less efficient firms. Leftwich (1980) showed that monopoly control of information by management is one of the main reasons for this. In general, corporate accounting reports are considered to be the main source of information available to investors. As a result of this, it is argued that managers might be able to manipulate stock prices to their own interest. Hence, governmentally enforced disclosure improves the ability of capital market to distinguish between firms and to allocate capital appropriately.

Some may argue that accounting regulation affects the aggregate supply and demand for accounting information. The disclosure of information on business profitability can affect decisions on consumption, saving and investments, and therefore interest rates and the rate of capital accumulation. Other economic factors might be influenced by this, for instance, the rate of the economic growth as well as changes in productivity, costs and prices. Furthermore, accounting regulation can result in the reallocation of resources among different levels of expected risks and returns associated with investment opportunities.

It could be argued that regulation might increase the quality and the quantity of information disclosed to the extent that they improve the assessment of risk and return and the relationship between them. Since risk is the reflection of the supply of information, accounting information may affect the distribution of risks among individuals and the aggregate risk of the economy as a whole. Accounting information affects the risk underlying the agent–principal relation and therefore plays an important role in construction of incentive contracts. On the other hand, Beaver (1981) affirmed that regulation on public disclosure may create competitive disadvantage if the returns on innovation, research and development are adversely affected.

(c) *Market distortion*. To achieve optimal allocation of resources and consistent decision on production and consumption, producers and consumers should respond to an identical set of prices. Optimality may not be achieved if prices facing producers and consumers are not identical. The supply of accounting information is restricted by reporting enterprises which under legal obligations disclose information to users. Gonedes and Dopuch (1974) pointed out that, in the absence of a normal pricing system, demands for additional information cannot be made effective by consumers who are dissatisfied with the level of supply of accounting information and if additional resources are not allocated to information production. Bromwich (1981) contended that certain groups such as investment analysts or industrial investors, are expected to have access to more than the legal or conventional minimum amount of information, indicating more market power than individual shareholders. The costs of supplying accounting information are borne either by the supplying enterprise or some other economic units to whom costs are passed via the process of production or exchange. This invalidates the connection between costs and incentives to produce and consume accounting information. If information is not publicly available, some users will be informed more than others about market opportunities. This means that investments which have different characteristics may be offered at the same price in the capital market. Taylor and

Turley (1986) contended that unless all enterprises make voluntary disclosures of audited information, market distortion will remain. A requirement to make such a disclosure, either by law or by the rules of the capital market, may be a more effective solution.

Taylor and Turley (1986) discussed another problem of market distortion which arises where the cost of providing an incremental unit of commodity is very low. Such cases are normally associated with long-run declining average costs, spare capacity in production or jointness in supply. In each case, prices should reflect marginal costs (and distort market allocation) with no guarantee of profitable operation within the market. Accounting information appears to exhibit declining units costs of production and is supplied jointly to users at a very low incremental cost. According to this analysis, without regulation, accounting information would either be priced above marginal costs by monopoly suppliers, thereby distorting the market, or not be provided at all. Accounting regulation requiring minimum disclosure may be the only means of provision of information.

(d) *Externalities and public goods*. Accounting information is expected to give rise to externalities and have public goods characteristics. Public goods are commodities expected to be available to all without any restrictions. Accordingly, it is difficult to identify preferences for public goods and to maintain their preference by the market. In general, individuals tend to hide their actual preferences and try to become free riders at the expense of others. Thus, it becomes difficult to determine the actual demand for public goods. Hence, the demand is likely to be understated and underprovision occurs. The problem created by public goods leads to the result that non-market allocation methods are necessary to maintain the supply. In the case of accounting, information is publicly disclosed, every one may share in its consumption and it then becomes a public good. A rational person might not share in the costs unless exclusion is applied to its consumption. Gonedes and Dopuch (1974) showed that exclusion might be practised by allowing full property rights over accounting information and, in the absence of free riders, with perfect competition, market mechanisms can be demonstrated to produce an efficient allocation of accounting information. Insider trading can be taken as an example of the exercise of property rights over accounting information. In the case where insider trading is prohibited or exclusive property rights over accounting information do not exist, Pareto optimal allocation of resources in accounting information production is difficult to maintain.

Taylor and Turley (1986) deduced that, even if exclusion is possible in the consumption of accounting information, externalities are likely to be present in the exercise of the consumption right. An individual who gains access to additional accounting information might use this in trading decisions which will affect the prices of other securities. Others observe the trends of prices and may draw conclusions about the market. In this case, information may leak and this may result in a number of implications. Grossman (1977) believed that it may reduce the value of information and Foster (1980) believed it may weaken the incentive to purchase it, and may generate externalities. Hence, externalities may cause private and social costs to diverge, and non-optimal relations to result.

(e) *Merit and demerit goods.* Market failure may be associated with merit and demerit goods. Merit goods evidence important external benefits in consumption. For example, there might be high demand for a commodity which is not given expression in the market, such as health care and education. Likewise, there might be rejection of a specific commodity by those who do not directly consume it, as in the case of alcohol in many Islamic countries. So, the disclosure of accounting information at a minimum level of quality and quantity may be considered a merit commodity, while insider trading may be considered a demerit commodity. The reflection of the difference between individual preferences and those of the society might be seen through the recognition of merit and demerit goods. In the case where regulations are involved in the free process of the market in which merit and demerit commodities are traded, Taylor and Turley (1986) contended that governments may be seen as attempting to impose their interest on individuals by claiming to know better about what is good for them.

Watts and Zimmerman (1986) contend that management would not produce additional information because production costs exceed the revenue derived from the sale of information. Hence, Watts and Zimmerman believe that mandated disclosure can only be superior if its cost of production is less with the required disclosure and/or the social value of the information is greater than its market value. They concluded that managerial monopoly power over information leads to non-optimal ability of the market to distinguish between efficient and less efficient firms. In all cases this seems to support regulation.

On the other hand, Watts and Zimmerman argue that investors are price protected and, in an efficient market, managers cannot use diverse procedures to mislead investors systematically. Efficient market theory also suggests that managers and outside producers of information have the motive to reduce confusion due to the diversity of accounting procedures.

The proponents of non-regulation argue that, if information is not publicly available, some users will be more informed than others about market opportunities. This means that investments which have different characteristics may sell at the same price in the capital market. Akerlof (1970) contended that this will lead to the phenomenon of adverse selection whereby only poor quality commodities find their way to the markets. In the case of investing, only those of low quality may be offered for sale. This will cause investors to bear greater risk or to reduce their investment because they predict poor quality investment. Consequently, the holders of good quality investments (those investments which bear relatively low risk and high return) may voluntarily disclose information, which allow their quality to be assessed. If the information is endorsed and the endorsement is accepted, it would avoid investment with different characteristics selling at the same price.

On the other hand, market failure suggests that social welfare can be improved in a Pareto sense by the government regulation moving the private output closer to the social optimum. The ability of the government to increase welfare in a Pareto sense means it can induce an output change that makes at least one person better off at the expense of others. However, the absence of accounting regulation results, in non-optimal Pareto sense, in the output of information accounting and this will lead to a market failure. According to Burton (1974) accounting market failure exists because the resource allocation resulting from the market for financial information is inequitable, that is, unfair to some group of individuals. Watts and Zimmerman (1986) argued that this market failure has not been observed by market researchers who implement economics because it is not easy to define the optimality criterion of fairness that is acceptable to every one. In this respect, Arrow (1963) and Demski (1973) pointed out that each individual has his or her own preferences towards ranking the resource allocation and, in general, there is no point in believing that those preferences can be aggregated in a consistent social welfare function.

Equity and Distribution Problem

Under unregulated markets a means must be found to choose between efficient alternatives, that is, exercising social choice in matters affecting equity and distribution. Taylor and Turley (1986) considered two distribution issues: the distribution of accounting information between economic units, and the distribution of income and wealth which occurs as a result of the operating market. The latter is affected by the level of supply and allocation of accounting information when considering the presence of economic consequences of accounting information. A government may also be involved through taxation and subsidy policies in redistributing income and wealth.

However, redistribution of income and wealth may result from inequitable endowment of accounting information. In this case, governments may not become involved in regulating the supply and the distribution of accounting information but may deal directly with the result of unregulated market allocation. Alternatively, government may intervene to clarify the disclosure of accounting information through its policies in order to remove the cause of an inequitable distribution of income and wealth. In these circumstances, the accounting regulation takes place for distributional consideration.

The above analysis suggests that regulation is inevitable. There is a group of researchers who advocate what they called the 'equitable accounting policy'. Allingham (1976), Archibald and Donaldson (1979), Howe and Roemer (1981), Baumol (1982), Crawford (1977, 1979, 1980), Svensson (1980), Wilson (1975), and Lev (1988) all argued that a higher level of accounting information in equity results in a lower number of investors, high transaction costs, low liquidity of securities, low volumes of trade, and all these lead to less social gains from trade. The inequality of information results in adverse consequences in capital markets. To reduce the inequality (benefit held by informed investors) mandated policy regulation and timely public disclosure may be imposed. In this respect, Friedman (1980) showed that such a policy is desirable to help some persons but not at the expense of others:

> it is possible in our society to argue for a government programme to help the poor. ... But the argument is that by helping the poor we can make every one better off, that helping the poor is not merely a means to make the poor happier but a means to reduce crime, make us feel less guilty, make cities livable ... etc.

In fact, some disclosure rules might result in welfare redistribution particularly when some investors benefit at the expense of others. Glosten and Milgrom (1985) stressed that, if such redistribution exists, the possibility of the capital market breaking down due to severe information asymmetry exists with disclosure regulation. It might also be argued that regulation control protects the market against any breakdown which is more risky than welfare redistribution. Moreover, there is clear evidence that regulation will decrease inequality. Lev and Penman (1987) showed that voluntary release of information was found to be inconsistent. Thus, the assumption that non-regulatory disclosure will enhance equity in the capital market has no ground. Consequently, Lev (1988) argued that equity is considered to be one of the main justifications for regulation. Bromwich (1985) demonstrated that, to see the ASC successful in its activities, it is probably necessary that the ASC be seen as neutral between sections of the community and for its response to conflicting views to be as equitable and fully reasoned as possible.

The preceding discussion has been on the arguments for and against regulations. However, no matter how compelling the market for positive accounting theory arguments might be, few governments in the developed world have been prepared to run the risk of market failure. The social welfare arguments prevail that regulation in one form or another is a reality. The question that then emerges is, who should be responsible for accounting regulation?

WHO SHOULD ENFORCE ACCOUNTING REGULATIONS?

The above section argued that regulating accounting information is inevitable. However, the problem to be solved is who should enforce standard setting. Opinion is divided between the public sector, private sector or agency regulation as good candidates to enforce standard setting. Before examining each of the suggested alternatives, it is useful to report the present institutional framework which governs financial reporting in the United States and United Kingdom.

The common feature of financial reporting, in most countries, is the existence of public sector-based regulatory forces that influence the disclosure of financial information of the business entity. In some countries, specific legislation exists covering the contents of financial reports (Companies Acts in the United Kingdom and Commonwealth countries). In other countries, legislation is associated with corporate taxation as an important determinant of the contents of the financial reports (Germany, Japan, Sweden). In other countries, decisions by government regulatory bodies exercise an important influence (for example, the Securities of Exchange Commission (SEC) in the United States).

According to Foster (1986, p. 26), the US institutional framework for financial reporting can be categorized into four levels:

Level one includes the executive, legislative, and judicial branches of the US government. The executive branch exercises influence in a proactive way. The judicial branch exercises its influence by its rulings.

Level two consists of governmental regulatory bodies, such as the SEC and the Department of Treasury.

Level three includes private sector regulatory bodies such as the FASB, the American Institute of Certified Public Accountants (AICPA) and New York Stock Exchange (NYSE).

Level four consists of lobbying groups trying to affect decisions taken by the parties in the above levels, such as Financial Analysts Federation (FAF), Financial Executives Institutions (FEI) and other lobbying organizations.

A summary of US institutional framework for financial reporting is presented in figure 2.2.

It can be noted that the institutional framework in the United States is a joint effort between the public and the private sectors. The public sector governs levels one and two, while the private sector governs the other two levels. By the same token, in the United Kingdom the institutional framework for financial reporting operates at several levels:

1. *Parliament* – responsible for legislation underlying financial reporting (Companies Acts).

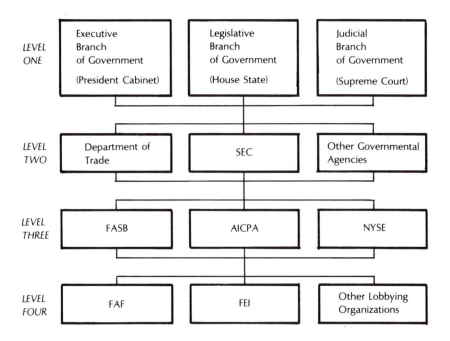

LEVEL ONE	Executive Branch of Government (President Cabinet)	Legislative Branch of Government (House State)	Judicial Branch of Government (Supreme Court)
LEVEL TWO	Department of Trade	SEC	Other Governmental Agencies
LEVEL THREE	FASB	AICPA	NYSE
LEVEL FOUR	FAF	FEI	Other Lobbying Organizations

Figure 2.2. Institutional framework ruling financial reporting in the United States
Source: Foster (1986)

2. *Government* – initiates the legislation process and exercises considerable influence through the involvement of the Department of Trade and Industry (DTI).

3. *Financial Reporting Council (FRC)* – it has two operating entities: the Accounting Standard Board (ASB) and the Review Panel. The Council has the responsibility for guiding the ASB on its planned work and acts as a source of counsel to it on broad matters of policy. The FRC also provides a forum for public advocacy and support for accounting standards. The ASB has the task of issuing financial reporting standards (FRSs) on its own responsibility. The ASB, through the Urgent Issues Task Force (UITF), has the task of tackling urgent matters not covered by the existing standards. The Review Panel has the task of examining and questioning departure from accounting standards by large companies. The Panel employs procedures to ensure that all parties concerned have a fair hearing.

4. *The International Stock Exchange, London (ISEL)* – produces rules concerning the financial information disclosed by quoted companies. The ISEL makes sure that quoted companies comply with the requirements of SSAPs and FRSs.

5. *Other influences* – include pressure groups which might influence the contents of the Companies Act, SSAPs and FRSs. These might include government

departments, employer organizations (CBI) and other professional bodies (the Law Society).

As in the United States, the institutional framework governing financial reporting is a partnership between the public and the private sectors. The public sector governs the first two categories, whilst the private sector governs the others.

Those who advocate an institutional framework, similar to those above, argue that accounting standards have economic consequences. In general, accounting regulation can affect the investor's wealth, and the magnitude of this effect varies across regulations. For example, Dukes, *et al.* (1980), and Horwitz and Kolodny (1980; 1983) showed how changes in the research and development rules affect reported profits/share value and therefore wealth. Ball and Foster (1982), Lev and Ohlson (1982) and Chow (1983b) found evidence consistent with the 1933 Securities Act having significant out-of-pocket compliance costs, or having reduced the firm's available investment, financing and product opportunities by tightening existing accounting debt covenants. Leftwich (1981), Collins *et al.* (1981) and Chow (1983a) demonstrated how selected accounting standards affect the wealth of the firm owners through their impact on debt covenants. Hence, the public sector can be seen as a qualified candidate to enforce accounting regulations if it counters the redistribution effects resulting from regulations. The argument for the public sector as the candidate to enforce standard setting lies in its ability to counter any redistributional effect (inefficient and inequitable resource allocation) by using its power of subsidies and taxation. Bromwich (1985) demonstrated that the government can meet any legitimate arguments concerning the economic effects of accounting standard setting without modifying what might be regarded as an accounting ideal. He added that the use of subsidies and taxation motivates the acceptance of promulgated accounting requirements. Moreover, accounting regulation by the legislature might be less open to pressure from the affected parties. Furthermore, governmental accounting regulation provided ultimate appeal mechanisms concerning extant accounting standards which is available in a sufficiently independent manner. Leftwich (1980) argued that it is far from obvious that a policy body such as ASC or the FASB can regulate information production so as to achieve an efficient allocation of resources. Yet, Ronen and Schiff (1978) reported the results of a survey that attempted to shed light on who should set financial accounting reporting standards, the public or the private sector? The sample survey (the sample contained corporations, practising CPAs, non-practising CPAs, accounting academics, financial analysts, corporate lawyers and financial reporters) showed a clear preference for financial accounting reporting to be standardized within the private sector.

In fact, regulating activities by a government suggests that there are problems which cannot be overcome by an ideally functioning legislative system. Some of these difficulties come from the fact that each individual has his/her own preference for options including various accounting treatments. Hence, if preferences could be identified, it is difficult to solve the problem by choosing among options. Arrow (1963) showed that it is difficult to find a social choice mechanism that would point at an option that is a Pareto–optimal in a liberal society. This view has been supported by Mueller (1979). He pointed out that it is difficult to find a generally acceptable conceptual framework of financial information. Sen (1970) and Mueller (1979) believe that the value judgement can be made to impose an acceptable mechanism on a society if no person in the group acts as a dictator. In addition, choices which favour some in the society and harm no one else should be accepted. A choice among alternative options should consider the impact of each option on the social welfare and the mechanism should accept the Pareto–optimal option as the rational and logical preference in the decision–making process and consider it as society's choice. According to Mueller (1979), the literature suggests that the government is more likely to be able to extract true preferences than any other sector. This is because the government can use subsidies and taxation to combat the impact of a newly issued standard. Ironically, it is difficult to assess preferences, particularly within a non-governmental body. On the other hand, Bromwich (1985) argued that the legislators might be seen as rubber stamping the ideas of the political party in power. This might point to the private sector as an alternative candidate to develop accounting standard setting.

However, private sector regulation faces two major problems: (1) the authority of standards setters, and (2) a consensus seeking. The nature of any mandate given to standard setters also determines the likely strength of any enforced powers which they can claim. The separation of profession from enterprise management and its clients may also provide a strong support for the acceptance of accounting standards. Moreover, because of their lack of formal authority, self-regulatory accounting bodies have to achieve a consensus for each standard among those who have the power to ignore the standards. In this respect, Sprouse (1983), the vice president of FASB, argued that the FASB is supported by other bodies with sufficient enforcement power.

One may argue that, in the private sector, standards may be set to please those who have strong bargaining power and thus standards will serve only the interest of influential parties. Standard setting might therefore be seen as unfair to other parties in society. To cope with this problem, sufficient authority should be given to the standard setting body, or the government should be invited to become more involved in accounting regulation.

Obviously, one of the criticisms directed to public sector standard setting is the possibility that the legislators are affected by the political party in power. On the other hand, the private sector lacks authority and consensus seeking. To overcome these problems, accounting decisions might be delegated to an agency which would derive its power from explicit legislative backing. Moreover, the agency approach might offer regulation without high cost and minimize the distributed costs of legislation such as tax and subsidy. Furthermore, an agency might be accepted as an independent body and perceived as better than a self-regulatory body. In general, such agencies have to provide a report on their activities to legislative masters. Nevertheless, Benston (1976) argued that the SEC in the United States represents a conservative force in the accounting area and acts in most of its judgement to its own personal interest. It is difficult to believe that the agency has an influential power more than those of private sector bodies. Horngren (1973) said that, despite the existing constraints, accountants believe that more progress can be achieved from some versions of the current decentralized set-up. He went on to say that to be successful the political role of the standard setters should be recognized no matter what standard setting structure is used, be it private, public or some combination thereof.

SUMMARY AND CONCLUSION

The early stage of accounting was unregulated and all reported accounting information was considered creative accounting. The next stage was characterized by a much wider spread of share ownership and a divorce between ownership and control occurred. As a result of this, financial accounting became important to meet the ownership requirement of monitoring managers' actions and it was thus an important element in the accountability process. It then became evident that these stewardship statements were also providing an input into decision making (lending/share trading) which had implications for capital market allocation and this led to much stronger pressure for regulation. Not every one agreed that such pressure was justified but, irrespective of the arguments that have been put forward against regulation, the reality is that most societies have opted to regulate in an attempt to minimize the impact of choice in accounting disclosure and measurement on capital market allocation. The question that then emerged was, who should be responsible for accounting regulation – public sector or private sector? It was argued that standards affect wealth redistribution, an argument which excludes the private sector as a candidate to be responsible of accounting regulation on the ground that it lacks the power to counter the redistribution effects. Logically, this pushed regulation towards the public sector, or, as is usually the case, a partnership between the public and private sectors.

In fact, the main thrust of imposed regulations (and also regulation through market forces) is to restrict flexibility in accounting measurement and disclosure. This is the paradox: regulation, either voluntarily through market force pressures, or, as is more usually the case, imposed by public and/or private sector regulatory bodies, is the response to the problem that a complete free-for-all in accounting measurement, reporting and disclosure requirements would lead to creative accounting. In other words, creative accounting would be unbounded. However, imposition of increasingly detailed and specific regulations has resulted in the search for ways to avoid the regulation or, more likely, avoid the intended impact of the regulations. Thus a different kind of creative accounting has emerged and manipulation becomes inevitable. How manipulation comes to be practised under the present accounting system is the main concern of the following chapter.

REVIEW QUESTIONS

1. It is argued that the divorce between ownership and management emphasized the importance of financial accounting. Explain, with reasons, if you agree or disagree with this argument.

2. Accounting information has been designed to benefit a diverse set of parties. Show how financial information will assist these parties in making decisions.

3. List possible parties that might be interested in financial information and what they need financial information for.

4. Although the users of financial information have a diverse set of needs, some of their needs may be common. Explain.

5. Give some examples of areas where the interests of the users of financial information are in conflict.

6. What are the major factors that affect the demand for financial information?

7. Critically analyze the arguments put forward against accounting regulation.

8. The proponents of market regulations believe that the lack of regulation may lead to market failure and may result in equity and distribution problems. Critically analyze this argument.

9. In the light of the argument for and against accounting regulation, state the extent to which you agree or disagree with accounting regulation.

10. In your opinion, who should be responsible for accounting regulation, public sector, private sector or a combination of both? Why?

CHAPTER 3

Creative Accounting Under Different Accounting Systems

INTRODUCTION

Financial statements are a product of cumulative historical influences. In the stage before the industrial revolution, financial statements were prepared as arithmetical checks of ledger balances. In the nineteenth century, periodic financial reporting emerged and this led to subdivision of accounts into current and long-term categories and accruals and deferrals. Each business firm had great freedom to develop the accounting methods or principles which best met its needs. This resulted in inconsistent outcomes. This was the situation in the past and yet a long period of regulation and attempts at greater uniformity in disclosure and measurement has done little to alter the situation. The main characteristic of present-day accounting is the freedom of preparers to choose measurement methods. Freedom of choice is axiomatic to Western accounting. In this respect, Watts and Zimmerman (1979) argued that the main common feature of the prescription and proposed accounting methodologies is their failure to convince all accountants and to be generally accepted by accounting standard setting bodies.

Turning back to the agency theory discussed in the preceding chapter, accounting procedures are designed to reduce the agency costs of contracts. However, the costs are different from one firm to another and this will give rise to different accounting techniques and information. In this context, Watts and Zimmerman (1979) concluded that the incentive function of the accounting theory is now to supply excuses which satisfy the demand created by the political process. As a result, accounting theories have become increasingly normative. One obvious example of a period when reporting enterprises were free to choose any accounting measurement and procedures was the nineteenth century and earlier. The main difference, far more than today, is that the accounting behaviour in the nineteenth century was a response to the objective of the industrial manager and accounting information (financial statements) were prepared without any regulatory constraints.

Indeed, potential freedom gave managers the opportunity to adopt accounting and reporting practices that met their requirements. This means that creative accounting existed in every aspect of accounting. Therefore, inventory valuation, depreciation methods, fixed assets revaluation and so on could potentially be considered as creative accounting. While 'creativity' may not be the intended objective because such a concept was not then in vogue, the reasons given were much more socially acceptable, probably because these were typical examples of the operation of a market for excuses (Watts and Zimmerman 1979).

Probably because the freedom to choose measurement practice permits the production of a more acceptable 'bottom line' figure, there was a patent reluctance to clamour for corporate reporting regulation and this provides a screen behind which most of the creative accounting schemes hide. The rest of this chapter provides some early examples of creative accounting schemes and the allocation problem.

SOME EARLY EXAMPLES OF CREATIVE ACCOUNTING

Before 1830 cost accounting was a product of changing social and economic environment. Edwards (1989) shows that, after they decided what they wanted to do, managers in this period structured their cost accounting accordingly. The disclosed accounting information used to be adjusted as companies' plans were changed. Edwards classified the costing procedures used at that stage as an *ad hoc* one.

The industrial revolution made an essential physical change towards the concentration of production and factories using powered equipment and large firms emerged. According to Pollard (1965), industrialization created the need for the development of industrial accounting, and the appointment and training of management staff. Brief (1966) states that during the industrial revolution accountants first tried to cope with the major problem which concerned them at that time when each firm had great freedom to amplify whatever accounting methods and principles suited its particular needs. At that time, the accounting profession lacked influence over the preparation of financial reports. Moreover, the accounting behaviour was a response to the objectives of individual managers. In each business, managers would largely make the rules by which assets were valued and income was determined.

In the eighteenth century many large English industrial firms merged into partnerships. This required an accounting system which facilitated precise allocation of profit. Industrialists wished to prevent errors, control thefts, and be able to estimate their net worth at any time. They had to ensure that money for payments to creditors was made available and needed a systematic record of transactions in dealing with customers and for their own use (ledger balances therefore provided a useful record to which reference could be made). Industrial accounting brought into existence two new factors of mercantile bookkeeping:

1. the use of large acquisition of fixed assets, and

2. an increased need for periodic reporting.

Indeed, most accounting problems revolved around fixed assets, depreciation, maintenance and overhead expenses. According to Chatfield (1977) Pacioli, writing in 1494, made no provision for financial statements and no serious attempt to determine the profits earned during any given period of time. Since business in his days was typically a series of discrete ventures, there were few of the modern reasons for assigning the cost and revenue to specific periods. Moreover, owners were in personal contact with their affairs, operations could easily be observed and profits were not hard to estimate. Statements were normally prepared only at the end of each major project. Accounting periods were unnecessary and the base of operations dictated the accounting process. However, once a firm's life lasted through many ventures it no longer became workable to wait till dissolution before preparing financial statements. The provision of accounting information at regular intervals was only one aspect of a new sense of timeliness which emerged from the industrial revolution. Pollard (1965) demonstrated that the adoption of periodic reporting enabled management to handle details and to regulate operations too extensive to be easily supervised. In addition, periodic reports helped in solving the problem of management from a distance, when a company's plants were located in different places. Many expense items (salaries and wages paid weekly or monthly, interest, etc.) dictated the use of calendar intervals as a useful basis for reporting financial information. Moreover, the adoption of mechanized techniques made operational time more important and emphasized the need for a uniform reporting of the company's accounts.

During the nineteenth century, it became generally accepted that the calculation of annual income available for stockholders was the primary accounting task. The key to income measurement was usually assets valuation, not the matching of costs and revenues. Litherland (1951, p. 475) pointed out that 'the expressed purpose of accounting at that time was to show a true balance sheet with capital maintenance intact and policy, if any, clearly indicated.'

Even though diversity and inconsistency in asset valuation practices characterized the nineteenth century, two viewpoints predominated. Public service railways and utility corporations used some type of replacement costs. In contrast, manufacturing companies accounted for depreciable assets as if they were unsold merchandise. They used to revalue assets at the end of each accounting period and charge any increase or decrease directly to the income statement. Original investment was to be capitalized while assets maintenance and replacement changes were to be expensed.

Brief (1966) pointed out that, while asset valuation had many variations in practice, assets had to be appraised or revalued at the end of each accounting period. The new value was debited and the old one credited to the asset account, the difference being charged to the income statement. In these terms, depreciation was a product of a valuation procedure. However, valuation methods of depreciation have always been difficult to standardize. There was no agreement on best practices, nor was there a definite answer to the question, what is value? Thus the growth of corporations with large fixed assets investments made it essential for accounts to deal directly with the problem of capital. This was especially true after the increasing use of manufacturing compensation costs, which made it necessary to know the cost as accurately as possible. On the other hand, the railways were the first industrial sector to demonstrate the whole range of asset valuation problems. Requiring large capital investments and more long-lived equipment than most nineteenth-century businesses, they were forced to make methodical distinctions between assets expenditures and their maintenance accounts. However, there was concern for capital maintenance through depreciation.

During the boom of the 1840s many railways paid large dividends out of capital, ending with a windfall for short-term speculators at the expense of long-term investors and creditors. In response to the resulting scandals, some firms adopted cost-based depreciation, but in most cases it was abandoned when such depreciation provision was to be found inadequate to replace fixed assets. Norton (1976) showed that the usual approach was to relate depreciation to assets maintenance, on the assumption that original investment capital was permanently maintained in good working order by repairs and renewals. Thus, long-lived assets purchased from stock issues and proceeds of bonds were capitalized at the original cost and never depreciated. Consequently, the cost of replacement of these original assets as well as repairs were charged directly to expense; only expenditure on additional assets was capitalized. Littleton (1933) believed that railway operations encouraged replacement accounting because most of the assets involved had long lives, and because maintenance was the railway's main operating problem. This resulted in many variations in practice and permitted creative accounting. Littleton also reported that, in the nineteenth century, some railways charged all capital costs to expense if repair charges were thought to cover depreciation. Some formed a depreciation fund by setting amounts aside for repairs at an annual percentage rate above ordinary charges. Others ignored depreciation only if repairs were sufficient to make good wear and tear. However, replacement accounting was simple and flexible in practice to make managers able to choose a wide range of accounting options. It avoided the problem of estimating the useful life of fixed assets. More importantly, since most of the companies had followed the approach of not allocating any expense of the original investment in fixed assets until they had been replaced, this enhanced the attractiveness to investors (railways incurred high depreciation expenses in the early years of an asset's life cycle but did not charge them to the income statement and therefore inflated their profits). May (1936) argued that the rapid development of American railroads would probably have been impossible if periodic costs depreciation had been required.

However, replacement accounting developed serious creative accounting problems. Railway assets valuation policies had two conflicting purposes: to attract investors with the prospect of high earnings and dividends, at the same time they were working on accumulating capital to replace assets. Thus, dividends were paid from the inflated income of the early years and they relied on the future income to obtain cash for asset replacements. They also supposed that repairs and maintenance would keep rolling stock in working order, while this might not always be true: obsolescence as well as usage decreased asset values. One of the purposes of interweaving repairs, replacement and depreciation was to assist the progress of internal financing by allowing managers to create secret reserves.

Brief (1965) considered the replacement as an essentially unstable offshoot of cash basis accounting. This inconsistency was the characteristic of nineteenth-century accounting and the variety of valuation methods which followed made comparison between published accounts difficult. Stockholders were misled as to actual income, future earnings potential and management efficiency. It seems that the businessmen of the nineteenth century were in some doubt as to the essential purpose of depreciation: to refine income calculation; finance asset replacements; reflect the asset value; maintain capital intact; or to secure dividends payment. Hence, each party from the standpoint of its own interest wanted something different from depreciation. Creditors hoped to be assured that capital was maintained intact. Management wanted cash reserves to finance assets replacement. Stockholders needed an accurate consistent statement of income available for dividends. If management did not plan to replace assets, or if profits were not available for dividends, they saw no reason for depreciation.

Thus, accounting theory became important and according to Hendriksen (1970) the indirect effects of industrial technology were: (1) a greater adherence to cost as a valuation basis; (2) greater significance of the distinction between capital and income; and (3) the development of a going concern concept. It might be useful to point out that continuity, periodicity, historical costs and conservation emerged in their modern form after being adopted by nineteenth-century manufacturers. On the other hand, continuous industrial production produced a demand for accounting reports at intermediate points of operation. Periodicity in turn affected other accounting concepts. To make the going concern principle possible, transactions of each accounting period needed to be classified. This was followed by the idea of matching cost and related revenue (matching principle).

However, the transition from venture to going concern made record keeping more subjective. Differences of opinion about depreciation could lead to large variations in reported profits. Managers could deliberately obscure periodic results by shifting income from one period to another, by over-depreciating assets and charging capital goods to expenses. This was essentially brought about by the contradiction between the going concern principle and the periodicity principle. The former assumes the operations as a continuous flow, the latter assumes the break of flow into comparable time segments.

Turning back to the period following 1850, a tendency to understate profits began to replace the deliberate overstatement which had characterized the speculative inception of railways. Beside safeguarding legal capital against excess dividends payments, the convention of understatement strengthened the rise of the prudence convention, and the use of lower of cost or market inventory valuation and of historical cost in fixed assets accounting. In this respect, Brief (1965) considered the accounting literature of the time and other evidence which suggested that conservatism was widely ineffective in the face of management desire to equalize income over the phase of the business cycle. Since depreciation expense was not recognized until assets were replaced, there was often a motive to expense betterment or to keep income high by not replacing equipment. A systematic overstatement of income and assets permitted managers to maintain the appearance of stability which was attractive to investors, while distorting the analysis of management effectiveness and future earnings potential. Thus, Brief (1966) demonstrated that the unstable accounting treatment influenced resource allocation, prices and output, the business cycle and economic growth in general.

In return, complete flexibility characterized the fixed asset values of the nineteenth century. Assets were the backbone of businesses, providing a basic framework which allowed them to carry out their operations. Yet, despite their importance, the rules which governed the reported values of fixed assets were remarkably flexible. Their flexibility was the more remarkable given the starting point for evaluation processes. There would, in the large majority of cases, be the cost of assets which was rarely open to manipulation. There was little scope for playing with the original cost of fixed assets but after that there was unlimited scope for making fixed assets work for the business in every sense of the phrase. Brief (1966) demonstrated that the scope was more pronounced because the value placed on the assets could be adjusted upwards or downwards almost at will. The justification for this creativity was embodied in the adoption of revaluations of fixed assets, depreciation, maintenance and overhead expenses. A careful juggling of valuation and depreciation will usually allow a company to arrive at a combination which will maximize the impact on the balance sheet and minimize its effects on the income statement. Thus, replacement accounting left railway financial statements with good-looking high earnings and dividends that helped to attract investors. As mentioned earlier, dividends were to be paid from inflated income of early years and management relied on the future income to secure cash to replace scrapped assets. Shareholders were misled by information disclosed on actual income, future earnings, potential and management efficiency.

Thus, nineteenth-century accounting failed to have a consistent approach towards the allocation of costs. This resulted in various accounting measurements and presentations. Today, of course, accounting does take into consideration the allocation case ignored in the nineteenth century. A discussion of the extent to which the allocation system employed at the present time is useful is the task of the next section.

THE ALLOCATION PROBLEM

One of the basic principles underlying the preparation of financial statement is the matching principle. In recognizing expenses, accounts attempt to follow the approach of 'let the expenses follow the revenues' (Kieso and Weygandt, 1980). Hence, expense recognition is tied with revenue recognition. In other words, costs are analyzed to determine whether a relationship exists with revenues. Where this association holds, the costs are expensed and matched against the revenue in the period when the revenue is recognized. If no connection appears between costs and revenues, an allocation of costs on some systematic and rational basis might be appropriate. However, if this method does not seem obtainable, the costs may be expensed immediately.

In fact, the problem of cost recognition is as complex as that of revenue recognition and the conceptual validity of the matching principle has been a subject of debate. A major concern is that matching permits certain costs to be deferred and treated as assets on the balance sheet when in fact the costs may not have future benefits. If abused, this principle permits the balance sheet to become a dumping ground for unmatched costs. In addition, there appears to be no objective definition of 'systematic and rational basis' that could be used to allocate costs in situations where no connection appears between revenue and cost. For instance, various depreciation methods might be used to allocate the costs over a depreciable asset's useful life. What criteria should guide the accountant in determining what portion of the cost of assets should be written off each period? Hence, it might be argued that even that procedure is well nigh impossible, given that the revenue flow from any given asset is interrelated with the remaining asset structure of the enterprise.

Actually, the roots of the allocation problem which concerns its critics lie in the freedom allowed in selecting from alternative procedures for matching expenses and revenue in determining net income. Most of the criticisms are directed at the different methods employed to allocate costs and revenues. With respect to this, Thomas has published two studies on allocation made in financial accounting. In the first (1969), *The Allocation Problem in Financial Accounting Theory*, he concluded that the allocation traditionally made in financial accounting is arbitrary and should cease. In the second (1974), *The Allocation Problem Part Two*, he concluded that financial accounting's allocations are not only arbitrary but also incorrigible (incapable of verification) and again that they should cease. This leads him to conclude that the incorrigible nature of accounting makes it improbable that consensus can ever be achieved on the best allocation scheme in any area where acceptable alternatives exist. According to Thomas, allocations are to cease, if they are not verified by reference to the market value. His conclusions are based on the position that allocations do not refer to the economic phenomenon of the real world. However, Eckel (1976) argued that this statement is true in one sense only, and it is one that is neither surprising nor new. Contrary to his proposal, allocations do refer to real world economic phenomena; depreciation is intended to reflect the decline in value due to the use in generating revenue. Eckel believes that the quest for verifiability or objectivity is an old one and the lack of verifiability by reference to current market values has not been found so compelling as to result in the abandonment of the historical cost allocation model. The labelling of that lack of verifiability as incorrigibility is unlikely to change things.

Thomas structured his treatment of the problem so that depreciation allocation is used as a representative example of all financial accounting allocation concerning multiperiod goods. The entire enquiry in Studies in Accounting Research (SAR 3) is based on the reasoning that, if the depreciation allocation can be shown to be arbitrary, then all financial accounting's allocations are arbitrary. To justify allocation, Thomas believes, the following must be met:

1. The method should be unambiguous, it should yield a unique allocation and provide in advance clear instructions as to how the allocation should be conducted.

2. The method should derive what is available for allocation, and the result must be additive.

It seems that the critical aspect of the Thomas criteria is that an allocation method must be defensible. This is a subjective and abstracted word which carries different meanings.

Eckel (1976) believed that Thomas incorrectly concluded that allocations are generally arbitrary, while he should conclude that, as accounting is presently defined, accounting allocations are arbitrary. Meyers (1976) indicated that changes in GAAP would inevitably be a part of any complete solution to the allocation problem. On the other hand, Thomas himself (1980) concluded that allocation can be useful, in the sense that it can help achieve the objective of the organization. Even so, Skinner (1987) believes that Thomas's argument has never been explicitly refuted; the attempt to do so by Eckel (1976) was a very weak one. He demonstrated that the problem with Thomas's argument is that it is by no means clear to what extent his claims that allocations are incorrigible and arbitrary are true. Thomas' claim is not justified for the purpose of decision making; for example, it is necessary that allocation should be of some help in the estimation of incremental costs. There has never been any serious doubt about its usefulness in the case of allocation of variable costs in the estimation of short-run incremental cost. In the same fashion, Dixon (1953) argued that allocated full cost is likely to be the best available estimate of the long-run incremental cost of any additional activity. A justification of Dixon's view point is that a rationally operated business functions in the long run at balanced full capacity since any permanent increase or decrease in an activity is likely to be accomplished by an appropriate scaling up or down of capacity and, therefore, by an appropriate increase or decrease in all those costs that are, in the short run, fixed. Zimmerman (1979) made a point similar to that of Dixon. He argued that allocation can act as a useful and inexpensive substitute for a number of hard to observe costs, including the costs involved in the expansion of internally provided services. In this respect, Fremgen and Liao's (1981) survey found that 49% of those who allocated costs did that for decision analysis purposes. Yet, Skinner (1987) stated that:

> We know that many accountants believe allocated full costs are the best available estimates of long run incremental costs. However, there is no direct evidence available as to whether that belief is correct either for all long run decisions or just for expansion decisions.

The earlier discussion of nineteenth-century accounting systems illustrated how they failed to adopt a consistent approach to the interval accounting, (allocate costs to the related revenue among periods), and therefore ended up with inconsistent financial reporting. An environment in which creative accounting could thrive was then in evidence. The present day accounting system is characterized by its widespread adherence to the allocation system. However, as the discussion in the preceding paragraph has shown, allocations are essential and this means that there is also scope for creative accounting. In fact, allocation employed by conventional accounting systems distorts the usefulness of the prepared accounts. Sterling (1979) argued that the presence of time-period allocation invalidates financial reporting schemes. An accounting system which avoids any doubtful accounting allocations and provides relatively clear measures of financial performance is required. A cash flow accounting system is often suggested as a means of overcoming the conventional allocation problem. The usefulness of the cash flow accounting system as a feasible alternative to the use of conventional accounting allocation is the subject of the following section.

CASH FLOW ACCOUNTING SYSTEM

One characteristic of assets is their liquidity, that is, the amount of time expected to elapse until the asset is realized or is otherwise converted into cash. Liquidity is an indication of an enterprise's ability to meet its obligations as they become due. Cash represents the most important feature of business activities, the ability of the enterprise to pay its obligations, make distributions and provide for future continuity. More importantly, cash flow accounting is characterized by its avoidance of allocations. Therefore, it is not surprising to see that the cash flow accounting system is suggested as an alternative to the conventional allocation accounting system.

The history and the nature of the cash flow accounting system, the case for cash flow accounting and the case against it are discussed in this section.

1. The History and Nature of Cash Flow Accounting

Cash flow accounting is an old concept. Winjum (1972) showed that the cash flow accounting system was the main system of accounting up to the beginning of the eighteenth century. Before this stage accounting allocation and profit measurement were relatively unimportant, income statements being used to close off ledger accounts at the end of each accounting period. After this stage, the advent of the concept and practice of business continuity resulted in a growing need to produce periodic measurements of income and statements of financial position (balance sheet). Thus, cash flow accounting became the basis for the allocation system of accounting in use today.

Cash flow accounting is the term used to represent a system of financial accounting which reports the financial performance of an entity in cash terms. Under a strict cash basis, revenue is recorded only when the cash is received and expenses are recorded only when the cash is paid. Thus, cash flow accounting is based on matching cash inflows and outflows within a specific period of time. The question to be raised is, why is cash flow accounting suggested as an alternative to the conventional accounting allocation system? This is the task of the next section.

2. The Case for Cash Flow Accounting

The importance of cash flow accounting lies in the avoidance of allocations. Cash flow accounting also has secondary advantages in that it provides information on a firm's liquidity.

The advocates of cash flow accounting argue that it solves the main two problems associated with the conventional accounting system; first, it is free of arbitrary conventional accounting allocation. Second, since its attention is to the time value of money, it is the only proper basis for measuring the value of the entity as a going concern.

Ashton (1976) pointed out many advantages of the cash flow statement; the first advantage is that cash flow accounting provides information on which management's view of the future will be projected, which is of considerable importance to investors who are connected with evaluating the desirability of being part of the future. Another advantage where Ashton describes it as the most important is what he called price/discounted cash flow ratio (price per share/discounted cash flow per share). He considers this ratio as a reliable investment indicator, more than price earning ratio which is based on arbitrary allocation used in determining the earning per share. Another advantage claimed by Ashton is that the investors can determine from the cash flow the ability of the company to pay its money in the future and also its planned financial policy. The Research Committee of the Institute of Chartered Accounts of Scotland (1988) regarded the cash flow statement as essential for any board of directors and for investors.

Cash flow accounting seems to be an objective system which avoids most of the subjective allocations. It also provides comparable data free of subjective allocations and measurements of different purchasing power. More importantly, cash flow accounting is capable of producing data which are needed for a variety of decisions. Lee (1980) showed that bankers and lenders would be provided with data relevant to their assessment of the reporting entity's quality of financial management. Lee reported in 1981 that there is an argument that the stock market (at least in aggregate) would be more efficient and derive more accurate share values as a consequence. Lee also reported that the utility of cash flow accounting in the area of corporate tax has been recognized in the report of the Mead Committee (1978) in which it is recommended that company tax in the United Kingdom be based on measured cash flow. This was considered tangible evidence of cash flow accounting, particularly utility and importance. The importance of cash flow accounting has been emphasized by the FASB of the United States in 1987 after the issuance of SFAS No. 95 and by the ASB of the United Kingdom in 1991 after the issuance of FRS No. 1. This was followed by Exposure Draft 36 issued for comments by the International Accounting Standards Committee in July 1991, which requires all firms to make use of the cash (or near cash) concept of fund. Before the end of 1992, the IASC published cash flow statement standard IAS 7 (revised).

FRS 1 requires that a reporting enterprise should issue a cash flow statement instead of a statement of sources and application of funds. The standard applies for all reporting periods on or after 23 March 1992. The objective of FRS 1 is

> to require reporting entities, falling within its scope, to report, on a standard basis, their cash generation and cash absorption for a period. To this end, the cash flow statements should provide cash flow information under the standard headings of 'operating activities', 'return on investment and servicing of finance', 'taxation', 'investing activities' and 'financing'. This structure aims to assist users ... in their assessment of the reporting entity's liquidity, viability and financial adaptability. (FRS 1)

The publication of FRS1 represents a departure from accrual accounting upon which the profit and loss account and the balance sheet are based. In this case, FRS 1 is expected to avoid measurement problems associated with profit determination. Lee (1992) views the issuance of FRS 1 as an important step forward. He believes that FRS 1 will avoid the effect of the periodic accounting accruals and cost allocation. Harvey (1992) contends that FRS1 has potential 'to provide extra dimension to corporate reporting and hence corporate performance appraisal'.

Clearly, cash flow accounting gives investors different impressions of the company's performance than the conventional annual financial statements.

Be that as it may, cash flow accounting cannot alone provide a complete picture on the company's performance and one may argue that cash flow accounting is an incomplete reporting statement because it concentrates on flows rather than stock. Hence, some writers suggested other statements to support cash flow statements. Lee (1992) warned against relying solely on cash flows to predict the success or failure of an entity and conclusions can only be reached over an extended period of time.

However, cash flow accounting is not without its critics. The case against cash flow accounting is given in the following section.

3. The Case Against Cash Flow Accounting

Cash flow accounting is being advocated on the grounds that it avoids the subjective allocation problems associated with conventional accounting. The argument against cash flow accounting is led by Rutherford. Rutherford (1982) stated that:

although it is true that cash flows are not tainted by metrical allocation, under normal circumstances cash flow accounting does not overcome the underlying measurement problem caused by economic interaction.

He argued that cash flow accounting is not allocation free and therefore contains many judgement problems similar in nature and impact to those associated with the conventional allocation based system of accounting. At all events, Lawson (1971) illustrates that cash flow accounting is free from most of the controversial problems of conventional accounting and Lee (1972) contended that cash flow accounting avoids allocations but does not avoid all allocations. In the same manner, Thomas (1980, p. 220) argued that: 'cash flow accounting avoids dubious accounting allocation, and thus, unlike period income measurement, cash flow provides relatively unambiguous measures of entity financial performance.'

Indeed, the first point raised by Rutherford was related to the segmental cash flow statement suggested by Lee. Lee (1972) suggested that a firm's manufacturing and/or trading transactions flow should be analyzed according to a significant economic unit group. Rutherford (1982) contended that, in the face of economic interactions, it will not be possible to apportion a group cash flow completely by using simple rules. The interaction will affect cash flows as well as costs and the total cash outflows of the group cannot be apportioned between segments without performing distributional allocation. In addition, Lee's proposal gives rise to transfer prices and joint cost problems. Thomas (1980) also stated that at best all that can be done is to live with the problem. Lawson (1976) also recognized the problem when he suggested that divisional performance on a cash flow accounting basis should only be measured if the division was independent.

Another area of cash flow accounting that might give scope for allocation problems is the distinction between capital expenditures and revenue expenditures. Rutherford (1982) argued that the economic interaction will be likely to occur in the distinction between capital and revenue flows. In this respect, Thomas (1969) found difficulties in distinguishing between depreciable assets from any other economic goods when he examined the depreciation methods as a case for an allocation problem. This problem is valid in the case of cash flow accounting. Lee (1981) suggested that the major worry was that cash flow accounting was being used for decision-making purposes as a substitute for income, and the cost for durable assets was not being taken into account. Meyers (1976) agreed that this distinction between capital and revenue flows itself requires allocation. On the other hand, Glautier and Underdown (1976, p. 664) stated that:

> the problem associated with the distinction between capital, revenue, income and expenditures or of allocation of costs between a series of arbitrary time periods, do not arise under cash flow accounting.

Lee contended that the distinction between revenue and capital transactions and developing criteria classifying business assets are not necessary, although Lee (1981) did not discountenance the problem when he suggested the link between cash flow accounting and net realizable value accounting for income and capital.

As a matter of fact, any cash flow which results from a transaction affecting more than one accounting period might be subject to economic interactions. Hence, capital flows are categorized under this framework. Therefore, a high proportion of cash flows might be subject to interaction, thus leaving a great number of flows unappropriated to a time period and giving scope for creativity.

Another problem raised by Rutherford relates to transactions which take place in a form of by-passes of cash (exchange transactions, i.e. exchanging assets with shares and netting payables with receivables).

A further problem also raised by Rutherford (1982) is what he called the window dressing of cash flow accounting reports caused by management responsible for cash flow by cutting off, accelerating, or delaying cash receipts or payment. Thus, the fixed or short nature of the financial reporting period may create cash flow variability which needs to be smoothed in an attempt to improve the financial reports of a particular period, or the trends of financial results over a number of periods. Lee (1982) believed that such window-dressing procedures can only have a short-term effect in most cases and one accounting period will benefit on the account of others. To cope with this problem, Lee suggested a multiple period cash flow accounting system to avoid any attempt of window dressing.

In the same fashion, Watts and Zimmerman (1979) argued that cash flow profit is susceptible to short-run manipulation. The manager can reduce repairs and maintenance expenditure and increase cash inflows and profits which increase the manager's compensation. In addition, reducing maintenance expenditures increase the ability of the corporation to pay current dividends. In this case, they will reduce creditors' claims and increase the shareholders' wealth.

Ashton (1976) pointed out other problematic areas associated with the cash flow accounting system. He contended that, since the income measures provide information on how the company performed and how it is likely to perform in the future, then they are important measures. Hence, cash flow accounting provides the investors with very little information on profit margins, gearings or interest coverage, or how quickly assets were turned over.

Harvey (1992) argued that the allocation of cash flow made by FRS 1 is subject to discussion. He questioned whether repair and renovation expenditure should be classified as an operating activity or investing activity for a property company. He believes that the FRS 1 fails to settle three issues, namely: how can a company report its cash flow when it faces restrictions on its cash and cash equivalent? What will be the case if exchange restrictions impose many years' waiting before profit can be accessed as a result of shortage of foreign currency in a subsidiary operating in a foreign country? FRS 1 fails to make prescription for what Harvey called its borrowing facilities, that is, when a company involves in high level of debt and asks for overdraft facilities and another has healthy gearing ratios and borrowing options. In this situation the reader of the companies' accounts will find it difficult to compare the liquidity of the two companies. As mentioned earlier, the cash flow statement suggested by FRS 1 ignores vital information relating to exchange transactions (exchange of shares for assets). This type of information may be of considerable use for the readers of the statement.

Whatever the argument for or against cash flow accounting, introducing a new standard related to cash flow accounting by the US Financial Accounting Standard Board (FASB) and the ASB of the United Kingdom may reflect the usefulness of the cash flow accounting for decision makers. Yet, the system is still open to manipulation.

SUMMARY AND CONCLUSION

The extent to which any accounting system is to be considered acceptable depends on its ability to counter any attempts to adopt creative accounting. The preceding discussion illustrates how the main characteristic of the nineteenth-century accounting system was the ignorance of the time period allocation as a basis for financial reporting. Hence, it failed to counter manipulation. On the other hand, the most popular assumption underlying the present-day accounting system is the time period allocation used to report on discrete periods of business activities. The conventional system proved to be subject to arbitrary allocation since the concepts upon which prepared financial statements are based are neither consistent nor logical. A cash flow accounting system was proposed as free of arbitrary allocation, but it was demonstrated that even here there is scope for allocation and consequent manipulation. The following chapters illustrate that creative accounting is likely to occur under conventional and cash flow accounting systems and both systems can do little to avoid the creativity problem.

REVIEW QUESTIONS

1. It is suggested that creative accounting is likely to occur with or without regulation. Discuss this suggestion (support your answer with some practical examples).

2. Explain how the emergence of the industrial technology produced a demand for accounting regulation.

3. In response to the going-concern assumption, financial transactions of each accounting period need to be classified. This should be followed by the idea of matching cost and related revenue within the accounting period. However, this may result in subjective decisions and therefore creativity. Show how the going-concern, periodicity and matching concepts might be used as a screen behind which to hide schemes of creative accounting.

4. It is claimed that flexibility in accounting measurement and disclosure is considered the strength and yet the weakness of the conventional accounting system. Critically discuss this claim.

5. The main weaknesses of the accounting system of the nineteenth century were the failures to distinguish between revenue expenditure and capital expenditure and to have a consistent approach towards the allocation of costs. Show how this resulted in various accounting measurements and disclosures and therefore creative accounting.

6. It is contended that allocation traditionally made in the conventional accounting system is not only arbitrary but also incorrigible and it should cease. Explain the meaning of arbitrary and incorrigible allocation and state the extent to which you agree or disagree with this opinion.

7. To avoid the allocation problem of the present-day accounting system, a cash flow accounting system is suggested. Discuss the ability or otherwise of the cash flow accounting system to avoid the allocation problem.

8. Although a cash flow accounting system provides useful information on the company's liquidity position, the user of the accounting information may still need more information to enable them to take financial decisions. State how this is likely to occur.

9. State the strengths and weaknesses of the cash flow accounting system.

10. 'Since allocation is likely to occur under the conventional accounting system as well as the cash flow accounting system, creative accounting can be employed under either of these'. Discuss.

CHAPTER 4

The Accounting Profession's Response to Creative Accounting

INTRODUCTION

Previous chapters have discussed the inevitability of the use of creative accounting. The accounting profession has responded by publishing known opportunities or actual schemes of creative accounting and seeking ways of limiting their use. This chapter examines these responses and, in particular, critically evaluates pronouncements (or indications of attempts to) limiting the use of creative accounting such as TR 603 (1986), ED 42 (1988) and ED 49 (1990). In addition, an attempt is made in this chapter to explain the reasons for the growing popularity of creative accounting.

CREATIVE ACCOUNTING DISTORTS THE PURPOSE OF PREPARING THE ACCOUNTS

In 1985 the President of the Institute of Chartered Accountants in England and Wales (ICAEW) drew attention to what he described as the 'potentially very serious problems of window dressing and off-balance sheet financing'. (*Accountancy*, October, p. 4). There had then been concern about a number of devices which could be used to remove debt from the balance sheet. Wild (1987a) quoted Bullen, the American FASB manager responsible for a project on creative accounting, as saying 'the project will be one of the largest and most complex... that the Board has ever addressed'. Bullen considers creative accounting as another accounting problem, while Wild (1987a) believes that it is more than that. It casts doubt on the purpose of preparing the accounts. Morgan (1989) demonstrated that the main target of the off-balance sheet financing form of creative accounting is to remove assets and related liabilities from a company's balance sheet to improve the company's perceived financial position and to keep the true economic benefits of assets and the economic costs of liabilities undisclosed.

Thus, it seems that both in the United Kingdom and the United States, there is concern at the professional level. In both countries it is accepted that creative accounting has the potential to mislead users of financial statements. Unless the problem is considered and a conceptual framework set which addresses criteria for recognizing assets, liabilities, revenues, expenses, gains, losses and investment, the purpose of accounting reports might be distorted.

Even with such a treatment the accountants might still face difficulties in distinguishing between 'plain' business transactions that can be impounded in the balance sheet and complex transactions that are not presently within the confine of items that may be reported in the balance sheet. For example, if a company agrees to sell specific assets at the end of its fiscal year (this might appear to be a genuine business transaction), and if this is followed by an arrangement to repurchase these assets in the next accounting period, this will give birth to creative accounting. This difficulty was demonstrated by the chairman of the working party, set up to look into the creative accounting problem, when he was quoted by *Accountancy* (October 1985, p. 4) as saying 'if you do not look at the two [i.e 'plain' versus 'complex' transactions] together then the cases you're aiming at drop into a hole between the two.'

Undoubtedly, creative accounting represents a challenging problem and it requires an active solution. The next section will discuss the UK accounting profession's responses to the problem.

THE ACCOUNTING PROFESSION'S RESPONSE

According to Peasnell (1989), the American accounting profession has been dealing with the creative accounting problem for the last two decades. In the United Kingdom, since the issuance of SSAP 21, the accounting profession's interest in creative accounting has increased. In (1985), the ICAEW set up a working group to look into the creative accounting problem. The first task of the working group was to try to define off-balance sheet financing and window dressing. In February 1986, the ICAEW issued Technical Release TR 603. The technical release argued that the economic substance rather than the legal form of a business transaction should be considered when determining its true nature and thus the appropriate accounting treatment. A business transaction should be included in the financial statements on the basis of its economic substance, but with the legal form of the transaction also being disclosed. However, the release is intended to be persuasive in considering whether a company's financial statement showed a true and fair view as required by section 228 (2) of the *Companies Act 1985*. This requirement overrides that of schedule 4, which contains detailed rules on the form and content of a company's financial statements, and all other requirements of the Act as to the matters to be included in a company's financial statements. Where a 'true and fair view' override is used to depart from other provisions of the *Companies Act 1985*, the financial statements must disclose particulars of the departure, the reasons for it, and its effects in accordance with section 228 (6). Hence, the release proposes that, in order to present a true and fair view, it is important to recognize the substance of a transaction in the financial statements. Consequently, to ensure compliance with section 228 (6), the release stated that the legal form of the transaction will need to be disclosed in the notes to the financial statements. However, it is important to mention that there is no definition in the Companies Act as to what is meant by 'a true and fair view'.

To stress the strength of problems associated with the use of creative accounting techniques, in April 1988 an Exposure Draft ED 42 entitled *Accounting for Special Purpose Transactions* was issued for comment by the Accounting Standards Committee. The title to ED 42 is what the ASC previously referred to as 'off-balance sheet financing and window dressing'. ED 42 tried to answer the questions that followed the issuance of TR 603 by the ICAEW's Technical Committee. The ASC chairman (Michael Renshall) stated (*Accountancy Age*, 10 March 1988) that:

> We are trying to establish the types of analysis we expect preparers and auditors to carry out when they identify one of these special purpose transactions. They need to analyse the commercial effects of these transactions with special care. So the solution we have provided is a conceptual one.

Although there are many examples of creative accounting in existence, only SSAP 17 *Accounting for Post Balance Sheet Events* (1980) provides an answer for one type of window dressing and SSAP 21 *Accounting for Lease and Hire Purchase Contracts* provides a solution for leasing as a form of off-balance sheet financing (the preceding chapter suggests that, even after the issuance of SSAP 21, off-balance sheet financing is still being practised).

Unlike almost every other accounting standard, ED 42 did not prescribe specific treatments which must be adopted by all companies. The Exposure Draft dealt with special purpose transactions whose true intention and commercial effect may not be immediately obvious. The draft placed emphasis on identifying the substance of the transaction, and on the aspects and implications of the transaction that are likely to have commercial effect in practice. To determine the commercial effect, the draft suggested that it is important to view how a special purpose transaction affects the recorded assets and liabilities. Regarding the company's assets, it is important to identify whether a special purpose transaction has affected the company's control of future benefits or future risk underlying the benefits. Likewise, it is important to identify what effect the special purpose transaction has on liabilities and whether the transaction results in a possible future sacrifice of economic benefits by transferring assets or providing services to other enterprises in the future. Assets and liabilities relating to special purpose transactions should be re-assessed using generally accepted accounting and measurement criteria and, if appropriate under these criteria, should be re-included in the company's balance sheet. Hence, to ensure that the effects of the special purpose transaction on the assets, liabilities, or profit and loss accounts, can be appreciated by the users of the financial statements, additional disclosure to the financial statements is necessary. In addition, the Exposure Draft indicated that the existence of a controlled non-subsidiary creates a presumption that there are special circumstances that need to be treated in the group's financial statements in the same way as a legally defined subsidiary. The Exposure Draft also suggested that a summary of non-subsidiary financial statements should be given in the notes to the group's financial statements. On the other hand, if a special purpose transaction does not need to be reported in the financial statements, the Draft stated that it is necessary to include in the notes information on the nature of the transaction to make sure that the financial statements are giving a true and fair view. The preliminary consideration of the ASC is to support the following basic issues:

1. Consolidation of all entities that are effectively controlled without looking at their activities.

2. Accounting transactions should be dealt with in accordance with substance not their legal form.

3. Disclosure in the notes can contribute to a distorted balance sheet.

4. Accounting effects should be consistent with economic effects.

ED 42 attempted to reduce the amount of assets and liabilities that have been excluded from a company's financial statements. However, ED 42 adopted a broad approach intended to apply to many transactions rather than deal with individual cases like SSAP 21. In this respect, Mitchell (1988) contended that the UK proposal ED 42 is radically different from the US approach which provides more detailed requirements for specific financial issues. It recommended that disclosure should reflect the true commercial effect of such transactions and not be dictated by their strict legal form. ED 42 stated that:

> the purpose of this proposed statement is to clarify principles and particularly the essential characteristics of assets and liabilities in order that a general body of recognition and measurement criteria can be applied in determining appropriate accounting treatment.

It attempts to help financial report readers understand a company's progress and its financial position. Its interest to the reader of financial reports is obvious in its definition of substance. According to ED 42 accounting for substance means that 'a transaction's accounting treatment should fairly reflect its commercial effect'. The focus of interest is the stock of assets less liabilities reported by the company. The ED states that:

> a key element in determining the substance of a transaction is to identify whether the transaction has increased or decreased the various assets of liabilities previously recognized in the accounts of the enterprises and whether it has given rise to assets or liabilities not previously recognized.

Therefore, determining the substance is related to the interest of readers in the stock of assets.

The preference of 'substance' over the form of transactions in assets and liabilities as a basis of constructing and reporting financial statements becomes more apparent when, in May 1990, the ASC published Exposure Draft 49 (1990) *Reflecting the Substance of Transactions in Assets and Liabilities*. ED 49 does not seek to replace ED 42, it supplements and enhances the principles enunciated in ED 21.

The new draft requires that the accounting treatment of complex transactions in assets and liabilities should reflect fairly their commercial effects. Since the publication of ED 42 the ASC has chosen to adopt the IASC's conceptual framework. Hence ED 49, like the IASC's framework, chose to define an asset as a resource controlled by an enterprise from which future economic benefits are expected to flow and a liability as a present obligation likely to result in the outflow of future economic benefit for the enterprise. The Draft also addressed the concept of control over assets and liabilities as well as over subsidiaries. According to the Draft, the control over a source (assets or liabilities) can be determined through the ability to obtain future economic benefits or bear economic costs associated with the source. On the other hand, control over subsidiaries is defined as the ability to exercise the required power necessary to determine the financial and operating policies of the subsidiary. However, ED 49 admitted that, in many off-balance sheet financing schemes, it is difficult to identify control. Hence, evidence on the source of control may be related to the ability to restrict others' access to future benefits.

ED 49 also adopted a generic approach rather than the provision of specified rules which can be manipulated. This approach has been criticized by Whiteley (1990) who believes that it would be difficult to implement. Pimm (1991) shows that the implementation of ED 49 would result in three main difficulties concerned with exposure to risk. First, accountants will put more emphasis on risk associated with ownership. Second, this may require recognition from the ASB in the accounting standards that follow ED 49. Third, theoretical analysis is needed to make sure that accountants can portray risk. Hence, the ED 49 test of control over future economic benefits may result in a wrong answer. In Pimm's opinion, the accountant's task is the determination of profit not the portrayal of risk. Gibbons and Freedman (1991) argue that the implementation of ED 49 may result in a conflict between the accounting and legal analysis of a transaction.

Another source of misunderstanding in ED 42 is the accounting treatment of financing schemes with or without recourse. According to ED 42,

> an accounting treatment results in the inclusion of an item in the profit and loss account or balance sheet in such a way as to affect the amount stated under the appropriate heading and the total.

In the United Kingdom there is a little professional guidance on how to assess a transaction and to identify off-balance sheet financing and window dressing and what should be included in the balance sheet. In this respect, Morgan (1989) illustrated that the question of recourse can be used as a central factor in classifying off-balance sheet accounting schemes. Schemes without recourse are straightforward because the effect is to take one asset off the balance sheet and replace it with another (e.g., the factoring of receivables means that debtors are removed and replaced by cash). Schemes which allow recourse are more problematical because of the need for adequate provision or contingent liability recognition.

Peasnell and Yaansah (1988) consider an off-balance sheet financing scheme as:

> a transaction with two characteristics. Firstly, the events involved in setting up such a scheme are 'similar' in some respects to a conventional decision to purchase resources with borrowed money. Secondly, the liability does not have to be reported on the company's balance sheet.

However, in examining accounting for off-balance sheet financing and window dressing a true and fair view must be considered and ED 42 showed two possible approaches which the ASC (now ASB) could adopt in a future standard on the issue. It could specify an accounting solution or it could require an accounting disclosure of the transaction or the arrangement concerned. The reporting company should be aware of the provisions of the Companies Act (1985) on the need to assure that any such information presents a true and fair view of the underlying transaction or arrangement.

In rare cases, where the accounting treatment would not comply with the Companies Act, the arrangement or the solution should be reflected in the financial statement by means of full disclosure. This should include not just the nature of the transaction but also the full extent of any assets from all or a substantial part of the economic benefit and the corresponding liabilities, actual or contingent, which are created. ED 42 went on to show that in certain cases this may best be achieved by presenting performance accounts. Nevertheless, one may ask whether the true and fair view requirement solves the problem associated with creative accounting.

Grace (1988) demonstrated that creative accounting is inconsistent with the obligation to give a true and fair view. In *Accountancy* (1987) the Law Society agreed with the objectives of Technical Release 603 (discussed below), but not with the proposed solution. They contended that the use of substance over form would give rise to unacceptable subjectivity, resulting in accounting treatments that contradict the law and make legal analysis of financial statements difficult. Hence, lawyers prefer what they call 'adventurous restatement' to be kept at a bare minimum. The justification of this is shown in the Law Society's analysis of the purpose and the functions of accounts. In contrast, Tweedie and Kellas (1987) argued that if the Society's views were to be accepted, financial reporting would be set back to the era before the advent of a true and fair concept. Actually, the corporate report (ASC 1975) was clear in this respect. It stated that corporate reports should give recognition to economic substance over legal and technical forms. Because many substance and form issues coincide and few do not, accountants stress substance rather than the form to offer information which reflects the economic activities reported. The focus on substance is more realistic than that of the legal form. However, as Tweedie and Kellas (1987) affirm, if the Law Society's advice concerning the treatment of creative accounting is accepted, creative accounting would grow; accounting development in the United Kingdom would be paralysed for years to come; the reader of financial statements would be provided with misleading information; and accountants would be brought into disrepute.

Indeed, the question to be asked is not whether the true and fair view obligation would solve the problem associated with creative accounting, but whether the true and fair view obligation permits substance over form. It depends on how you define true and fair view. The legalistic approach would say that unless something is legally owned (e.g. an asset) it should not be reported as though it were. On the other hand, a true and fair view might not mean 'legally' true but true in terms of economic reality. In this case legal ownership of the asset would be irrelevant and the test of economic benefit would determine whether to include the asset in a company's balance sheet or not.

THE ARGUMENTS FOR AND AGAINST TR 603, ED 42 AND ED 49

The Law Society's Standing Committee on Company Law issued memorandum (1987) *Off-Balance Sheet Financing and Window Dressing* that disagreed with the solution proposed by TR 603 for two primary reasons:

1. The argument about substituting substance over form is dangerous and undesirable.

2. The juxtaposition of off-balance sheet financing and window dressing leads to a misleading impression; such transactions are likely to fall foul of the true and fair requirements. To treat all off-balance sheet financing in the same way as misleading window dressing is deemed to be confusing.

The Law Society goes further to explain its views and identifies three categories of transactions incorporating creative accounting:

(a) Transactions which if reflected in the accounts at face value will result in the account not showing a true and fair view;

(b) Transactions in respect of which it is considered that strict compliance with sch.4, Companies Act 1985 will result in inadequate information being given in the accounts; and

(c) Transactions where the true legal effect is different from what it appears to be.

The accountant will find it difficult to obtain clear guidance on how to identify creative accounting from the Law Society's three categories. Tweedie and Kellas (1987) argued that in category (a) the Society insists on a true and fair view and in category (b) asks for more information, but they gave no indication as to which particular circumstances require disclosure in note form rather adjustment of balance sheet figures. Tweedie and Kellas went on to say that category (c) is simply confusing, 'we do not fully understand the term true legal effect'. Be that as it may, the Law Society believes that additional disclosure is the remedy to creative accounting without specifying the sort and quality of information and how it promotes the function of the accounts. On the other hand, the IASC's framework (1989) states that if information is to represent faithfully the transactions and other events that it purports to represent, it is necessary that they are accounted for and presented in accordance with their substance and economic reality and not merely with their legal form. In this respect, it is important to mention that in the United States, Canada and Australia the reporting requirement is only for faithful representation.

Aldwinkle (1987) responds to Tweedie and Kellas' criticisms. He affirmed that the issue is not a simplistic one of a battle between accountants and lawyers. The Law Society's disagreement is not with the objectives but with the actual solution proposed. Aldwinkle proceeds further to say that the technical solution was an opening shot and, as Tweedie and Kellas themselves admit, it is not perfect. What matters is that imperfection is recognized so that a satisfactory and workable solution can be found. Wild (1987a) supported the argument of Tweedie and Kellas and rejected the Law Society announcement on the Institute Technical Release 603. Wild (1987a) believes creative accounting is more difficult than any accounting problem and it puts the purpose of preparing the accounts under attack. Accordingly, the accounting profession body is attempting to stop something being taken away (off-balance sheet financing) which they expect to be there. Wild continues to say that:

> The Law Society's call for objectivity and certainty in accounts indicates, I believe, a desire to protect the integrity of accounts. But the extent of its emphasis on objectivity is misplaced. Unless we can find a way forward together, both the accountants and the lawyers are likely to leave the accountants easy prey to those with no real interest in the law.

The debate on how to form an accounting standard to cope with off-balance sheet financing and window dressing seems to attract the Accounting Standard Committee towards setting a well-defined conceptual framework. This can be seen in the issuance of ED 42. ED 42 addresses those transactions associated with artificial devices designed by companies to achieve the special purpose of keeping debts hidden, and the aim of the Exposure Draft is to prevent such schemes. The main thrust of ED 42 and ED 49 is the suggestion of operational guide-lines that can help in resolving individual creative accounting problems. The questions then are, whether it is effective to have a conceptual approach as a regulatory instrument; whether the application of the conceptual basis would exclude the need for dealing with specific issues; and whether the ED would generate more and new issues.

Walton and Wyman (1988) believe that some answers may be inferred from the US experience and this does not give ground for optimism. The experience of the conceptual framework concept was that it created problems for accountants. This can be clearly noted when dealing with deferred tax as a type of liability. After liabilities have been defined, it became evident that deferred tax did not meet the definition. Subsequently, the deferred tax standard was revised. However, Peasnell and Yaansah (1988) describe the issuance of ED 42 as a bold attempt to address the conceptual issues, but they believe that such an approach will raise more questions than answers. Walton and Wyman (1988) argued that:

> 'if the conceptual framework is to serve a useful purpose, it should inform accounting decisions. But if the conceptual framework does not avoid the need for very specific standards and is regularly set aside on individual questions as the

US experience suggests, it inevitably falls into disrepute – and considerable resources have been wasted in debating, adopting and disseminating it.

Peasnell and Yaansah (1988) demonstrated that the problematic area of the proposed standards is the reliance placed on a true and fair view, particularly where this requires a departure from the provision of the Companies Act. A related difficulty is the attempt to deal, in one standard, with both types of off-balance sheet financing schemes, i.e. those involving the use of related companies, and those that do not. They suggested the possibility of dealing with the related company schemes by an amendment to the relevant scheme of Companies Act 1989 and the revision of SSAP 1 and SSAP 14. Samuels *et al.* (1989) considered the Draft as a brave step at dealing with a complicated problem, but they believe that there will be situations where the Draft cannot be applied. In choosing a more general approach, the proposed ED 42 is in harmony with European legal attitudes and practices as well as continuing the UK tradition from which the idea of the true and fair view derives. Similarly, Cook (1989) stated that:

> ED 42 represents one attempt to grapple with an old but newly proliferating problem by newly elaborated concepts and principles in the context of a new framework of European law.

Cook (1989) went on to report that some 200 pages from 55 respondents were received as comments on the ED 42 proposals and the most frequent comments were that the Draft does not include sufficient guidance, its disclosure requirements are too broad and the consideration of controlled non-subsidiary is best left to statute. In addition, the proposal only considers balance sheet items and does not discuss profit and loss account items. The DTI, according to Cook (1989), gives strong support to the inclusion of passages dealing with controlled non-subsidiaries, not withstanding that the implication of the Seventh Directive would shift the boundary between what is and what is not subsidiary. This issue has been clarified in the CA 1989.

In fact, if the disclosures requirements of ED 42 are accepted, differences will remain on whether they should be reported by way of notes to the accounts, or whether their financial effect should appear in the income statement or balance sheet. The Law Society, which represents the disclosure school, believes that reference to the transaction by using a note is quite sufficient. The argument they used is that objectivity in accounting can be maintained by complying strictly with the legal form of the transaction rather than dealing with the transaction as a whole. Strict disclosure by way of a note might be a simple task compared with the attempt to quantify the financial effects of transactions Aldwinkle (1987).

It is also argued that special purpose transactions should be reported in the income statement and balance sheet because they are important to assess the firm's financial position and also that the account's users might not expect to find important information in the notes to the accounts. Moreover, users give more attention to the information reported in the income statement and balance sheet. Furthermore, the main task of the accounts is to provide the reader with the best possible simple understanding of the company's progress and financial position. This cannot be attained by simply noting transactions in the small prints of the 'notes' section and leaving the financial effect of such transactions to the readers' predictions.

More importantly, Peasnell and Yaansah (1988) pointed out that ED 42 and the accounting literature neglect the issue of recourse (provision of a guarantee or options on another entity) which arises in many off-balance sheet schemes. ED 42 also failed to answer the question 'should the off-setting of liabilities against assets be permitted?'

However, the ASB seem determined to minimize the use of creative accounting. In July 1992 the ASB issued a proposal *The Elements of Financial Statements and the Recognition of items in Financial Statements*. According to *Accountancy Age* (July 1992) the proposal defines assets as 'rights or other access to future tangible economic benefits controlled by an entity as a result of past transactions and events'. Liabilities are defined as 'obligations to transfer economic benefits as a result of past transactions or events'.

The ASB definition of assets and liabilities and when to report them in the financial statements will make it difficult to distinguish between operating and finance lease where the former is not reported now on the balance sheet. The ASB proposal will also force companies to write off reorganization costs on acquisition directly to the profit and loss account rather than to the acquisition reserves.

Accountancy Age (July 1992) believes that the suggested proposal will force many companies to report contracts for full performance where the related parties have the rights and obligations under the contract.

In short, current legal uncertainty in the United Kingdom is preventing accountants from doing what they feel is essential and right to ensure that the financial statements give useful information to the users. The key solution appears to be the adoption of the concept of substance of transaction prevailing over the form, and setting specific standards for particular devices of creative accounting. Thus, the accountants are not merely permitted, but required, to look through the legal or the structured form of the transaction to the economic substance. This is superseded by the IASC's conceptual framework (1989).

However, at this stage it might be beneficial to define creative accounting and to bring up the causes of its growing popularity. This is the intention of the next section.

CREATIVE ACCOUNTING DEFINITION AND THE CAUSE OF ITS GROWING POPULARITY

1. Creative Accounting Definition

Creative accounting is an activity that defies easy definition. The flexibility in accounting measurement and disclosure rules have always permitted some degree of creativity. Thus, creative accounting can range from a genuine attempt to present a true and fair view, through to the more doubtful practices of off-balance sheet financing and window dressing. However, creative accounting may be defined as (1) the process of manipulating accounting figures by taking advantage of the loopholes in accounting rules and the choices of measurement and disclosure practices in them to transform financial statements from what they should be, to what preparers would prefer to see reported, and (2) the process by which transactions are structured so as to produce the required accounting results rather than reporting transactions in a neutral and consistent way.

2. The Cause of the Increase in the Practice of Creative Accounting

The flexibility and the inconsistency of the existing accounting conventions coupled with legal requirements are merged together to permit a variety of alternative practices to co-exist. This can result in tailor-made accounting to meet the individual needs of a company, so that the financial statements give a misguided or unrepresentative impression of its financial position. An innocent observer might ask why a company would want to do such a thing. The answer gives the key to creative accounting's growing popularity.

The following factors may motivate managers to adopt creative accounting schemes:

(a) Misinformation, signalling and financial motives

Peasnell and Yaansah (1988) distinguished between the misinformation and signalling motives and financial motives to establish creative accounting schemes. Misinformation means being economical with the truth by reporting correct but incomplete information.

On the other hand, as Peasnell and Yaansah (1988) argued, creative accounting schemes are far from being uninformative, and give management a cost-effective way of signalling certain kinds of information to the capital markets. Companies might report their superior information if, and only if, they feel it is beneficial to do so. As discussed below, preparers of accounts, as agents in charge of company's resources, have economic and political incentives to disclose financial information concerning their progress and financial position in order to maintain the confidence of the users of their accounts. Companies may have the incentive to hide information so as to help their financial statements. The balance sheet provides, among other things, information concerning the total economic resources available to the company and how these resources are financed. Companies can finance their resources through debt or equity sources. The proportion of companies' debt to equity is generally referred to as capital structure. The gearing ratio derived from the balance sheet and the interest cover from the income statement are used for the purpose of assessing the capital structure of the company. A company can employ creative accounting to improve its financial ratios.

(b) The agency and the political cost incentives

The cause of creative accounting can also be explained by using the political and contracting (agency) costs, as discussed in the section on the positive accounting theory in Chapter 2. The positive accounting researchers apply economic theories which assume non-zero cost of contracts. The costs associated with contracts explain the differences in accounting procedures used by a firm. The costs also explain the time of adopting specific accounting procedures. The positive accounting researchers argue that any adopted accounting procedure will affect the cash flow of the firm's manager. Hence, the choice of procedures depends on the political process of cash flow effects and contracting. In general, researchers use the compensation plan and debt contracts to generate hypotheses about the difference in the accounting procedures used by firms and industries. Compensation plans are usually based on earnings. In this case, one should expect management to use procedures which affect reported earnings. The management will try to play around with accounting figures to meet its requirements in maintaining high levels of compensation. However, any attempt to play around with accounting figures is expected by the stock market and consequently restrictions might be imposed on the accounting procedures used by the manager.

In fact, it is difficult to totally restrict a manager's choice of accounting procedures. The manager could justify the use of any accounting procedure on the grounds that the adopted procedure provides better information to the users. The manager may also justify the use of specific accounting procedures on the grounds that the cost associated with government regulation is different from one procedure to another and he adopts this procedure to minimize the firm's costs.

Thus, creative accounting is likely to occur, as far as the compensation plan is concerned, and the only possible solution to this problem is to restrict the use of accounting procedures available to management. However, this might not be consistent with the flexibility feature of the present accounting system which takes into consideration the varied nature of businesses. In addition, the contracting and monitoring methods that are used to restrict the manager's choice among accounting procedures might prove to be expensive and thus any attempt to eliminate manipulation becomes difficult. Moreover, managers have the ability to adopt accounting procedures that affect earnings without attracting the auditor's attention. Furthermore, the incentive schemes in the compensation plan are often related to a stated accounting standard of performance determinable by an agreed accounting framework. If earnings exceed the stated standard, the manager is more likely to defer part of the earnings to increase the expected future bonuses (reporting high earnings might raise the standard). If the earnings are below the standard, the manager will take what is called 'a big bath'. Healy (1985) demonstrated that, if the firm has sustained losses, managers may increase losses by including all possible future losses that they can wipe off, that is, take a big bath to generate high levels of earnings in the future and therefore good bonuses. Thus, creative accounting is likely to occur if the earnings are below or exceed the stated standard.

Another reason which may motivate the manager to employ creative accounting is the covenants that use accounting numbers. In this respect, Watts and Zimmerman (1986) demonstrated that such covenants put restrictions on the manager and the manager tries to avoid these restrictions. The contract may put a restriction on dividends. The constraint prevents the manager from paying liquidating dividends. The contract may put a restriction on merger activities. This prevents the manager from entering into a merger with a riskier firm. In other cases, the contract might allow the manager to enter into a merger (if the tangible assets after the merger meet a minimum threshold of long-term debt). This prevents the manager from increasing the level of debts and puts a limit on the debt levels. The contract may also require the maintenance of working capital (the current assets exceed current liabilities). In addition, the contract may prevent the manager from investing in other firms – but to change the firm's risk the manager may need to invest in other firms. However, in some cases constraints allow for investment until the net tangible assets reach specific levels or do not exceed specific levels of equity and long-term debt. Furthermore, covenants may put restrictions on the disposition of assets. If disposition is allowed, it might be restricted to a specific amount, or there might be a requirement that the proceeds should be used to buy new fixed assets or retire liabilities. These constraints are used to prevent the management from changing the firm's risks and reducing its ability to pay liquidating dividends. Covenants may also restrict additional debt (a covenant may not permit the debt of higher priority) or, if it permits, the existing debt priority should be equal to that of newly issued debt.

Ironically, loan covenants pose significant stumbling blocks for accounting for financial arrangements according to their substance. A loan covenant imposes specific restrictions on any additional debt a company may incur (in the case where the covenant specifies a debt to equity ratio). To help raise new capital or finance new acquisitions, a company may employ off-balance sheet financing schemes. The company may also adopt off-balance sheet financing instruments to improve the financing options and flexibility. However, similar to the accounting-based compensation plans, the accounting-based debt covenants will be effective only if some restrictions are placed on the manager's abilities to control the calculation of accounting numbers (manager's choice of accounting procedures to be restricted). For instance, companies with debt contracts are more likely to choose earnings- and assets-increasing accounting procedures (e.g. the straight-line method of depreciation) than firms with no debt. If the restriction put on the firm is to control the ratio of interest to earnings, it is more likely that the firm will adopt the straight-line method of depreciation on the assumption that the straight-line method increases earnings.

Watts and Zimmerman (1986) provided examples of hypotheses that explain how managers might react to restrictions. For this purpose bonus and debt to equity ratio are examined. The bonus hypothesis expects that managers with bonus plans are likely to choose procedures which will increase earnings. Similarly, the debt to equity hypothesis expects managers to choose procedures that increase earnings.

Accounting procedures can also affect the firm's cash flows via the political process as well as the contracting process. As mentioned earlier, the political process is a competition between individuals for wealth transfers. The firm is subject to wealth transfers under this process. In this situation, the manager is likely to adopt accounting procedures that reduce the reported earnings to get away from any political pressures. The question to be raised is, 'If accounting numbers are used in this process, then what incentives are available for the manager when choosing among accounting procedures?'

Watts and Zimmerman (1986) presented examples of incentives produced by the political process regarding choice of accounting procedures. One of these incentives is the asymmetric loss function. This leads economists to believe that the motive to create information in the political process and the cost of information cause a bias in the pronouncements issued by standard setters. The asymmetric loss can be seen if a company went bankrupt and its assets were over-valued. In this case, the standard-setters (SEC, FASB, ASB) are likely to be blamed. On the other hand, in a case where the company operates successfully and its assets were understated, it will generate little attention from investors. This asymmetric loss may lead the (ASC and SEC) bureaucrats to eliminate the potential source of overstatement of assets and to keep the source of understatement. This constraint might motivate the firm's manager to choose accounting procedures that raise the value of assets (straight-line method of depreciation). Thus, the asymmetric loss is a product of information costs.

The use of reported earnings by politicians and regulators is hypothesized to provide corporate managers with an incentive to adopt accounting procedures that reduce reported earnings (accelerated method of depreciation). Lower reported earnings reduce government pressure (tax) on the company and may increase its subsidies to the firm. As long as monitoring procedures used to restrict the reporting company's choice between accounting procedures is an expensive one, the company is expected to continue adopting accounting procedures that would reduce the reported earnings. Likewise, income tax affects the manager's choice among accounting procedures. In this respect, Morse and Richardson (1983) stated that, because inventory valuation affects income taxes, the corporate manager takes into consideration the tax effects when making his choice. This might give an explanation as to why companies tend to switch from the FIFO to the LIFO method of inventory valuation at the time of inflation. In this respect, Argenti (1976) pointed out that companies do not want their results to look better. The more profits a company reports the more tax it pays and the unions will put pressure on the company to increase wages. However, Argenti (1976) demonstrated that a company tries to improve its results in order to maintain high stock prices or to get a loan.

Similarly, where the prices or rates that can be changed are regulated this might affect the manager's choice among accounting procedures. Where accounting numbers are used to determine the prices or rates there is an incentive for the corporate manager to adopt accounting procedures which result in favourable rates and prices.

The political process might also produce an incentive to reduce the variance of reported earning changes. In general, the outsider computes the percentage change in earnings over the same past periods and therefore corporate managers will have the incentive to reduce the variance of reported earnings by adopting appropriate accounting procedures.

The accounting researchers in this area (e.g. Gagon, 1967; Watts and Zimmerman, 1978) assume that large firms are more politically sensitive than small firms and therefore practise various incentives in their choice of accounting procedures. Alchain and Kessel (1962) and Jensen and Meckling (1978) suggest that large firms with high profits fear greater government action. Accounting researchers use the firm size to test the firm's political sensitivity and the manager's incentives to choose procedures which reduce earnings (the size hypothesis in the positive accounting theory context). The size hypothesis assumes that large firms are more sensitive and relatively larger wealth transfers (political costs) are imposed on them than smaller firms. Zimmerman (1983) considered this assumption by examining the empirical relationship between corporate tax rate (a component of the political costs) and the firm's size. He found that large firms incurred high tax rates (political costs). Yet, large firms may receive more political benefits (such as government contracts, import restrictions on competing products, etc.), that offset higher tax rates. Ball and Foster (1982) indicated that, beside the firm's size, its industry may affect the political process. Thus, finding a statistical association between the firm's size and the accounting procedures employed may be due to the industry. In addition, Peltzman (1976) believes that government regulation tends to vary over the business cycle, and this could be another factor that affects the size hypotheses.

The above discussion illustrates that the incentives provided by the political process are in direct opposition to the incentives provided by management compensation contracts to increase earnings. However, both sets of incentives are used to reduce the variance in the reported earnings and managers trade off the costs and benefits of alternative procedures. In this respect, Zimijewski and Hagerman (1981) studied the firm's portfolio of procedures. They found evidence consistent with three simple variables that have been relatively widely tested: the bonus plan, debt to equity and the size hypothesis. If a firm has an earning-based compensation (bonus) plan, a large debt to equity ratio or big size (assets), it is more likely to choose current-earnings increasing procedures. Studies of single procedure choice also found evidence consistent with debt to equity and size hypothesis. Their evidence on the bonus plan hypothesis is mixed.

(c) Poor Management

In his study of corporate collapse, Argenti (1976) connected the use of creative accounting with poor management. He believes that poor management tends to neglect the system of accounting information and it will not respond to change. Poor management is likely to involve high levels of gearing so that a crisis becomes a continuous threat. As a result of that, financial ratios deteriorate. When a company reaches this stage Argenti believes that it will start using creative accounting to reduce the predictive nature of these ratios.

Be that as it may, the mechanism that brings creative accounting into play is simple. If a company failed to maintain good performance then it is likely to expect lenders to move towards tightening their credit terms, suppliers may ask the company to pay cash on or before delivery, and customers may run away. In this situation, the manager will try to put up a smoke screen by presenting his/her accounts in the most optimistic shape possible. By employing creative accounting, Argenti believes that the manager is taking a defensive position and his refusal to admit any failure is possibly part of the normal psychological tool, which accounts for his refusal to accept any advice or his belief that 'clouds will roll away'. However, Argenti (1976) presented 18 examples of creative accounting a company may employ to make it look better than it really is (see Argenti, 1976, pp. 141-2). Argenti concluded that creative accounting becomes one of the symptoms of impending failure. He contended that the creative accounting phenomenon is almost invariably associated with failure and companies adopt it to postpone the evil day.

(d) Reducing Uncertainty and Risk

According to Goodfellow (1988) creative accounting schemes are employed as a result of increased volatility in the related market elements, interest, inflation, and exchange rates. The movement, by market forces, from fixed currency to floating exchange rates resulted in greater uncertainty. In addition, the sharp increase in inflation rates merged together with the growing change of interest and currency rates fuelled the problem. In fact, one may argue that, without the related uncertainty associated with the exchange markets, the traditional financing methods (issuance of bonds or equity) may still be in use and companies would have no need to use forward contracts. It is obvious that, when a company is facing volatility and uncertainty, it becomes highly motivated to adopt instruments to reduce the associated risks.

(e) The Weakness of the Current Accounting Concepts
Particularly Under Inflation

It can be argued that the most important incentive for creative accounting is the weakness of the current accounting concepts underlying the preparation and presentation of accounts. In this respect, Dieter and Watt (1980) argued that the main reason for the growing popularity of off-balance sheet financing schemes is that the existing concepts underlying accounting for liabilities are ill-equipped to deal with the increasingly sophisticated financing methods being practised today. Stewart and Neuhausen (1986) took the same position when they argued that off-balance sheet financing schemes arise because the financial arrangements associated with these schemes are not addressed in the accounting literature. Samuels *et al.* (1989) demonstrated that some creative accounting techniques are designed to take advantage of the lack of accounting rules or the conflict between existing rules. Hence, off-balance sheet financing schemes are likely to be adopted to take advantage of the current accounting concepts.

Another possible motive for the use of off-balance sheet financing schemes (under the historic cost accounting system) is the failure of historic cost accounting to deal effectively with inflation. Argenti (1976) indicated that accounting is a somewhat flexible set of rules made even more flexible by inflation. Under inflation, the historical cost balance sheet figures are below their current values. For instance, during inflation, companies employ the LIFO method to account for inventory costs, to lower tax and to eliminate the effects of price fluctuations on inventory and profits. Under LIFO, the carrying amount of inventory during the period of inflation diverges increasingly from their current values. The carrying value of the depreciable assets shows similar disparity under inflation. Companies that use LIFO costing for inventory and accelerated methods for depreciation will often carry amounts for inventory, property, plant and equipment that are much lower than their current values. As an offset to these lower values, some managements believe that part of the debt does not have to be reported. In other words, if assets were reported at current values, less pressure would exist for off-balance sheet financing arrangements. In this case, the difference between the current values and the carrying values will be added to the stockholders' equity section of the balance sheet. As a consequence, using the debt to equity relation, firms would have an additional capacity to carry increased liabilities. In the same fashion, to the extent that the loan covenant is related to the debt–equity ratio, such a covenant would be easily met if the current values are used to report the accounting figures and this tends to permit companies to embark on new capital replacement or expansion programmes by adopting traditional arrangements.

(f) Pressure from Big Institutional Investors

It could be argued that the users of financial statements may contribute to the use of creative accounting. Pressure from big institutional investors, and the move to attract wider share ownership by more investors, may encourage the companies to manipulate their performance to satisfy the demand of the stock market. The stock market looks for a steady growth in retained earnings. To live with stock market expectations, companies may become involved in the use of creative accounting (Griffiths, 1986).

SUMMARY AND CONCLUSION

The ill-defined concepts that underlie the preparation and the presentation of financial reports together with the agency costs associated with the political process are the main factors which motivate the use of creative accounting. The existing standards still fall short because of the free choice of treatment permitted and the absence of standards on certain topics. In an attempt to tackle the problem, either detailed standards rules or general guidance standards are suggested. The former leaves no room for interpretation, although preparers argue that particular cases are outside specific rules. On the other hand, judgement allows more cases to be brought within a standard, but allows individuals the freedom in application of guidance (this is to apply the true and fair over-ride).

REVIEW QUESTIONS

1. It is argued that creative accounting casts doubt on the purpose of preparing financial statements. Discuss the consequences of the continued use of creative accounting.

2. The accounting profession has been dealing with the issue of creative accounting for the last two decades. Critically analyze the accounting profession's attempts to combat the problem.

3. Discuss the contents of the TR 603 and highlight its weaknesses.

4. One of the main shortcomings of ED 42 is that it adopts a broad approach to the solution of complex transactions accounting. Show how this represents a problem for ED 42.

5. Evaluate the argument used by the Law Society to criticize TR 603, ED 42 and ED 49.

6. Show how the flexibility and the inconsistency of the existing accounting principles, coupled with the legal requirements, combines to permit the use of creative accounting.

7. Use agency theory to explain the use of creative accounting.

8. Creative accounting is looked upon as a symptom of poor management. Discuss.

9. Show how companies may use schemes of creative accounting to reduce uncertainty and risk.

10. Schemes of creative accounting are encouraged by the conventional accounting system operating under inflation. State the extent to which you agree or disagree with this opinion.

CHAPTER 5

Accounting for Short-term Investment and Trade Debtors

INTRODUCTION

Investments are usually classified as short term (temporary, marketable) and long term. Short-term investments consist of marketable government securities and marketable equity securities (preferred and ordinary). They are reported on the balance sheet as current assets. Short-term investment should meet the following two conditions:

1. Be readily marketable.

2. Be held with an intent to convert them into cash within one year or the operating cycle, whichever is longer.

VALUATION OF SHORT-TERM INVESTMENTS

As with other assets, short-term investments are recorded at cost when acquired plus any brokerage or tax fees. According to FAS Statement No. 12,

> Cost refers to the original cost of marketable equity security unless a new cost basis has been assigned based on recognition of an implement that was deemed other than temporary or as the result of a transfer between current and non-current classification.

Because short-term securities are traded regularly, their historical costs are not as important as their market value prior to sale. The market price of a marketable security usually changes as transactions involving the security occur. The main problem facing the accountant is how to reflect the value of such securities in the balance sheet. In general, one of the following methods might be employed:

1. Cost

2. Market

3. Lower of cost or market (LCM)

1. Valuation at Cost Price

FASB Statement No. 12, when strictly applied, does not apply to debt securities held as short-term investments. Such securities can be accounted for at cost. When debt security is acquired as a short-term investment, accrued interest from the last interest date of acquisition must be recognized.

2. Valuation at Market Value

Many accountants are unhappy with FASB No. 12. They argue that market value whether higher or lower than cost should be recognized in the accounts. It is inconsistent to reduce the value of the securities to a value below cost without increasing their carrying value when the market value is above cost. The supporters of the market value approach believe that gains and losses occur when the value of the investments change and only when investments are sold. Thus, recognizing only losses is too conservative and does not reflect the economic reality when prices increase.

3. Lower of Cost or Market Price (LCM)

FAS statement number 12 states that

> the carrying amount of the marketable equity security portfolios be reported at the lower of its aggregate cost or market value determined at the balance sheet date. The amount by which aggregate cost of the portfolio excess the market value shall be accounted for as the valuation allowance.

In applying the concept of LCM the FAS distinguishes between unrealized and realized gains or losses. An unrealized gain or loss is the difference between the cost and the market value of the securities. A realized profit or loss is the difference between the proceeds from the sale of securities and their costs. In line with the conservatism principle, the drop in the prices of the investment should be reported in the profit and loss account.

Evaluation of the Methods

The main weakness of the LCM method is that it is inconsistent. When the aggregate market price drops below the aggregate cost of securities, LCM correctly reflects the realizable value of a portfolio securities. However, when the aggregate market price exceeds the aggregate cost, the LCM results in an understatement of the securities value.

The cost method is criticized because it results in an overstatement of the securities' value and profit when the market price drops below costs. Identical securities would be reported at different values because they were acquired at different times. When the cost method is employed, it is easy to manipulate assets and profit figures by selecting which securities are sold if they are reported at different costs. Another opportunity for manipulation exists if the company sells its securities just before the close of the accounting period and replaces them immediately after the start of the next period. On the other hand, the main strength of the cost approach is its objectivity. Indeed, this approach is in line with the valuation basis used for most other assets which guarantees uniformity.

The market value approach is criticized on the grounds that the market values are not always readily determined. Market values are not relevant unless sales occur. However, the market value approach does not have the advantage that it eliminates inconsistencies resulting from the use of the LCM approach and it assigns profit or loss maintained during the accounting period, rather than delaying them until the time of sale, as is the case with the cost method. In addition, the market value approach informs the users of the financial statements of the real value of the company's assets.

Scope for Creative Accounting

Creative accounting is likely to occur in the exercise of corporate discretion to classify investments in the balance sheet. Classifying investments as current assets will improve the liquidity ratio. In addition, the choice between different methods of short-term investment valuation provides an opportunity for creative accounting.

To illustrate possible schemes of creative accounting suppose ABC Company has the following balance sheet at 31 October, 1992.

Fixed assets		£100,000	Ordinary shares £1 each	125,000
Current assets			Long term liabilities	50,000
Stock	10,000		Short term liabilities	25,000
Debtors	15,000			
Cash	75,000	100,000		
Total assets		£200,000		£200,000

In addition, the following transactions took place.

1 January 1992, 10,000 ordinary shares of X Corporation purchased at a market price of £3.5 per share plus a brokerage conversion of £250.

20 November 1992, 5,000 shares of X Corporation sold for cash at a market price of £4.5 per share, less commission, tax and fees of £250.

At the end of 1992 the market price of the ordinary shares of the company was £5.

(a) The effect of the classification of the investment (short-term or long-term) on the liquidity ratios can be shown in the following balance sheet.

The Balance sheet after the acquisition of the investment

		The investment classified short-term		The investment classified-long term	
Fixed assets			100,000		£135,250
Stock	10,000			10,000	
Debtors	15,000			15,000	
Short-term investment	35,250			—	
Cash	39,750		100,000	39,750	64,750
			200,000		200,000
Current liabilities			25,000		25,000
Long-term liabilities			50,000		50,000
Ordinary shares £1 each			125,000		125,000
			200,000		200,000
Working capital			75,000		39,750
Current ratio			4.00		1.59
Acid test ratio			3.6		2.19

(b) The effect of the use of different valuation methods of short term investments on the financial ratios can be shown as:

$$\text{Cost of shares sold} = \frac{5,000}{10,000 \text{ shares}} \text{ shares} \times £35,250 = £17,625$$

The short-term investment balance should be reduced by this amount and the cash balance should be increased by the same amount (see below).

		LCM £100,000			Cost £100,000			Market £100,000
Fixed assets								
Current assets								
Stock	10,000			10,000			10,000	
Debtors	15,000			15,000			15,000	
Short-term investment	17,625			17,625			25,125*	
Cash	62,000	104,625	62,000	62,000	104,625	62,000	112,125	
		204,625			204,625			212,125
Current liabilities		25,000			25,000			25,000
Long-term liabilities		50,000			50,000			50,000
Ordinary shares 1 each		125,000			125,000			125,000
Unrealized gain								7,500 **
Realized gain on sale		4,625			4,625			4,625
Working capital		79,625			79,625			87,125
Current ratio		3.185			3.185			4.485
Acid test ratio		3.785			3.785			3.085
Total liabilities/equity		0.58			0.58			0.55
Equity/total assets		0.63			0.63			0.65

* Market value of the retained investment and brokerage cost paid on the acquisition of the investment (£5 × 5,000 shares + £125). **Unrealized gain = (Marker price − cost) × No. of shares remaining. (£5 − £3.5) × 5,000 shares = £7,500.

The realized gain on sale of the investment should be reported on the profit and loss account. Hence the profit figures will be identical under all these methods. However, the situation will be different if the investment value drops below the market price. For example, suppose that at 31 December 1992 the market price was £3. The account would show the changes indicated in the next balance sheet.

	LCM		Cost		Market	
Fixed assets		£100,000		£100,000		£100,000
Current assets						
Stock	10,000		10,000		10,000	
Debtors	15,000		15,000		15,000	
Short-term investment	15,125		17,625		15,125	
Allowance for short-term						
investment	(2,500)		—		—	
Cash	62,000		62,000		62,000	
		102,125		104,625		102,125
		202,125		204,625		202,125
Short-term liabilities		25,000		25,000		25,000
Long-term liabilities		50,000		50,000		50,000
Ordinary shares £1 each		125,000		125,000		125,000
Unrealized loss on evaluation		(2,500)				(2,500)
Realized gain on sale		4,625		4,625		4,625
		127,125		129,625		127,125
		202,125		204,625		202,125
Working capital		77,125		79,625		77,125
Current ratio		3.085		3.185		3.085
Acid test ratio		2.685		2.785		2.685
Total liabilities/equity		0.59		0.58		0.59
Equity/total assets		0.628		0.633		0.628

In an attempt to see how European companies report their short-term investments on the balance sheet, a random sample of 25 companies from each of Britain, Germany, France, and Holland has been surveyed. The result of the survey is reported in Table 5.1.

It is evident from Table 5.1 that most of the surveyed companies from Germany and France use the lower of cost or market approach to report their short-term investment and marketable securities. However, the British and Dutch companies seem to use the market value.

ACCOUNTING FOR TRADE DEBTORS (SHORT-TERM RECEIVABLES)

The term 'trade debtors' encompasses the entity's claims for money, goods or services from other entities. Largely trade debtors consist of an amount due from customers arising from normal operations.

Table 5.1. Method used to report short-term investments and marketable securities.

	British companies (No)	British companies (%)	German companies (No)	German companies (%)	French companies (No)	French companies (%)	Dutch companies (No)	Dutch companies (%)
Acquisition cost	5	20	5	20	3	12		
Lower of cost or market	4	16	12	48	10	40	4	16
Market value	7	28			1	4	6	24
Net realizable value	1	4						
No information given or no short-term investment reported	8	32	8	32	11	44	15	60
Total	25	100	25	100	25	100	25	100

Valuation Problems

Once debtors' transactions and their dates of occurrence have been identified, the appropriate amount to record must be determined. The accountant must consider the face value of the trade debtors, the probability of future collection, and the length of time debtors will be outstanding.

Determination of Face Value

Valuation of debtors is an attempt to estimate the amount which will actually be collected from debtors. Customers are often quoted prices on the basis of list or catalogue price that may be subject to a trade or quantity discount. The normal practice is simply to deduct the trade discount from the list price and bill the customer the net amount. Cash discount is offered as an inducement for quick payment and communicated in terms that read 2/10, n/30, meaning 2% discount if it is paid within 10 days and the gross amount is due in 30 days.

In accounting for cash discount, accountants have the choice between recording the net amount of trade debtors (*net approach*) and the gross amount (*gross approach*).

Some accountants believe that cash discount is not actual discount but a penalty added to an established price to encourage quick payment. That is, the seller offers sales on account at a slightly higher price than if selling for cash, the increase being offset by the cash discount offered. Thus, customers who pay within the discount period purchase at the cash price, while those who pay after expiration of the discount period are penalized because they must pay an amount in excess of the cash price.

On the other hand, the most commonly used approach of recording trade debtors discount transactions is to enter debtors and sales at the gross amount.

Under this approach sales discounts are recognized in the account only when payment is received within the discount period. Sales discount would then appear in the profit and loss account as a deduction from sales to arrive at net sales.

Probability of Uncollectible Trade Debtors

When trade debtors are extended on a continuing basis, there are some inevitable losses due to uncollectability. These losses are considered a normal expense of business. According to the matching principle, these expenses should be matched with the sales revenue of the period in which transactions occurred, rather than in the period when the specific trade debtors are found to be uncollectible. Since it is difficult to know bad debtors in advance, the bad debt expense must be predicted in advance. It should be recorded in the accounts and reported on the current financial statement.

Two methods are commonly used to determine the adjustment to the allowance for uncollectible debtors.

1. Some small entities use *a specific charge off method* whereby a loss arising from an uncollectible debt is deferred until it becomes positively known that the particular account is bad. Supporters of this approach contend that facts, not estimates, are recorded. It assumes that good trade debtors result from cash sales, and that later events prove certain accounts to be uncollectible and worthless. The approach is also simple and practical.

   Although this approach has the advantage of greater certainty, it is subject to two major criticisms, namely (a) debtors are overstated and (b) the period in which the write off occurs is often later than the period in which debtors were created. These result in an incorrect matching of costs with revenues of the period.

2. An estimate is made of the expected uncollectible accounts from all sales made on account and deducted from the total of outstanding trade debtors. This is usually called *the allowance method*. The supporters of this method believe that in order to obtain a proper matching of expenses and revenue and to achieve a proper realized value of trade debtors at the end of the accounting period, bad debt expenses should be estimated and recorded in the same period as the sale. Although estimates are involved, the percentage of uncollectibles can be predicted from past experience, market conditions, and analyzing the outstanding balances.

   Because non-collectibility of trade debtors is considered a contingent loss, the allowance approach is appropriate only in cases where it seems obvious that the credit worthiness of a debtor has been impaired and the uncollectible amount can be reasonably estimated. Accountants have accepted the challenge of estimating the proportion of uncorrectable accounts. Debtors are a prospective cash inflow and the probability of their collection must be considered in assessing this inflow. The estimates are made either on the basis of percentage of net sales or on the basis of outstanding debtors.

The *net sales approach* may be regarded as *the profit and the loss (P and L) account approach* to estimating uncollectible expenses. Bad debt expense can be estimated as a percentage of sales or credit sales. This approach emphasizes the expense side of the adjustment and does not consider any existing balance in the allowance for bad debt account.

The *outstanding trade debtors approach* may be regarded as the *balance sheet approach*. Bad debt expense can be estimated as a percentage of the outstanding debtors. This approach consists of adjusting the valuation account to a new balance equal to the estimated uncollectible position of the existing trade debtors. The approach rests on ageing the outstanding trade debtors. The adjusting entry takes into consideration the existing allowance of the uncorrectable bad debt accounts.

Evaluation of Allowance Methods

Both methods of estimating bad debts are acceptable under generally accepted accounting principles. Each method has certain strengths and weaknesses. The P and L account approach is generally preferable because it complies with the matching convention by matching current bad debt expenses in relation to the revenues of the current period that caused the bad debt account. Thus it focuses on matching current revenues with current expenses and emphasizes the profit and loss account rather than the balance sheet. The use of credit sales rather than total sales (i.e. cash + credit sales) as the basis for adjustments is preferable because cash sales do not cause credit losses.

The balance sheet approach suffers from the probability that bad debt expense reported on the profit and loss account for the period may not be related to the credit sales of the current period which would violate the matching convention. It favours balance sheet over profit and loss accounts. In using this approach, ageing the debtors at the end of each period is preferable to the use of a simple estimation.

Scope for Creative Accounting

Adjustment of Allowance for Bad Debt
How a company manages its receivables influences its cash flow position. A company's liquidity performance and prospects can be derived from the

relation between receivables and payables. Unfortunately, receivables management also forms an important part of window dressing. The most obvious source for manipulating accounting figures is the allowance for bad debts. For one reason or another, customers are occasionally unable to pay for goods and services with which they have been provided. Although companies take steps to make sure that bad debts are kept at minimum levels, this problem is inevitable.

The attraction of the allowance for bad debts to the creative accountants is that it can affect the balance sheet and the income statement and it can be changed from one year to another. In the year when carrying of receivables appear to be higher than required they can be reduced, and when the values are smaller than desired they can be increased. As the bad debt allowance on receivables is reflected in the income statement, it can also be used to smooth the reported income so as to improve efficiency ratios.

For instance, if a company expects to report high levels of income in a particular year, it may charge high levels of allowances, and this can be reduced gradually in future years. Hence, the auditor will find it difficult to challenge the levels of allowances for bad debts, especially if the company can relate the levels of adjustments to sales levels.

Creative Accounting Associated with Adjustments of Allowances for Bad Debts

For example, suppose that the Western End Plc balance sheet of 31 December 1991 is as follows:

Western End Plc Balance Sheet 31 December 1991				
Fixed assets		5,000	Short-term liabilities	1,500
Current assets:				
Debtors	1,100			
Allowance	(100)		Long-term liabilities	2,500
Stock	2,000			
Cash	2,000	5,000	Ordinary shares £1 each	6,000
		10,000		10,000

During 1992, Western End Plc purchased merchandise for £3,000, paid £2,000 and the rest was to be paid at the beginning of 1993. In addition, merchandise was sold for £5,000 terms 2/10, n/30. A payment of £2,000 was received within the discount period. The other payment was received by the end of the period. The stock on hand was valued at £1,500. Western End has the choice between the net method and the gross method to account for the cash discount. The allowance for bad debt can be calculated as 2% of credit sales or 3% of the outstanding trade debtors.

The following two balance sheets show how the choice among the above methods affect the profit and loss account, balance sheet, and key financial ratios.

	P & L Account Net approach allowance as a percentage of credit sales	P & L Account Net approach allowance as a percentage of outstanding debtors
	$(\pounds)$	$(\pounds)$
Sales	5,000	5,000
Cash discount	(40)	(40)
Net sales	4,960	4,960
Cost of sales		
Opening stock	2,000	2,000
Purchases	3,000	3,000
Closing stock	(1,500)	(1,500)
	3,500	3,500
Gross profit	1,460	1,460
Expenses		
Bad debt expense	(60)★	(23)★★
Net Profit	1,400	1,437

★ $2\% \times \pounds 3,000 = \pounds 60$
★★ $(3\% \times \pounds 4,100) - \pounds 100 = \pounds 23$

	Balance sheet Net approach allowance as a percentage of credit sales	Balance sheet Net approach allowance as a percentage of outstanding debtors
	$(\pounds)$	$(\pounds)$
Fixed assets	5,000	5,000
Current assets		
Debtors	4,100	4,100
Allowance	(160)	(123)
Stock	1,500	1,500
Cash	1,960	1,960
	12,400	12,437
Current liabilities	2,500	2,500
Long-term liabilities	2,500	2,500
Ordinary shares $\pounds 1$ each	6,000	6,000
Profit and loss account	1,400	1,437
	12,400	12,437

	P & L account Net approach allowance as a percentage of credit sales	P & L account Net approach allowance as a percentage of outstanding debtors
	(£)	(£)
Sales	4,900	4,900
Cost of sales		
Opening stock	2,000	2,000
Purchases	3,000	3,000
Closing stock	(1,500)	(1,500)
	3,500	3,500
Gross profit	1,400	1,400
Expenses		
Bad debt expense	(58.8)★	(21.2)★★
Net profit	1,341.2	1,378.8

★ $[£4,900 - (£2,000 \times .98)] \times 2\% = £58.8$
★★ $(£1,100 + £2,940) \times .03 = 121.2$
    $£121.2 - £100 = £21.2$

	Balance sheet Gross approach allowance as a percentage of credit sale	Balance sheet Gross approach allowance as a percentage of outstanding debtors
	(£)	(£)
Fixed assets	5,000	5,000
Current assets		
Debtors	4,040	4,040
Allowance for bad debt	(158.8)	(121.2)
Stock	1,500	1,500
Cash	1,960	1,960
	12,341.2	12,378.8
Current liabilities	2,500	2,500
Long-term liabilities	2,500	2,500
Ordinary shares £1 each	6,000	6,000
Profit and loss account	1,341.2	1,378.8
	12,341.2	12,378.8

	Gross method allowance as a percentage of credit sales	Gross method allowance as a percentage of outstanding debtors	Gross method allowance as a percentage of credit sales	Net method allowance as a percentage of outstanding debtors
Net profit	1,400	1,437	1,341.2	1,378.8
Current assets	7,400	7,437	3,311.2	7,378.8
Current liabilities	2,500	2,500	2,500	2,500
Total assets	12,400	12,437	12,341.2	12,378.8
Total equity	7,400	7,437	7,341.2	7,378.8
Working capital	4,900	4,937	4,841.2	4,878.8
Current ratio	2.96	2.97	2.94	2.95
Acid test ratio	2.36	2.37	2.34	2.35
Liabilities/equity	0.676	0.672	0.681	0.678
Equity/total asset	0.597	0.598	0.595	0.596
Return on equity	0.189	0.193	0.183	0.187

Transfer Debtors with Recourse to An Unrelated Third Party

In the normal operating cycle of a business, cash needed for current operations is provided through the collection of accounts receivable. It is possible to accelerate this process by selling receivables. A person or a financial concern which buys receivables is often called a factor. A factor may buy receivables *with or without recourse*. 'Without recourse' means that the factor assumes full risk of failure to collect the accounts purchased. Hence, it is in the sale of receivables with recourse that the off–balance sheet financing problems lies. When receivables are sold with full recourse, the seller in effect guarantees the collectibility of receivables and the company buying the receivables is assured of earnings at a stipulated rate of return on its investment. In this situation, the question is whether or not factoring receivables with recourse is a sale transaction in which a gain or loss should be recognized immediately. Or is it a borrowing transaction, in which the difference between the carrying value of receivables and proceeds from the sale of the receivables is a financing cost (interest) that should be amortized over the duration of the 'recourse' sale? In 1983, US FASB 77 *Reporting by Transferor for Transfers of Receivables with Recourse* suggested two methods of accounting for the transfer of receivables with recourse, either by treating the transfer as a sale transaction or as borrowing.

A transfer of receivables with recourse can be accounted for as a sale, recognizing any gain or loss, if all three of the following conditions are met:

1. The transferor surrenders its control of future economic benefits relating to receivables

2. The transferor can reasonably estimate its obligation under the recourse provisions.

3. The transferee cannot return the receivables to the transferor except pursuant to the recourse provisions.

If the transferor with recourse does not meet these conditions, the amount of proceeds from the transfer of receivables should be reported and accounted for as a liability. However, if a company adopts the sale approach a contingent liability arises since there is a possibility of defaulting. In general, the contingent liability is taken off the balance sheet. This technique can be used by British companies treating the transfer of receivables with recourse as a sales transaction without providing any information on the expected liabilities associated with this approach.

After all, ED 42 considered the main problem associated with the transfer of receivables with recourse; the main issue being the scope of recourse. If there is a full recourse, ED 42 suggests that the debt should be retained on the balance sheet. In many factoring agreements treated as off-balance sheet, there is only limited recourse to the transferor company. The Exposure Draft proposes that, where there is only limited recourse, such debt should be excluded from the balance sheet with provision being made for expected doubtful debt. Any remaining risk should be disclosed as a contingent liability.

There appears to exist an element of inconsistency here. The Exposure Draft suggests that for other special purpose transactions even a limited amount of recourse might mean that the item should be brought back onto the balance sheet. However, Walter (1986) demonstrated that employing factoring arrangement schemes provides the company with the cash generated from sale. Similarly, Hutson (1988) showed that factoring overcomes cash flow constraints resulting from a combination of rapid growth and late invoice payment. Many companies cannot expand because their receivables are growing faster than their capacity to borrow under traditional banking criteria. Hutson went on to add that these constraints, along with flexible off-balance sheet financing, show factoring as a highly cost effective management tool. Indeed, factoring receivables with recourse improves the balance sheet. Receivables are converted into cash which can be used to pay off liabilities. The problem is that they overstate the assets by not making adequate provision or they fail to show contingent liabilities. Hence, the company can grow without needs for equity capital. What is more important is that factoring also improves specific balance sheet ratios (current ratio, total debt to stockholder's equity ratios).

Brindle (1986), in the *Survey of UK Published Accounts* (1985–1986), provided examples of UK companies disclosing information on debt factoring. He reported more examples in the *Survey of UK Published Accounts* of (1986–1987).

In one of the examples, a company that employed the factoring scheme was less informative since it did not separate the bills from debtors and it left the reader to presume that there are recourse provisions relating to the debtors disclosed. In the same manner, Pimm (1991b) in the *Survey of UK Published Accounts* reported two examples of companies factoring their debt. The companies treated the factoring as sales and disclosed the total outstanding amount of factored debt.

Discounting Notes and Bills Receivable

The term 'discounting' applies when a company borrows against notes receivable and endorses them on a recourse basis, which means that the borrowing company must pay the note if the original drawer does not.

However, the question to be asked is whether the discounting of the note is a sale with gains and losses which is to be recognized and a contingent liability disclosed. Or is the borrowing transaction that is accounted for by retaining the notes receivable in the accounts, reporting the endorser's obligation among the current liabilities and recognizing interest expense or interest revenue? As discussed in connection with accounts receivable, if the factoring with recourse meets all three of the conditions listed earlier, FASB 77 requires that the transfer (discounting) of notes receivable with recourse be accounted for and reported as a sale and that a gain or loss be recognized. However, some accountants contend that the position in FASB 77 often legitimatizes what is actually a form of off-balance financing.

Likewise, if the transfer with recourse does not meet the three conditions, the transaction is accounted for as a borrowing with the value of the note recorded and reported along with interest expense.

Where the discounted transactions were recorded as sales, the endorser would disclose its contingent liability on the discounted notes with recourse by reporting the contingent liability in a note to the accounts. Alternatively, the endorser could not credit 'notes receivable discounted'; instead, the notes receivable discounted can be reported as a contra asset deducted from notes receivable in the current assets section. This would serve to disclose the endorser's contingent liability for default by the maker of the note. However, Dieter and Watt (1980) considered the sale of receivables with recourse as off-balance sheet financing since receivables and liabilities are eliminated from the balance sheet.

Brindle (1986), in the *Survey of UK Published Accounts* (1985–1986), demonstrated that discounting notes receivable is probably one of the earliest forms of off-balance sheet financing. He showed that discounting notes receivable is associated with contingent liabilities because the person discounting usually has recourse to the endorser of the bill in the case of default. In the *Survey of UK Published Accounts* (1986–87), Brindle found that many of the companies he reviewed reported a contingent liability for receivables discounted. However, he believes that the amount of contingent liability disclosed did not appear to be very significant and was probably related to bills drawn on export against delivery of products since debt factoring did not appear to be a more convenient method of financing local sales. He also observes that the value attached to a contingent liabilities disclosure is debatable when the amount involved is not disclosed.

In the 1986–87 *Survey of the UK Published Accounts*, Brindle provided examples of off-balance sheet financing associated with accounting for discounted notes receivable. Some of the companies disclosed an insufficient amount of contingent liabilities, others disclosed no information. The Beecham Group reported in the notes to their 1986 accounts that among the contingent liabilities of the group were £13.7 million 'mainly of bills discounted and bank guarantees for which no provision is considered necessary'. Pimm (1991b) in the *Survey of UK Published Accounts* (1990–1991) provided two examples of off-balance sheet financing associated with the accounting for discounted bills receivable.

Insurance of Collateralized Mortgage Obligations (CMOs)

CMOs are bonds, issued by a special purpose subsidiary (or organization) established by a sponsorship parent company, that are secured by mortgaged-backed securities or mortgage loans. The mortgage loans are acquired by the special-purpose company usually from the parent company and then pledged to an independent trustee until the special purpose company issuing the CMOs fulfils its obligation under the bonds (CMOs). The investors, i.e. the persons acquiring the bonds, can look only to the special purpose company's assets (primarily the trusted assets–mortgage loans) or third parties (such as investors or guarantors) for repayment of the obligation under the bond. The sponsorship payment has no financial obligation under the instrument, although the parent or its affiliate may retain responsibility for servicing the underlying mortgage loans. Thus, a CMO is a debt security that is collateralized by a pool of mortgage loan receivables. The interest and the principal payments of mortgages are accumulated and then used to pay interest and principal to the credit of the borrower; the holder may look only to the cash for the mortgage collateral for their interest and principal payments.

FASB Technical Bulletin No. 85-2, *Accounting for Collateralized Mortgage Obligations*, allows assets and debts to be removed from the balance sheet (with gain and loss recognition) in a CMO transaction if the cash flow from the assets is irrevocably passed to the creditors and if the borrower cannot be required to make any future payment to the creditors. In the United Kingdom, the National Home Loans Corporation (NHLC) (1987) sold a £50 million bundle of mortgages as marketable securities. The corporation argued that to show these securities as liabilities in the accounts would be misleading, as the holder of securities has no right of recourse against the NHLC (the parent company) if the mortgages are sold to a controlled non-subsidiary company which in turn sells the mortgages as marketable securities to third parties or investors.

REVIEW QUESTIONS

1. Distinguish between long-term and short-term investments.

2. Discuss the effects of adopting different methods of valuation of short-term investments on the profit and loss account and balance sheet.

3. Evaluate the methods of evaluation of short-term investments.

4. Explain the difference between the gross approach and the net approach of recording trade debtors and explain how the choice between the two approaches affects profit and loss account balance sheet figures.

5. Critically analyze the methods used to overcome the uncorrectable trade debtors problem; state their impact on the profit and loss account and balance sheet.

6. Show how factoring receivables with recourse represents an opportunity for off-balance sheet financing.

7. Explain what is meant by discounted notes receivable and illustrate how this may represent an opportunity for off-balance sheet financing.

8. Insurance of collateralized mortgage obligation is considered to be an opportunity for off-balance sheet financing. Explain.

9. In December 1992, John Enterprises had the following short-term and long-term investments:

Short-term portfolio
Security original 31/12/1992

	Cost (£)	Market value (£)
JCT Inc.	10,000	12,000
ARBC Co.	5,000	6,500
MDA Co.	2,000	1,500
USS Inc.	5,500	6,000
KHM Co.	3,500	3,000
	26,000	29,000

Long-term portfolio
Security original 31/12/1992

	Cost (£)	Market value (£)
P & H Inc.	5,000	3,500
M & H	6,500	5,000
W & I	10,000	7,000
J & L Co.	6,000	8,000
I & F	5,500	6,500
	33,000	33,000

There were no sales of securities during 1992.

(a) Assuming that John wishes to maximize the reported loss from short-term and long-term investments, what is the maximum loss for 1992?

(b) Assuming that John wishes to maximize the reported profit from short-term and longer-term investment, what is the maximum profit reported in 1992?

(c) Show the effects of the approaches you used in requirements (a) and (b) on the balance sheet and on some key financial ratio.

10. Webster Bookbinder's major customer, Anto Publishers, is in financial trouble. To avoid bankruptcy, Webster has agreed to accept an interest bearing note on several outstanding invoices as follows:

Invoice number	Date of invoice	Invoice amount
101	20/01/92	£50,000
102	25/06/92	£30,000
212	20/09/92	£70,000

On 1 November 1992, Webster accepted a 1 year note with a face value of £150,000 and interest rate of 12% when it became obvious that the invoices would not be paid in a timely manner. On 1 December 1992 Webster discounted the note at the bank at a discount rate of 15%. In an event of default by Auto, the discounting agreement requires Webster to pay the full value plus interest of 5% of the face value penalty. The bank uses a 365 days yearly basis to complete its discounting calculations and its debtors assume that each month equals 1/12 of a year.

(a) Show the effect of discounting the note on the profit and loss account and the balance sheet if Auto paid the note on time.

(b) Show the effect on the profit and loss account and the balance sheet if Auto default.

(c) Briefly explain the benefit Webster might gain from discounting the note and how the discounting may represent an opportunity for off-balance sheet financing.

CHAPTER 6

Accounting for Stock

INTRODUCTION

One of the largest assets in a retail store, as in a wholesale business is the stock of merchandise. Hence the sale of this stock at prices in excess of cost is the major source of income.

Stocks are assets consisting of goods owned by the business at a particular time held for future sale or for utilization in the manufacture of goods for sale.

The major problem associated with accounting for stock is the fact that goods sold during a financial period seldom correspond exactly to those produced or bought during the period. As a result of this, it becomes necessary to allocate the cost of goods available for sale between those goods that are used or sold and those that remain on hand. This solution causes two main problems: *identifiability* and *measurement* of the quality of physical goods that should be included in the flow of stock; measurement of accounting values assigned to the flow of stock.

IDENTIFICATION OF GOODS THAT SHOULD BE INCLUDED IN THE STOCK

In identifying the goods that should be included in the stock, the accountant should adopt the general rule that goods which the business owns at the stock date should be included. Goods purchased but not received should be included. In addition, goods under contract for sale but not yet segregated and supplied to the contractee should be included. Furthermore, goods held out on consignment (by agents and/or branches) should be included in the stock. On the other hand, goods held for sale on commission or assignment and those rejected and awaiting return to the supplier should be excluded.

EFFECT OF STOCK MANIPULATION ON THE PROFIT AND LOSS ACCOUNT AND BALANCE SHEET

An overstatement of the opening stock understates profits by the overstated amount and the understatement of the opening stock overstates profit. Conversely, an overstatement of closing stock overstates profit by the overstated amount and the understatement of closing stock understates profit.

Different approaches used to account for stock will affect both profit and loss account and balance sheets not only for the current accounting period but also for future periods.

Incorrect inclusion or exclusion of physical units in stock will affect the financial statements. In identifying items that should be included or excluded in stock, the accountant must exercise judgement in light of particular situations on whether ownership has passed. In this case, the right title of the goods must be acknowledged. However, a strict legal conversion is often impossible.

An overstatement or understatement of closing stock for the current period will cause a counter-balance effect in the next period because the closing stock of this period is the opening stock for the next period. However, the use of different approaches does not affect the life time of the profit of the business.

MEASUREMENT PROBLEM IN ACCOUNTING FOR STOCK AND COST OF SALES

In accounting for stock and cost of sales accountants have two main problems, namely (1) stock unit, and (2) stock flows. Below we shall look at these in more detail.

Stock unit cost

The first problem facing the accountant is to select an appropriate unit cost of each type of stock. The main bases of the stock valuation methods are as follows.

1. Cost Basis
The unit cost is measured by dividing the total amount spent to acquire, make goods, or to prepare goods for sale, by the number of units acquired. The cost includes not only the possible price but also all the costs incurred on the goods up to the date they are ready for use or sale (i.e. purchase tax, freight, storage, insurance while in transit or storage).

Administration and distribution expenses and interest expense are not included in the unit cost because they are not directly related to the purchase or manufacture of goods. Under the cost principle, the net cash equivalent paid for specific items is cost. In theory, all cash discount permitted, whether taken or not, should be excluded from cost. Any discount not taken constitutes interest expense. However, accountants can record the gross amount of purchases and justify them on the grounds that cash discount is immaterial.

2. Departure from cost basis
Under specific circumstances, generally accepted accounting principles allow exceptions to the cost principle in measuring the unit cost of stock. The exceptions may be classified as follows.

a. Lower of cost or market
Under this rule the unit cost used is the lower of the original cost when purchased or made, and market cost at the end of the accounting period. This rule is used on the basis of the matching principle which states that the decline in utility of goods on hand should be recognized as loss in the period in which the decline in utility occurred. It is also justified on the basis of the concept of conservatism which states that an asset (such as stock) should be reported at lower figures.

b. Net realizable value and replacement cost
Many accountants believe that stock should be reported as either a net realizable value or a current replacement cost whichever is clearly determinable rather than the actual cost. This would provide more relevant and meaningful information for decision makers using financial statements.

c. Selling price
Under certain circumstances stock items may be valued at their selling price (see the Accounting Research and Terminology Bulletin No. 43, chapter 4, para 16). Under this method, if there is an increase in the selling price, a holding gain would be reported; conversely, when there is a decrease, a holding loss would be reported.

The methods discussed above represent the generally accepted departure from cost in specific circumstances. Hence it is not difficult for the accountant to find justification for adopting any of the above methods.

Stock Cost Flow Methods

When goods are purchased or manufactured, there is an inflow of cost; when the goods are sold, there is an outflow of cost. The net difference between cost inflow and outflow represents the cost of closing stock. Since it is expected to buy goods at a different unit cost, the accountant faces a problem of determining the appropriate unit cost for units remaining on hand.

Any stock flow method should comply with the cost principle and reflect the matching principle. In general, four cost flow methods are used.

Specific Cost Identification Method

Under this method each item of stock and its cost needs to be identified and retained until sold. Items still on hand can be easily costed to arrive at the value of closing stock. For example, suppose the Electricity Board purchased three Hotpoint washing machines at costs of £500, £450 and £600, respectively. During the year two washing machines sold for £1,500. At the end of the year it is noted that the £500 washing machine is still on hand. In this case the cost of sale will be £1,050 (£450 + £600) and the cost of closing stock is £500.

This approach is workable where the trade involves the sale of relatively large and expensive items where their individual costs can be easily identified (cars, TVs, videos, fridges, washing machines, pianos and organs, tables, cabinets, etc.). Hence, this approach is ideal when specific identification is possible and therefore may require the creation of detailed records. Thus, this may limit its use in practice. Another disadvantage also associated with this method is the possibility of manipulating the cost of sales and therefore profit figures. In our example, since the products are identical, the company can report its cost of sales at £950 (£450 + £500) instead of £1,050. In this case the profit figure will be overstated by £100.

Average Cost Method

This approach takes into consideration fluctuations in prices during the accounting cycle. The idea of the average cost is adopted in two different ways depending upon whether the stock system adopted by the company is the periodic or perpetual stock system. Under the periodic stock system, *the weighted average unit cost* is used. Under the perpetual stock system, however, *the moving average unit cost* is used.

In the weighted average method cost is computed by multiplying the cost per unit of opening stock and purchases with the number of units of opening stock and purchases to arrive at the cost of goods available for sale. This amount is then divided by the number of units available for sale to determine the weighted average cost per unit. The weighted average cost per unit can then be used to calculate the cost of sales and the cost of closing stock (multiply each of the number of units sold and the number of units of closing stock by the weighted average cost per unit).

With respect to the moving weighted average cost method under the perpetual stock system, the cost is determined at the time of sale. However, the weighted average approach can only be calculated at the end of the accounting cycle. Therefore, this approach cannot be used here. Thus, the moving average approach is used to calculate the new cost per unit after each purchase.

First In, First Out (FIFO)
This method assumes that the cost of the earliest units purchased or manufactured are the first to be included in the cost of sales.

Last In, First Out (LIFO)
This approach assumes that the costs of the latest goods acquired or manufactured are the first to be included in the cost of sales.

Evaluation of methods

Weighted Average Cost Approach
The weighted average cost is frequently adopted because of its simplicity and objectivity. It minimizes the effect of the fluctuations in prices. The approach is also systematic and difficult to manipulate. It is particularly good if the company adopts the periodic stock system where the average cost can be determined at the end of the accounting cycle. However, the weighted average approach cannot be implemented in a company using the perpetual stock system. Hence, the moving weighted average approach is introduced.

The main weakness of this approach is that the unit cost used to determine cost of sales does not match the current sales. Thus, this approach, in general, provides cost of sales between the FIFO and LIFO.

First In, First Out (FIFO)
This approach is widely used because of its simplicity and adaptability under any of the stock systems (periodic or perpetual systems). The value of the closing stock is very close to the value of the current replacement cost. In addition FIFO observes the physical flow of stock. Furthermore, it is systematic and difficult to manipulate.

The major shortcoming of this approach is that it matches the oldest unit cost with the current revenue. During inflation, this approach produces overstated profit figures, whereas, when prices are falling, it produces understated profits.

Last In, First Out (LIFO)
Similar to FIFO, this approach can be used under any of the stock systems. It matches the more current cost per unit with the current revenues. During periods of rising prices, LIFO will result in the lowest profit. Therefore, companies may employ this approach to pay less tax. However, although this approach results in better matching of current cost with current revenues, it does not observe the physical flow of stock. In addition, this approach can be subject to heavy

manipulation. For example, an enterprise can reduce its profit sharply by heavy buying at the increased prices at the end of the accounting cycle.

Estimating the cost of the closing stock

On specific occasions, companies try to estimate the value of their stock.

1. In case it is difficult to make a physical count, for example if an entity is interested in producing monthly or quarterly financial statements and the entity takes physical count at the end of the accounting cycle.

2. In the case of fire, theft or any other type of casualty, physical count is difficult to maintain.

In these circumstances, estimate techniques are used to compute the value of the stock.

a. *Gross Profit Approach*

Under this approach, the cost of closing stock is estimated by applying a gross profit rate to net sales. Past experience can be used to estimate this rate. This approach can be adopted if information on sales, cost of goods available for sale, and gross profit are available.

For example, suppose Z plc wishes to estimate the cost of closing stock without taking a physical count. The company's records show that the net sales are £50,000, opening stock £5,000, and the cost of purchases £30,000. Past experience indicates that the company realizes 40% gross profit rate and it is expected to earn the same rate this year. From this information the company can estimate the cost of the closing stock without taking physical count.

Gross profit	40% × £50,000 = £20,000	
Cost of sales	60% × £50,000 = £30,000	

Now the cost of closing stock can be derived as follows:

	(£)	(£)
Net sale		50,000
Cost of sales		
Opening stock	5,000	
Purchases	30,000	
Less: closing stock	(?)	
Cost of sales		30,000
Gross profit		20,000
Cost of goods available for sale		35,000
Estimated cost of sales		(30,000)
Estimated value of closing stock		5,000

Retail approach

This approach is used by big supermarkets and departmental stores who have thousands of different types of merchandise at low unit costs. The use of the physical count under these circumstances is extremely difficult. Thus, the retail approach of estimating the value of closing stock is used. Under this approach, the closing stock is determined at the retail price. This amount is then converted to cost by the use of the relationship between cost and the retail price. To illustrate, suppose the following information was extracted from Z plc records:

	Cost ($£$)	Retail ($£$)
Opening stock, 1 January 1992	20,000	30,000
Net purchases	100,000	120,000
Goods available for sale	120,000	150,000
Cost / retail ratio (120,000–150,000)	80%	
Net sales		110,000
Estimated closing stock at retail		40,000
Estimated closing stock at cost ($£40,000 \times 80\%$)	32,000	

Thus, the estimated cost of the closing stock is $£32,000$.

Variable Costing Versus Absorption Costing

Fixed manufacturing overhead costs represent a special problem in costing stock because *two concepts* exist relative to the costs that attach to the product as it flows through the manufacturing process. These two concepts are *variable costing (direct costing)* and *absorption costing (full costing)*.

Under variable costing only costs that vary directly with the volume of production are charged to products as manufacturing takes place. Under absorption costing, all manufacturing costs, variable and fixed, direct and indirect, incurred in the factory or production process, are included in the cost of stock. It should be mentioned that each approach produces different cost per unit of production.

The rules for accounting for stock and work in progress in the United Kingdom are contained in SSAP 9 *Stock and Work in Progress* and the *Companies Act 1985*. The overriding requirements of both SSAP 9 and CA 85 is that financial statements give a true and fair view. However, as is often the case, when two bodies attempt to regulate the same issue, conflict and confusion arise. The confusion and conflict are associated with whether or when to account for profits on long-term contracts, which valuation method to adopt, which overhead can be included in the cost, and the treatment of capitalized interest. Hence, each of these conflicting areas provides scope for window dressing.

Broadly speaking, CA 85 stated that inventory are to be valued at the lower of either purchase price or production cost and the net realizable value. In determining cost, the stock cost flow method can be either the first in first out method (FIFO), the last in first out method (LIFO), the weighted average method or any other similar method, which is not defined in any way and can therefore presumably cover any amount from the base cost at one extreme to the net realizable sale proceeds at another. Thus, it can be noted that various methods are applied in practice to determine the amounts which appear in the balance sheet and income statement and this can have a major effect on the results for the year. Creative accounting might well be the real underlying reason for switching from one method to another. However, the Efficient Market Hypothesis (EMH) would seem to suggest that the stock market would detect the consequences of such switching and there would thus seem to be little point in quoted companies using this technique for creative accounting purposes. However, unquoted companies might find it an attractive opportunity.

The Results of the Analysis of the European Sample Surveyed

An attempt has been made to see how European companies evaluate their stock. The annual financial reports of 25 companies from each of Britain, Germany, France and Holland have been used and the result of the analysis is included in Table 6.1.

It is evident that the use of the lower of cost or market, to report the value of the stock, is used regularly by the surveyed German companies. However, it seems that the lower of cost or net realizable value approach is in common use in France and Britain. Yet, surveyed Dutch companies seem to be using all the listed approaches, but not the lower of production cost, market value or replacement cost.

POSSIBLE SCHEMES OF CREATIVE ACCOUNTING

Circular Transactions

Circular transactions are identified by TR 603 as window dressing transactions where two or more companies enter into transactions with each other with equivalent values with the purpose of inflating the financial statements and therefore improving the gearings and the earnings per share ratios of one or more of the companies involved. Circular transactions can be seen if two companies operating in the same business have an identical stock balance of £1,000. Each of the companies agrees to buy the other's stock for £1,100. In each case each company will report £100 profit.

Table 6.1. The analysis of stock valuation methods used by the surveyed British, German, French and Dutch companies

	British companies (No)	(%)	German companies (No)	(%)	French companies (No)	(%)	Dutch companies (No)	(%)
Bases for determining cost								
FIFO							3	12
FIFO or average	1	4			4	16		
LIFO					1	4	5	20
Average cost			7	28	5	20	4	16
Current cost							4	16
Lower of cost or market			13	52	3	12	6	24
Lower of cost or net realizable value	24	96	1	4	12	44	3	12
Lower of production cost or market value or replacement cost			1	4				
No method disclosed			3	12				
	25	100	25	100	25	100	25	100

Completed Contract Method Versus Percentage of Completion Method

Construction in progress inventory is generally associated with long-run construction contracts. However, there appears to be an inventory measurement problem in the construction and ship building industry. The problem is peculiar to the industry because their construction period often covers a long period of time. In this case should income be recognised as construction progresses, or should income only be recognized when the contract is concluded?

The accounting profession has recognized two different approaches to deal with this issue: the *completion contract approach (CC)* and the *percentage of completion approach (PC)*.

Under the completion contract approach, income is recognized as earned only upon completion of the project. Under the percentage of completion approach, income is recognized as earned in each period based upon progress of the construction. For example, suppose Planet Construction received a contract to erect a shopping centre for £1,000,000. Construction is started in January 1991 and is to be completed 3 years from that date. The estimated cost of the project is £975,000. The cost incurred during the useful life of the contract was £250,000 in 1991, £350,000 in 1992 and £375,000 in 1993.

In this situation, income recognized under the PC method can be calculated as follows:

$$\frac{Cost\ incurred\ (current\ period)}{Total\ estimated\ cost} = \text{Percentage completed (current period)} \times \text{Total revenue}$$

$$= \text{Revenue recognized (current period)}$$

Using the above example income reported will be as follows:

1991 $\quad \dfrac{250,000}{975,000} \times 1,000,000 = £256,410$

1992 $\quad \dfrac{350,000}{975,000} \times 1,000,000 = £358,974$

1993 $\quad \dfrac{375,000}{975,000} \times 1,000,000 = £384,615$

Evaluation of Methods

The two methods are different in measuring and reporting the periodic income from construction and the closing stock during construction. By the end of the project, both methods would have recognized the same total amount of pre-tax profit.

The supporters of the CC method argue that it is more objective and more conservative since revenue is not recognized until all the revenue and expenses are known with certainty. However, it is sometimes viewed as useless since income measurement and recognition do not reflect the performance of the accounting period.

Advocates of the PC method assert that the construction company earns revenue as it performs the work on the contract. Hence, it is unreasonable to await completion before measuring and reporting revenue. The main defect of this approach is that the income is measured on the basis of the estimated work to be done and that income may be recognized in the early years of production, although in the end there may be an overall loss due to cost overruns.

In all events, the choice between the two approaches produces a different impact on the profit and loss account and on the balance sheet.

The Assignment of Work in Progress

Long-term construction contracts, for the construction of ships, bridges, dams and similar projects, often require several years to complete. Such contracts face problems in obtaining progress payments. One possible means of overcoming this cash problem, and of keeping the gearing ratios in check, is for a company to assign the work in progress.

Under this approach a company would sign an agreement with a bank or a finance company to assign irrevocably all the amounts which are payable under a major contract to a financier. In return, the construction company issues a bond which guarantees the completion of the contract. Accordingly, the financing company will guarantee regular cash advances to the company. The advances will help the company to obtain the necessary materials and other related costs. Hence, the financing company charges interest at a rate on which the two parties are agreed as part of the deal. Under the agreement, once the company has repaid the full amount of cash advances plus the accrued interest, the balance under the contract can be reassigned by the finance company to the construction company. Creative accounting is likely to occur before the recovery of advances plus interest. The company can control the rate at which the advances are repaid. The advances of cash can be used to pay the company's outstanding obligations. In this case, the advances drive part of the liabilities off the balance sheet and the construction company might not disclose the advances as liabilities in its balance sheet. In addition, cash receipt (advances, very liquid asset) are considered as a reduction in the value of the company's work in progress contract (less liquid assets).

In fact, the bond issued by the company to guarantee the completion of the contract represents a contingent liability that should be disclosed in notes to the company's accounts. Yet, the note can be presented in an abstracted way.

Schemes of Removing Debt from the Balance Sheet

A variety of approaches might be used in practice by an enterprise to finance its stock without reporting either the liabilities or the stock in its balance sheet. One of these approaches is considered by TR 603 in section (3.2) above *sale and repurchase of stock* (product financing arrangements). In this situation, the legal title is transferred but the economic substance of the transaction is that the risks of ownership are retained by the seller. These transactions are often described as *parking transactions*, because the seller simply parks the inventory on another enterprise's balance sheet for a short period of time. However, in 1981 the statement of Financial Accounting Standards (FASB) No.49, *Accounting for Product Financing Arrangements* has taken steps to curtail the product financing by requiring that, when a repurchase agreement exists at a set price and this price covers all costs of the inventory plus related holding costs, the inventory and the related liabilities remain in the seller's books. Nevertheless, there are other special sale arrangements used to finance inventory without reporting either the liabilities or the inventory on the balance sheet.

Sales with a high Level of Goods Returned

Formal or informal agreements often exist in such industries as publishing, records and tapes, and toys and sporting goods that permit goods to be returned for a full refund or allow an adjustment to be made to the amount owed. For example, suppose Book Publishers sells textbooks to university bookstores with an agreement that any books not sold may be returned for full credit. Past experience has shown that 25% of textbooks sold to university bookstores are returned. How should Book Publishers report its sales transactions? One alternative is to record the full amount and establish an estimated sale returns and allowance account. However, the contingent liabilities associated with the expected 25% returns and the inventory are derived off the balance sheet. Thus, the value of the inventory is transferred from the balance of the less liquid asset (inventory) to the balance of the more liquid asset (cash or receivables). In addition, the contingent liabilities that may result from returns would not appear in the balance sheet. More importantly, off-balance sheet financing is likely to occur if any cash collected (before the returns occurred) is used to pay the company's debts.

A second alternative is not to record any sales until circumstances indicate that the buyer will not return the inventory. The key question is: under what conditions should the inventory be considered sold and removed from Book Publishers, inventory? According to FASB (48) (1981) *Revenue Recognition When Right of Return Exists*, when the amount of returns can be reasonably estimated, the goods are considered sold. Conversely, if returns are unpredictable, removal of these goods from the inventory does not appear to be warranted. However, the possibility of moving the inventory off the balance sheet still exists.

Sales on Instalment

As in the case of a sale with a high rate of returns, sales on instalment cause income recognition problems. The sale of real estate may be made on a deferred payment plan whereby the seller receives a down payment and then receives the balance in a series of payments over a number of years. The instalment plan is commonly offered on sales of products ranging from automobiles to air travel. Selling on instalment basis raises questions regarding the appropriate patterns of revenue recognition. Although revenue is normally recognized on an accrual basis in the period in which a sale is made and an enforceable contract received, the uncertainty of collecting accounts to be received over an extended period of time may suggest the postponement of revenue recognition until the probability of collection can be reasonably estimated. In general, two approaches may be taken in recognizing gross profits on instalment sales: (1) the gross profit may be related to the period in which the sale is made (*accrual basis approach*) or (2) the gross profit may be related to the periods in which cash is collected on the instalment contract (*instalment method*). Since the risk of loss from uncollectibles is higher in instalment sale situations than in other sale transactions, the seller usually asks for forms of conditional sales contracts which withhold legal title to the merchandise until all the payments have been made. The question is whether the inventory should be considered sold, even though legal title has not passed. The economic substance of the transaction is that the goods should be excluded from the seller's inventory if the percentage of bad debt can be reasonably estimated. Hence, although legal title may not have passed, the goods should be removed from inventory.

Actually, the off-balance sheet financing problem is likely to exist if either of the two approaches (accrual or instalment) are used as a basis to recognize revenue. Before investigating off-balance sheet financing associated with the use of any of the two methods, the legal validity of each approach is considered. According to the Research Bulletin No.(43) 1953,

> profit is deemed to be realised when a sale in the ordinary course of the business is reflected, unless the circumstances are such that the collection of the sale price is not reasonably assured.

In 1934, the American Institute of Certified Public Accountants adopted this principle and it remains in force today. In the case of the instalment sales Scott and Scott (1979) argued that there was little theoretical justification for permitting some businesses to defer the recognition of their profits to a time in which the earning process is entirely completed. Hence, it might be argued that in the case of instalment sales the collection of the sale price is not reasonably assured and this might make them an exception to the general rule. Nevertheless, Scott and Scott wondered why sellers are consistently engaged in sale transactions where only an unreasonable level of assurance of collection existed, and whether it was possible to distinguish them from other reasonable levels of assurance sales on an objective basis?

In 1966, APB Opinion No.(10) *Omnibus Opinion* disposed of instalment accounting by proclaiming that it was no longer to be considered a member in good standing of generally accepted accounting principles. The board reaffirmed that revenue should ordinarily be accounted for at the time a transaction is completed, with appropriate provisions for uncollectible accounts. Accordingly, the Board concluded that the instalment method of recognizing revenue is not acceptable. However, the instalment method of accounting is still alive.

In 1973, the AICPA Committee on accounting for real estate transactions concluded that the sale was to be recorded as such only when certain circumventing provisions were absent. Furthermore, accruals of revenue at the time of a sale were to take place only when a substantial down payment (25% of the sales value of the property is usually sufficient, and it may be lower with less risky properties) was received and subsequent annual payments were scheduled by contract to service the balance due (over 20 years in the case of land and, for other types of real estate, the usual term of a first mortgage loan). If the buyer failed to demonstrate a sufficient initial and continuing investment, revenue recognition was to take place according to the timing prescribed by other accounting techniques.

Actually, under the instalment and the accrual basis approaches the inventory is driven off the balance sheet to be substituted by more liquid assets (receivables and cash). The contingent liabilities associated with the possibility of returns are not shown in any of the financial statements. Thus, the question to be raised is, do the accounting methods employed to deal with instalment sales result in off-balance sheet financing? The answer may become clear if the cash collected (before the return took place) is used to pay the company's outstanding debts or even used to secure a loan for the company.

Sale and Repurchase of Stock

Sale and repurchase of inventory is a type of off-balance sheet financing identified by TR 603. The technical release described a case where the inventory is sold for the option to buy it back (it is reasonably certain that the option will be exercised). The arrangement may last for months, or even years, during which time the company which sold the inventory will use the proceeds from the sale as a source of finance. The inventory and the related purchase obligation (liability to repay the finance provided by temporary holder of the inventory) are often excluded from the balance sheet, the difference between the original selling price and the buy back price (which is effectively a finance charge) being debited to cost of sales when the item is finally sold to an independent party.

In this respect, under the heading *non-monetary items*, Exposure Draft ED 42 deals with the sale and repurchase of stock and similar transactions. ED 42 proposed that the sale and repurchase agreement, where the repurchase price is predetermined and covers primarily interest and holding costs, should be treated as a financing arrangement. ED 42 also mentioned an example where this treatment would not be appropriate. It states that an agreement to sell commodity stocks at the spot market price applicable three months hence should be accounted for on the relevant separate occasions as sale and repurchase. This is because the seller is subject to market risk, rather than just interest cost, during the period. Hence, according to the proposal made by ED 42, the price differentiated in the sale repurchase transactions should be charged to the income statement as interest. During the existence of the scheme, inventory and other assets should be reported on the balance sheet and the related finance should be disclosed as a part of the liabilities.

Consignment Stock

Goods may be transferred by their owners to another party who is to act as sales agent, with legal title to the goods retained by the owner until their sale. Such a transaction is known as a consignment. The party who owns the goods in such a relationship is known as a consignor; the party who undertakes to sell the goods is known as a consignee. Hence, consignment inventory is a type of off-balance sheet financing described by TR 603. The technical release described the situation where dealerships frequently obtain inventory on consignment from the manufacturer. Under the consignment sale, the purchase price for the inventory might be paid immediately on sale or at a time after the inventory has been sold by the consignee. In the case where the purchase price is to be received after the sale of the inventory, the consignor is effectively financing the trading inventory of the consignee, but neither the inventory nor the loan is reflected on the consignee's balance sheet.

However, ED 42 referred to consignment inventory and stated that its accounting treatment will depend very much on the provisions of the consignment agreement. ED 42 distinguished between the arrangements where the consignee has no risks attached to the inventory holding, and other arrangements. For instance, the consignee can return the inventory to the consignor without incurring any penalties and, therefore, carries little or no risk in holding the inventory. In this case, it would not be necessary to include the relevant inventory in the balance sheet. Nevertheless, it might be necessary to present such an inventory and its related finance on the balance sheet of a consignee who is ultimately obliged to purchase a consignment inventory, and where he has to bear any inventory holding gains or losses.

ED 42 also pointed out that such transactions are complicated by deposit arrangements, but it maintains that the appropriate treatment under the proposal should still be determined by analyzing the rights and the benefits attached to the arrangement.

Scope for Creative Accounting

To illustrate the effect of the use of different methods of inventory valuation on the profit and loss account and the balance sheet, suppose that XYZ company was organized on 1 June 1992 and its balance sheet at this date was as follows:

XYZ Company Balance Sheet 1 June 1992

	(£)		(£)
Fixed assets	10,000	Amount falling due within a year	5,500
Current assets			
Debtors	3,000	Amount falling due after more than one year	6,500
Stock	8,000		
Cash	4,000	Ordinary shares £1	13,000
	25,000		25,000

The stock quantities, purchases, and sales of units for the year 1992 are summarized overleaf:

	No of units	Cost per unit (£)	Total cost (£)
Opening stock	200	40	8,000
First purchase	100	45	4,500
Second purchase	100	50	5,000
Third purchase	100	60	6,000
Fourth purchase	100	65	6,500
Available for sale	600		30,000
Units sold	360		
Units on hand	240		

The selling price per unit was £75. Suppose all the sales and purchases took place in terms of cash. The comparison will be as follows:

Comparison of alternative methods of pricing closing stock on the P and L account

	Average cost method (£)	FIFO (£)	LIFO (£)
Sales	27,000	27,000	27,000
Cost of sales			
Opening stock	8,000	8,000	8,000
Purchases	22,000	22,000	22,000
Closing stock	(12,000)	(14,500)	(9,800)
Cost of sales	18,000	15,500	20,200
Gross Profit	9,000	11,500	6,800

Comparison of the effect of alternative methods of stock pricing on the balance sheet

	Average cost method (£)	FIFO (£)	LIFO (£)
Fixed assets	10,000	10,000	10,000
Current assets			
Debtors	3,000	3,000	3,000
Stock	12,000	14,500	9,800
Cash	9,000	9,000	*9,000
	34,000	36,500	31,800
Amount falling due within a year	5,500	5,500	5,500
Amount falling due after more than one year	6,500	6,500	6,500
Ordinary shares	13,000	13,000	13,000
Profit and loss account	9,000	11,500	6,800
	34,000	36,500	31,800
Working capital	18,500	21,000	16,300
Current ratio	4.36	4.82	3.96
Acid test ratio	2.18	2.18	2.18
Liabilities/equity	0.55	0.49	0.61
Equity/total assets	0.65	0.67	0.62
Return on equity	0.41	0.47	0.34

*(Sales − Purchases + Cash balance)
£27,000 − £22,000 + £4,000 = £9,000

REVIEW QUESTIONS

1. Discuss the main problems facing accountants in accounting for closing stock.

2. At the balance sheet date, the XY Company held title to goods in transit amounting to £6,500. This amount was omitted from the purchase figures for the year and also from the closing stock. Discuss the effect of this omission on the profit and loss account and the balance sheet.

3. First in, first out; weighted average; and last in, first out methods are often used for stock valuation purposes. Compare these methods and discuss the theoretical validity of each method in the determination of profit and asset valuation.

4. A company has engaged in a manufacturing business with a relatively large stock of finished goods and proportionally large fixed costs. The company has a departmental cost accounting system that assigns all manufacturing costs to the product each year.

   The controller has informed you that the company is considering the use of direct cost methods of accounting for plant operations and stock valuation. The management asks for your opinion of the effects, if any, that such a change would have on the profit and loss account and the balance sheet.

5. Why is stock valued at the lower of cost or market? What are the arguments for and against the use of the lower of cost or market method of stock valuation?

6. Compare the profit and loss account and balance sheet effects of FIFO and LIFO when prices are rising and when prices are falling.

7. Why is the closing stock of construction in progress larger in amount when the percentage of completion method is used compared with the completed contract method?

8. The balance sheet of XYZ Company at 31 December 1992 is as follows:

	(£)	(£)		(£)
Fixed assets		25,000	Trade creditors	20,000
Current assets			Creditors falling	
Stock	20,000		due over one year	10,000
Debtors	3,000		Ordinary shares	20,000
Cash	2,000	25,000		
		50,000		50,000

Stock has been financed by trade creditors.

The manager of XYZ is concerned about the high level of stock and thinks that this would affect XYZ's liquidity ratios. The manager believes that there should be a way to improve the Company's financial ratios.

(a) Explain to the manager how he can get round his problem.
(b) Show the effect, if any, of your proposal on the liquidity and gearing ratios.

9. Book Makers and Sons sell textbooks to many university bookstores with an agreement that any books not sold may be returned for full credit. Past experience indicates that 30% of the textbooks sold to the bookstores were returned. Assume that Book Makers and Sons made sales of £100,000 to university bookstores, show how the company will report its sales highlighting the possibility of off-balance sheet financing.

10. Discuss the approaches that may be employed in accounting for sale on instalment and how they result in a revenue recognition problem. In your discussion point to any opportunity for off-balance sheet financing.

CHAPTER 7

Accounting for Tangible Fixed Assets

INTRODUCTION

Many organizations invest a large amount of money on assets that are used to manufacture products or provide services. Assets with long lives acquired for use in business operations are referred to as *fixed assets*. They are also called plant assets or plant and equipment. Those assets are of durable nature in their operations and include land, building structures (offices, warehouses, factories) and equipment (machinery, furniture, tools).

The discussion of fixed assets will focus on how to determine their costs, the treatment of interest used to finance the construction or the development of fixed assets, cash discount, depreciation methods and revaluation of fixed assets.

DETERMINING THE COST OF PLANT ASSETS

Historical cost is usually used as the basis for valuing property, plant and equipment. Historical cost is measured by cash and the cash equivalent price of obtaining the asset and getting it ready for its intended use. Hence, costs consist of all expenditures necessary to acquire an asset and make it ready for its intended use.

Initial Components of Cost

1. *Land*. The cost of land includes the cash purchase price, closing costs such as title and attorney's fees, real estate broker's commission, property tax, costs incurred in getting the land in condition for its intended use, assumptions of any mortgage, or encumbrance on the property and any additional land improvements that have an indefinite life.

2. *Buildings*. The cost of building includes all necessary expenditure relating to the purchase in construction of a building, such as materials, labour and

overhead costs incurred during construction, and fees (attorney's and architect's and building permits).

3. *Equipment.* The cost of equipment consists of the cash purchase price, freight charges, insurance during transit paid by the purchaser, cost of special foundation if required, assembling and installation costs, and the cost of conducting trial runs. In other words, the cost includes all expenditures incurred in acquiring the equipment and preparing it for use.

4. *Self-constructed assets.* Accountants face problems in determining the cost of machinery and equipment when companies construct their assets. Direct costs (materials and labour) used in construction pose no problem because the costs can be traced. However, the assignment of indirect costs poses an accounting problem. These indirect costs, overheads, include heat, power, light, insurance, property tax on factory building and equipment, factory supervisory labour and depreciation of fixed assets.

The indirect costs may be handled in three different ways.

1. *Assign no fixed overhead to the cost of the constructed asset.* The supporters of this approach believe that the indirect overhead is generally fixed in nature. Hence by including the indirect overhead to the cost of the constructed asset the company will reduce the reported current expenses and consequently overstate its profit figures. Thus, it is argued in this approach that variable overheads costs, which increase as a result of production, should be assigned to the constructed assets costs.

2. *Allocation on basis of lost production.* Under this approach the cost of any curtailed production that occurs as a result of asset construction rather than purchase are allocated on the construction project. This approach is based on the opportunity cost. Hence the approach suffers from valuation problems.

3. *Assign a proportion of overheads to the construction process.* Some believe that self-constructed assets should bear the same proportion of overhead costs as would regular production. This method is used because accountants believe that it represents a better matching of costs with revenue. In the view of the opponents of this approach, if the overhead is assigned on the basis of labour hours and 10% of labour hours accounted for and associated with self-construction, then 10% of overhead should be charged to the self-constructed assets. Those advocating assigning overheads on the same basis of production contend that self-constructed assets should be subjected to the same treatment as stock. Hence, if the company chooses not to assign the same overheads to the self-constructed assets, this will result in an overstatement of cost of sales and stock.

The opponents of this approach argue that allocating overheads to self-construction assets when idle capacity exists does not affect normal production, and therefore by reporting overhead, the cost of the construction assets will be overstated and the cost of stock understated. Consequently, profit will be temporarily overstated since the self-constructed asset has a longer life than stock.

The Results of the Analysis of the European Sample Surveyed

The annual financial report of 25 companies from each of Britain, Germany, France and Holland have been analyzed and the result of the analysis is disclosed in Table 7.1.

Although most of the surveyed companies seem to use the historic cost to report the value of the tangible fixed assets, many French companies employed the current value. Similarly, the table illustrates that few Dutch companies use the replacement cost to report the tangible fixed assets.

Table 7.1. The value used to report tangible fixed assets

	British companies		German companies		French companies		Dutch companies	
	(No)	(%)	(No)	(%)	(No)	(%)	(No)	(%)
Historic cost or acquisition cost	7	28	20	80	13	52	17	68
Part of the fixed assets reported at the historic cost and the other part at the revalued cost	16	64			11	44		
Current value	1	4					6	24
Replacement cost	1	4					1	4
Historic cost assigned for specific type of fixed assets and current value for other types			3	12	1	4	1	4
No information given			2	8				
	25	100	25	100	25	100	25	100

CAPITALIZATION OF INTEREST USED TO FINANCE THE CONSTRUCTION OR THE DEVELOPMENT OF FIXED ASSETS

In certain cases, a company may construct a plant asset for its own use in the operation of the business. The costs that are directly related to the construction process should be included as part of the cost of assets. The primary problem associated with the determination of cost is the treatment of any interest cost incurred during construction. This issue has created considerable controversy within the accounting profession. In fact, self-constructed assets pose a problem in identifying relevant costs. IAS 16 (1982) required that:

> the cost of self constructed property should comprise those costs that relate to specific assets and those that are attributable to the construction activity in general and can be allocated to specific assets. Cost inefficiencies should not be included as part of such cost.

The explanatory part of the standard states 'it is usually appropriate to have regard to a comparison with the cost of equivalent purchased assets.'

As far as the capitalization of interest cost incurred during the construction of assets are concerned, two basic approaches have been considered:

1. Expense interest charges as they are incurred; or

2. Capitalize interest charges on debt during the construction period.

Whichever alternative is adopted the effect over the life of the asset will be to change the timing of income recognition rather than the total amount of income recognized. The proponents of capitalization argue that interest represents the cost of funds used to construct the property, and that all costs incurred prior to the time the assets are utilized are part of the cost of the assets. If interest costs are necessary for creating the assets, then they should be capitalized in the same way as labour and materials. If costs were calculated according to the principles of opportunity cost then this would include the cost attributable to any equity finance tied up by the establishment of relevant costs. Rickwood (1983) summarized the major argument for capitalization. The interest cost should not be charged on the financial cost of assets before these assets are used in production. Since costs are spread over the assets productive life by charging depreciation in the annual income statement, then the depreciation of capitalized interest is consistent with this and with the underlying principle of matching. Moreover, capitalization helps in reducing fluctuations in profit behaviour and the return on invested capital of the period in which financing costs are high. Furthermore, capitalization provides a better basis for comparison between companies which have constructed their own assets and companies which buy ready to use assets. The latter set their prices in the hope of recovering financing costs in addition to the cost of labour and materials, and therefore the former should include financing costs to make comparison possible. In this respect, Philip (1984) pointed out that capitalization of interest is a well-established practice in many parts of the world.

The opposing view is that interest is a cost of financing, rather than a cost of constructing the assets. Rickwood (1983) demonstrated the reasons underlying the rejection of capitalizing the interest costs. Writing off the interest expense results in better matching of the cost of funds supplied with the period of supply. In addition, costs of holding assets should be treated as period costs. Not using the assets results in an increase in value with capitalization. Capitalization may distort comparison because the policy depends on arbitrary allocation, depreciation policies, company gearing position, method of financing, and company risk. Hence, capitalization increases discrepancies between profits and cash flows. IAS (23) specifies the circumstances under which interest may be capitalized and the means of measuring the amount of interest to be included in the cost of an asset. FASB (24) indicated that interest cost incurred during the period of time in which an asset is brought to the condition and location that is necessary for its intended use would be capitalized as part of the cost of the asset. In the United Kingdom capitalization of interest costs was allowed by the Companies Act 1981 and para. 26 sch. 4 of the Companies Act 1985 states that: 'interest of capital borrowed to finance the production of that asset, to the extent that it accrues in respect of the period of production ....' This statement is open to abuse since the period of production is not defined. By capitalizing interest, the amount capitalized will be allocated over the life of the assets. The life is subject to manipulation. In some cases where interest is used to finance undepreciable assets (i.e. land) interest charges are entirely avoided. Thus capitalization of interest will result in better gearing ratios.

Boersema and Helden (1986) surveyed the 1984 annual report of 125 of the top ranked companies in the *Financial Times* 1000. Their sample includes 86% of the top 50 and 73% of the top 100. They found that almost half of the companies surveyed do capitalize interest. They also found that the extent of the disclosure among companies that capitalize varies significantly and 21% of those companies did not disclose the amount capitalized. Some of the companies did not meet the requirement of FASB (34) and IAS (23) in disclosing information related to capitalization of interest. Around 25% of companies which capitalized disclosed how they determined their rate of interest. Companies that disclosed how they determined their rate did not restrict themselves to the methods permitted by FASB (34), that is, the rate of interest applicable to debt specifically associated with the qualifying asset, or a weighted average of all borrowing rates. Boersema and Helden believe that the most compelling argument against capitalization is that it provides no useful information to the financial statement users. Also useful to this assessment would be the usual footnote information on the principal amount of debt outstanding at various interest rates and the maturing dates of various issues. To the extent that users assess a company's ability to meet its commitments by employing ratios such as the interest coverage ratio, then this requires the use of actual interest obligations not actual interest less capitalized interest. Boersema and Helden concluded that the argument for interest capitalization is unconvincing and that the practice would needlessly add more arbitrary allocation to financial accounting. Yet, Swanney (1983) in the *Survey of UK Published Accounts* (1982–1983), referred to the practice by property companies of capitalizing interest costs. He found that the property companies often either disregard the normal accounting practice of writing off interest in the period, or compensate the profit and loss account by transferring an equivalent amount of reserves to relieve the revenue account of these and other charges. In the same fashion, Mellows and Hudson (1988), in the *Survey of UK Published Accounts* (1987–1988), found that a majority of property companies capitalize interest as part of development costs. They also found that there is great disparity between companies, both in the extent of disclosure of the period for which outgoings, and especially interest, are taken into account and in the policies adopted. Derwent (1991) in the *Survey of UK Published Accounts* (1990–1991) provided three examples of companies capitalizing interest.

On the other hand, in the survey of the European companies (25 from each of Germany, France and Holland) only the Dutch company Nedlloyd capitalized what it referred to as 'Seagoing and drilling units under construction are included at time aggregate of the instalment payments made, including interest on loans during the construction period.'

To illustrate the affect of interest capitalization on the profit and loss account and the balance sheet, suppose Company A and Company B have identical profit and loss accounts and balance sheets (as shown below) before adjusting their accounts for interest incurred in financing self-constructed assets. The self-constructed assets cost was £100,000. Each had borrowed £50,000 to finance the construction at 20% p.a. cost of borrowing. While Company A opted to capitalize the interest, Company B chose to write it off.

Indicate the effect of different approaches used by each company on their profit and loss accounts, and the balance sheets, and some key financial ratios.

Profit and Loss account

	Company A	Company B
Turnover	£150,000	£150,000
Expenses	£ 80,000	£ 80,000
Profit	£ 70,000	£ 70,000

Balance sheet

	Company A	Company B
Fixed asset	£500,000	£500,000
Current asset	400,000	400,000
	£900,000	£900,000
Ordinary shares	750,000	750,000
Short-term liabilities	100,000	100,000
Long-term liabilities	50,000	50,000
	£900,000	£900,000

Profit and Loss account after considering interest

Turnover	150,000	150,000
Expenses	80,000	90,000
Profit	70,000	60,000

Balance sheet after considering interest

Fixed assets	510,000	500,000
Current assets	470,000	470,000
	£980,000	£970,000
Ordinary shares	£750,000	£750,000
Short-term liabilities	110,000	110,000
Long-term liabilities	50,000	50,000
P and L account	70,000	60,000
	£980,000	£970,000

	Company A	Company B
Profit/ordinary shares	70,000/750,000 = 0.0934	60,000/750,00 = 0.080
Profit/Total asset	70,000/980,000 = 0.0714	60,000/970,000 = 0.062
Total liabilities/Total asset	160,000/980,000 = 0.163	160,000/970,000 = 0.165

CASH DISCOUNT

When fixed assets are purchased, they may be subject to cash discount for a quick payment. When discount is taken, it should be considered as a reduction in the purchase price of the purchased asset. However, if the discount is not taken then two approaches may be employed to determine the acquisition cost of the purchased assets.

The first approach considers the discount as a reduction in the purchase price since the real cost of the asset is the cash or cash equivalent of the asset (historical cost principle). Some argue that this failure to take the discount is a loss because management was inefficient. However, others argue that the discount should not be considered as a loss because the terms may be unfavourable or because it would not be purchased for the company to take discount. Thus, the choice between the two approaches provides scope for window dressing.

DEPRECIATION METHODS

The common feature of all assets is that they are acquired and utilized to generate revenue rather than for resale purposes. Hence their economic service values are used in generating revenue. A proportion of their cost should be allocated against revenues generated during the period in order to fulfil the requirements of the historic cost and profit measurement. Hence, the process of allocating fixed costs over the expected useful life of the fixed assets is called depreciation.

Accounting for depreciation is considered one of the rich areas which provides opportunities for creative accounting. The allocation process, estimated useful life, estimated residual value, in addition to the number of depreciation methods permitted which provide different patterns of allocation and therefore different impacts on the income statement, are all capable of manipulation.

The allocation process was discussed in the preceding chapter. The accounting for an asset's useful life and residual value are stated by SSAP 12 as: 'a business has a duty to allocate depreciation as fairly as possible to the periods expected to benefit from the use of the asset.' The standard also states that when

> as a result of experiencing changed circumstances, it is considered that the original estimate of useful life of an asset requires to be revised, the unamortized cost of the asset should be charged to the revenue over the remaining useful life.

In this respect, ED 18, para. (46), recommends that 'estimated lives of assets should be reviewed regularly'. This will result in a smaller percentage increase in depreciation charges. However, in (1987) SSAP 12 was revised: the general principle adopted in the revised standard is that, where a fixed asset has a finite useful economic life, its cost or revalued amount should be depreciated over that life.

Any change in the asset's useful life or residual value will be reflected on the financial statements and thus offer a considerable scope for manipulation. Egginton (1987) interviewed senior accountants in 12 large companies and questioned them about their fixed assets policies. On the basis of the cases which he has considered, he suggests that an average basis towards conservative life and tardiness in revising assets' lives go hand in hand. The effect on the company's balance sheet cannot be quantified in financial terms. He believes that there is evidence that hidden reserves may be substantial, and a suspicion in at least two of the investigated cases in his study that hidden reserves were down at a convenient time. Egginton demonstrated that, in an ideal world, companies would review asset's life as part of their overall investment planning, taking into consideration changes in demand and technology which affect the lives of their existing assets. His evidence suggests that such an approach is the exception rather than the rule. He recommended that the standard and the auditor should ensure that the needs of users of accounts are justified.

On the other hand, SSAP 12 leaves the choice open between the straight-line method and the reducing method for depreciation. In addition, there are a number of methods used which provide different patterns of allocation and therefore different impacts on the income statement and balance sheet. Depreciation methods and rates can materially affect reported income and the net assets value of fixed assets.

All of the above mentioned depreciation methods are generally accepted because they result in a systematic and rational allocation of the cost of an asset to the period that benefits from its use. However, it is not necessary that a company uses a single method of depreciation for all of its depreciable assets. The methods vary with management's expectations about the way the benefits incorporated in the assets are to be realized.

In fact, the yearly expenses to be reported in the income statement and the depreciable asset's net balance depends on the depreciation method used. When a company changes the method it uses from time to time, it becomes difficult to make any sense of the balance sheet values of fixed assets. However, changing the useful life does not require justification whereas changing the method does. Yet, the creative accountant will be prepared to justify his or her action.

Another problem associated with depreciable assets is the continued use of written-off assets. The SSAP tried to deal with this problem by requiring a regular review of assets' lives. If a company continues using the written-off assets this means it will generate revenue without charging any depreciation expenses to the income statement.

The Results of the Analysis of the European Sample Surveyed

The annual financial report of the some European companies (25 companies from each of Britain, Germany, France and Holland) has been surveyed to see which depreciation method(s) is/are commonly used in practice. The analysis of the survey result is shown in Table 7.2.

It is evident from Table 7.2 that the vast majority of the surveyed British, French and Dutch companies use the straight-line method to depreciate their tangible fixed assets. However, although many of the surveyed German

Table 7.2. Depreciation methods used by the European surveyed companies

	British companies (No)	(%)	German companies (No)	(%)	French companies (No)	(%)	Dutch companies (No)	(%)
Straight-line	23	92	3	12	21	84	25	100
Straight-line or declining balance	1	4	7	28	2	8		
Straight-line or declining balance or the maximum rate allowable for tax purposes			4	16				
Unit of output					1	4		
Unit of output and straight-line	1	4						
Straight-line or extraordinary methods			1	4				
Straight-line or declining balance or extraordinary depreciation			4	16				
Straight-line or declining which is higher			2	8				
Not disclosed			4	16	1	4		
	25	100	25	100	25	100	25	100

companies use both straight–line and declining balance methods, they still adopt many various methods.

REVALUATION OF TANGIBLE FIXED ASSETS

The practice of revaluing tangible fixed assets provides *considerable scope for window dressing* because of the many variables that can be introduced into the process. These include the amount of revaluation, the timing of its recognition, whether the original cost or the revalued amount should be used as a basis for depreciation and whether the original estimated life and residual value should also be used as basis for depreciation.

In May 1990 the ASB issued ED 51 *Accounting for Fixed Assets and Revaluation.* The Draft permits companies to report selected assets at their revalued values. The values of these assets should be kept up to date and carried out in a structured form as prescribed by the Draft.

The difference between the original cost and the revaluation value represents unrealized profit and should be included in the reserves of the stockholder's equity section of the balance sheet.

The revised version of SSAP 12 states that the effect of increase in value of depreciable fixed assets will be to reduce future profit. Yet, a creative accountant has the opportunity to benefit from the increased value without having to suffer the disadvantages. Revaluation increases assets and stockholder's equity balances in the balance sheet. When the balance sheet includes borrowing, the increase in the stockholder's equity will improve the company's gearing ratios. However, the side effect of revaluing fixed assets is the increase in depreciation expenses, which will be charged to the income statement. Even so, the company can control the reported figures by choosing which assets are to be revalued, at what time, what are their useful lives, and what are the justifications for revaluations. In this respect, Carty (1984), in the *Survey of UK Published Accounts* (1983–1984), showed that the valuation basis adopted by the surveyed companies was given as open market value in 17 cases, open market values for existing use in 9 cases and valuation with a view to disposal in 4 cases. In the other two cases, assuming 'vacant possession' was used as the basis for valuation. In addition, Carty found that 8 of the companies follow a revaluation policy of every three or five years. Three companies showed that they intended to carry out revaluation owing to uncertainty in market conditions. Moreover, Carty demonstrated that revaluation of plant and machinery is less frequent than revaluation of properties. Four companies revalued 100% of their plants during the year, one revalued 40% and eight revalued less than 20% . In the same fashion, in the *Survey of the UK Published Accounts* (1986–1987), Macdonald (1987) showed that most of the companies' accounts he examined incorporated the element of fixed assets revaluation, principally in connection with freehold and long leased land and building. In the *Survey of UK Published Accounts* (1987–1988), Tonkin and Watson (1988) showed that 5% of the surveyed companies, revalued their operating properties (investment properties are not included) during the current year in the proportion between 81–100%, 3% in the proportion between 61–80%, 1% in the proportion between 41–60%, 4% in the proportion between 21–40% and 8% in the proportion between 1–20%. In the *Survey of UK Published Accounts* (1989–1990), Tonkin and Watson (1990) concluded that the pattern of revaluation of operating properties illustrates an increase in the proportion of listed companies revaluing most or all of their operating properties. The companies justified their move on the grounds that they adopted this approach as a defensive reaction against takeover or mergers. Tonkin (1991) in the *Survey of UK Published Accounts* (1990–1991) showed that a substantial minority of companies revalue their operating properties. Of the sample companies he used 23% have revalued at least some of the operating assets.

In any event, it seems that the approach a company employs is affected by the profit profile appropriate to the company's needs. A company which had a good financial year does not take into consideration the reduction in profit associated with assets revaluation.

Scope for Creative Accounting

Specific examples of opportunities that the revaluation of fixed assets provided for window dressing are as follows.

Accumulated Depreciation

Two alternatives may be used to deal with accumulated depreciation after revaluation. To illustrate these alternatives, suppose a company has fixed assets which cost £2,000, which have been written down to £1,000, but now are revalued to £3,200. Paterson (1984) distinguished between two schools of thought as to the disposition of credit. Some hold the view that the £1,000 should be credited to retained earnings or income statement and the excess over cost of £1,200 to capital reserves, others believe that the whole £2,200 should go to capital reserves.

Those who advocate the former view believe that the revaluation has established that the depreciation charge was unnecessary, and that the retained earnings should reflect the position which would have existed as if no such depreciation had been charged. They argue that the excess of the valuation over cost represents unamortized surplus which should be regarded as undistributable and carried as revaluation reserves.

Those who defend the second approach believe that the function of depreciation is to allocate the cost of the asset over its useful life; this does not mean no depreciation should be charged. They contend that the revalued assets are not new assets but a half expired one, and accordingly the revaluation surplus should be measured as the difference between the valuation figures and its written down value, not its original costs. Thus, if a company has chosen the first approach its net income and the stockholders section in the balance sheet will be improved. This will have positive effects on the EPS ratio. Therefore, the abuse of the choice between the two approaches provides potential for manipulation.

Buildings Are Revalued and Depreciated For The First Time

In general land and buildings are shown as one figure in a UK company's reported balance sheet and they are bought and sold together. This results in practical difficulties in depreciating one without the other. Nobes and Akrikam (1977) found that 300 UK companies of the 1975 ICA survey did not depreciate freehold land and buildings. The most significant effect of SSAP 12 is its requirement that buildings should be depreciated. SSAP 12 makes it obvious in para. 14 that, where buildings have not previously been depreciated, adoption of SSAP 12 will constitute a change of policy which will require restatement of prior years. This affects the retained earnings of the company. To cope with this, companies may incorporate revaluation of the building in the year of the change of policy and allocate the difference over the remaining useful life.

This might be resisted in practice. The chapter by Brown (1983), in the survey of published accounts (1982–1983), raises a number of interesting points on non-compliance. He found that SSAP 12 is resisted most frequently by companies in the depreciation of all parts of their freehold and long leasehold property. The justification for non-compliance is that depreciation provision would not be material. Some of the surveyed companies implied that the depreciation charge would be immaterial because property as a whole is immaterial in relation to their operations, while others argued that the high market or residual value of property, often coupled with a long economic life, will make an annual depreciation charge an immaterial sum. In fact, what the companies advanced to defend their practice might be true for a single year, but the cumulative effect might well be material. Macdonald (1987), in the *Survey of UK Published Accounts* (1986–1987), noticed that some companies did not adopt the proposals laid down in ED 37 and the draft revision of SSAP 12 in dealing with accumulated depreciation balance after revaluation. Instead, some companies relied on the interpretation of the *Companies Act 1985* Sch.4 para. 31(1) to permit past accumulated depreciation to be released to distributable reserve instead of being added to the revaluation reserve. On the other hand, Tonkin (1991) in the *Survey of UK Published Accounts* noticed that there is a substantial and increasing minority of companies in the retail markets who do not depreciate freehold buildings or long leased property.

A further point of interest is that the standard specifically states that:

> it is not appropriate to omit charging depreciation of a fixed asset on the ground that its market value is greater than its carrying value, and also that an increase in the value of the land and building does not remove the necessity for charging the depreciation on the buildings on the buildings.

Ball *et al.* (1979) found that companies enjoyed a share price increase relative to the market as a result of receiving an audit qualification for non-compliance of depreciation of property. Thus, creativity lies in the amount of land and building subject to depreciation and the timing of the revaluation. The legal rule and the standard provide an opportunity for manipulation. The *Companies Act 1985* only requires depreciation to be deducted from assets that have a finite life, and the accounting standard SSAP 12 allows specifically for freehold land not to be depreciated. Many companies extend the exception to buildings. The justification is that the building has infinite economic life because it is continuously maintained and brought up to date. It might be also argued that the maintenance expenditures represent improvements to the property and should be capitalized rather than included in the expense of the income statement.

Depreciation in the Year of Revaluation

According to para. (9) of SSAP 12 when assets are revalued in the accounts 'the charge for depreciation thereafter should be based on the revalued amount'. Presumably this means that if the revaluation is made at the beginning of the year, the depreciation charge will be based on the revalued amounts. If the revaluation took place shortly before the end of the year, the income statement will carry depreciation charges based on the previous carrying value. However, if the revaluation took place in the middle of the year, depreciation should be based on the previous carrying values for the period up to that date and on the revalued amount for the remainder of the year. Thus, the difference in timing of revaluation can affect the figures reported in the income statement and on the balance sheet.

Split Depreciation

Split depreciation allows the company to revalue its assets and to base its depreciation charges on the historical cost amount. The company splits the depreciation into the portion related to the historical cost amount and that related to the revaluation adjustment. The former portion is charged to the income statement and the latter to the reserves in the stockholder's equity section of the balance sheet. On this occasion, the balance sheet will benefit from the increased value of assets and the income statement will incur the same amount of depreciation expense as before the revaluation. The justification for this approach is that since the unrealized profit of revaluation has not been shown in the income statement, this treatment complies with the matching principle. Even so, this approach contradicts the conservatism principle, which states that where acceptable alternatives for accounting measurements are available, the alternative having the lower immediate influence on the owners' equity should be accepted.

According to Councell (1984) in Woolworths' 1983–1984 accounts instead of charging the depreciation on the entire revalued amount to the income statement, they chose to split it, by charging the depreciation on the historical cost element to the income statement and the excess arising from revaluation to the revaluation reserve. This resulted in healthier profit figures and therefore earnings per share. Patient (1984) defended the split depreciation approach and claimed that the treatment is implicitly allowed by para. 32 (3), sch. 8, CA 1948. Even though Edey (1984) agreed that such a treatment is not forbidden under either SSAP 6 or SSAP 12 and is implicitly allowed by para. 32 (3), sch.8, *Companies Act 1948*, he went on to say: 'I am very doubtful whether the resulting "hybrid" accounts show a true and fair view as specified by s 149 of the same Act.' He added that he found it difficult to reconcile the split depreciation approach with the consistency concept set out in SSAP 2.

It has to be pointed out that, although revaluation of fixed assets in historical costs accounts has been practised in the United Kingdom for a long time and permitted by the *Companies Act 1985* and supported by the Accounting Standard Committee (ASC), it is not allowed in the United States and many other countries. Such differences make it difficult to compare companies in different countries. The ICAEW survey of published accounts for the years (1974–1975) to (1982–1983) shows that a majority of the firms surveyed revalued property and that a significant number revalued other fixed assets. A variety of reasons have been put forward for revaluation but many companies appear to have followed the advice of statement S20 (ICAEW 1974) that only existing use valuations or depreciated replacement costs are suitable for inclusion in accounts. The *Companies Act 1985* provided a choice between the market value and the current value and this will result in variations in accounting treatment. As a result of considerable variations in the periods that elapse between revaluation, further problems arise between companies and even within the same company. Grinyer (1987) believed that there is a need for an accepted rationale for revaluation. He went on to say that although unregulated variations in the timing of revaluation may often be justified, they do provide management with additional opportunities to manipulate information shown in the accounts. In this respect, the chapter by Brown (1983), in the *Survey of UK Published Accounts* (1982–1983), found that most of the companies do not provide any information concerning the revaluation of fixed assets.

Treatment of Gains or Losses on Sale of Revalued Fixed Assets

The practice of many companies is to calculate gains or losses by referring to the depreciated historical cost of the relevant assets. However, this practice is likely to be eliminated when ED 51 becomes a standard. ED 51 proposes that gains or losses on sale of revalued fixed assets should be determined by reference to the revalued carrying value. The difference between the two approaches can be illustrated by using the following example.

Assume XYZ Company purchased a fixed asset for £5,000 with an estimated useful life of five years. The company employs the straight-line depreciation method. In the second year of the asset's life, the asset was revalued to £6,000 and at the end of the same year sold for £6,000.

Table 7.3. Number of companies used the scheme of revaluation of fixed assets and the treatment they have adopted.

	British companies (No)	British companies (%)	German companies (No)	German companies (%)	French companies (No)	French companies (%)	Dutch companies (No)	Dutch companies (%)
Number of companies revalued their fixed assets	19	76	5	20	12	48	4	16
Treatment of revaluation difference								
Taken to revaluation reserves	18	72	3	12	8	32	2	8
Taken to retained earnings					2	8		
No information given	1	4	2	8	2	8	2	8

In this case £2,000 (£6,000 − £4,000) will be credited to revaluation reserves. If XYZ company calculates gains or losses by reference to the depreciated historical cost, it will report gains on the sale of fixed assets £2,000 (assume no depreciation charged to year two). On the other hand, if the XYZ company reported the gain in accordance with ED 51, it will show zero gain in its profit and loss account.

The Results of the Analysis of the European Sample Surveyed

An attempt has been made to how the scheme of revaluation of fixed assets and its treatment are reported by European companies surveyed. The results of the analysis are shown in Table 7.3.

It is evident from Table 7.3 that few German and Dutch companies adopted the scheme. By contrast, a relatively high number of the surveyed French companies employed the scheme. However, the result of the survey may point to variations in the treatment of the revaluation.

REVIEW QUESTIONS

1. What is the major uncertainty in accounting for self-constructed assets, and how can it be resolved?

2. What argument can you think of in favour of and against the capitalization of interest incurred in the self-construction of assets?

3. John and Mark own a winery. The vineyards from which the grapes are supplied to the winery was originally owned by their father. After the death of their father, John and Mark took his 300 acres for their perusal after paying £20,000 to the father's wife. John and Mark must decide now on the appropriate asset value for their accounting records. Discuss factors to be considered in establishing the book value for the vineyard.

4. Trainer Sports operate a new branch in Cardiff. All the structures are constructed by their employees during the off-season. In considering the cost of constructed assets, only the cost of the materials had been capitalized. The owner justified his policy of not capitalizing the cost of work done on the grounds that his staff were paid on a yearly basis. During the off-season, they have a lot of free time and the wages he paid for constructing the assets cannot be separated from wages relating to other work. He believes that no incremental cost had been incurred. Show whether or not the costs of the constructed assets were properly valued on the balance sheet.

5. Fresh Air Company decided to construct all of its machines. The construction required the company to borrow £100,000. The self-constructed assets' costs were £500,000. Suppose the cost of the loan was 15% per annum. Fresh Air is confused on which approach to adopt to deal with interest incurred on the loan. Although capitalizing the interest improves the book value of the company's shares, it increases income tax to be paid. On the other hand, while charging the interest to the profit and loss account reduces income tax to be paid, it reduces the book value per share. Explain to Fresh Air's manager the effect of the above suggested approaches on the profit and loss account, balance sheet and some key financial ratios.

6. Orange Corporation purchased equipment with a list price of £10,000. The vendor's credit term was 2/10, n/30. Orange paid cash for the equipment fifteen days after the purchase. The company's manager decided to record the cost of assets at £10,000. He justified his action on the grounds that the discount should not be considered as a loss because the credit terms were not favourable to the company and it was not prudent to the company to take that discount.

   (a) Discuss the effect of employing this approach on the profit and loss account, balance sheet and some key financial ratios.

   (b) Suggest another approach to Orange and show how it will affect the profit and loss account, balance sheet and some key financial ratios.

7. It is argued that accounting for depreciation is considered to be one of the rich areas providing opportunities for creative accounting. State if you agree or disagree with this argument and show the effect of alternative

accounting methods used for depreciation on the profit and loss account and balance sheet.

8. Baoum Company purchased an asset on 1 January 1990. It costs £50,000, and has an estimated useful life of 9 years and £5,000 residual scrap value. The company uses straight-line depreciation. At 31 December 1992, the company valued the asset at £65,000. Baoum's manager believes that the accumulated depreciation up to 31 December should be credited to retained earnings and the excess over cost to the capital reserves. Nevertheless, Baoum's accountant believes that the whole amount (accumulated depreciation + excess over cost) should go to capital reserves.

   (a) Discuss the justification for the use of each of the above suggested approaches and their effect (if any) on the earning per share ratio.

   (b) In the light of your discussion recommend the approach to be used by Baoum. Give reasons for the recommended approach.

9. In question 8 above discuss other opportunities of creative accounting that Baoum might adopt to deal with the side effect of asset revaluation. How will this affect the profit and loss account and balance sheet?

10. Explain what is meant by split depreciation and critically analyze its effect on the profit and loss account and balance sheet.

CHAPTER 8

Accounting for Intangibles

INTRODUCTION

The debate on the recognition of intangible fixed assets begins with the question of whether they should be capitalized. To recognize intangible fixed assets on the balance sheet, their historical cost ought to be known or readily ascertainable (see ED 52 *Accounting for Intangible Fixed Assets*).

Intangible assets are those properties without physical substance, their ownership confers some exclusive rights, they provide future benefits to operations and they are relatively long lived. ED 52 defined an intangible fixed asset as a fixed asset that is non-monetary in nature and without physical substance.

Accounting for intangible assets involves essentially the same accounting principles and procedures as for tangible property, plant and equipment.

MEASURING AND RECORDING INTANGIBLE ASSETS AT ACQUISITION

The cash equivalent price of the intangibles measured by considering the assets given or received, whichever is more objectively measurable, is the basis for the cost of intangibles. In addition, any element of loss incurred in the process of setting the asset to its intended use may be capitalized as part of the cost of intangibles.

Under the rules of ED 51 a fixed asset should be recognized when:

1. It is probable that any future economic benefits associated with assets will flow to the enterprise: and

2. The asset has a cost and, when carried at valuation, a value that can be measured with reliability.

ED 52 reveals that it is probable that many intangibles will fail to meet the above criteria, in which event intangibles can be recognized in the balance sheet if:

1. Either the historical cost incurred in creating it is known or it can be readily ascertainable: and

2. The characteristics can be clearly distinguished from those of goodwill or other assets: and

3. Its cost can be measured independently of goodwill or other assets and of the earning of the relevant business or business segment. In order for this to be possible when the historical cost of acquired assets is deemed to be their fair value, there will normally need to be an active market in intangible assets of the same kind independently of the purchase and sale of business or business segments.

These guiding concepts may look straightforward, but their application requires some degree of subjective judgement and this may give rise to creative accounting.

AMORTIZATION OF THE COST OF INTANGIBLE ASSETS

The cost of intangible assets should be deployed by systematic debit to expense over the estimated period of useful life as stipulated in APB Opinion No. 17. The opinion also stipulated that the maximum amortization period used in any given case should not be more than 40 years. In the United Kingdom, intangible fixed assets are considered by ED 52 to have a finite life. They are required to be amortized over their economic lives, a period which may not exceed 20 years unless it is clearly demonstrated that a longer period is appropriate. The amortization period should not in any event exceed 40 years.

DISPOSAL OF INTANGIBLES

When an intangible asset is sold, exchanged or disposed of the unamortized cost must be removed from the accounting record and the gains or losses on disposal recorded.

REVALUATION OF INTANGIBLES

As is the case with tangible assets, during the period of use an estimate of value and future benefit of an intangible asset may indicate that the unamortized cost exceeds the economic value. In this case the excess should be amortized over the estimated remaining useful life, not exceeding 40 years from the date of acquisition. (APB Opinion No. 17, para. 31). Where there is a write down because of impairment of value, disclosure is required in notes to the financial statements. In the United Kingdom according to ED 52 intangible fixed assets which satisfy the recognition criteria must be carried at an historic cost or valuation. To carry intangible assets at the valuation amount, the carrying amount must be based on the depreciated replacement cost and this should be measured with reasonable certainty. In addition, the replacement cost must represent current cost which means that it must not exceed the net recoverable amount of the asset.

IDENTIFIABLE AND UNIDENTIFIABLE INTANGIBLE ASSETS

A number of bases may be employed to differentiate one group of intangible assets from another. In the past, the accounting profession recognized two types of classification for intangibles: intangibles that had a limited life and intangibles that had an unlimited life.

The classification was changed by APB Opinion No. 17 to identifiable and unidentifiable intangible assets.

Identifiable intangible assets mean that cost associated with obtaining intangible assets can be identified as part of the cost of that intangible asset (patents, copyrights, leaseholds, trademarks, organization costs, franchises in research and development).

Unidentifiable intangible assets are like goodwill and brand names that may create some right or privilege but are not specifically identifiable. They have an indeterminable life, and their costs are inherent in a continuing business.

ACCOUNTING FOR GOODWILL

Accounting for goodwill is a complex and controversial issue. Goodwill is unique because unlike debtors, stock and patent, that can be exchanged or sold individually in the market place, goodwill can be only identified with the business as a whole. Goodwill is recorded only when an entire business is purchased because goodwill is a going concern valuation and cannot be separated from the business.

Methods of Measuring Goodwill

The methods of measuring goodwill are somewhat related to the two basic views of the nature of goodwill (see *Accounting for Business Combinations and Purchased Intangibles*, FASB Discussion Memorandum FASB 1976d, p. 48):

1. Goodwill represents intangible resources and conditions attributable to an enterprise's above average strength in areas such as technical skills and knowledge, marketing research and promotion that cannot be separately identified and valued.

2. Goodwill represents expected earnings in excess of anticipated normal earnings. According to this view, goodwill is the excess of the cost over the fair value of the identifiable net assets. Another view is one that determines the earnings, in excess of those that normally could be earned by tangible and identifiable intangible assets. These excess earnings are discounted to determine the present value of this extra inflow, which is considered the amount of goodwill.

In February 1990, in the United Kingdom, the ASB issued ED 47 *Accounting for Goodwill* which proposes that goodwill should be capitalized and amortized over its useful economic life. This prescription is one of two choices published in SSAP 22. The other choice of immediate write off against reserves would no longer be allowed if the draft became a standard.

To explain the idea of goodwill the following example is employed. Suppose that two businesses in the same line of trade were offered for sale and that the normal return of the fair market value of net identifiable assets in this industry is 20% a year. The relative earning power of the two companies during the past 10 years is shown below.

	Company A (£)	Company B (£)
Fair market value of net identifiable assets	600,000	600,000
Average annual net profit for past 10 years	120,000	150,000
Normal earnings, capitalized as 20% of net identifiable assets	120,000	120,000
Earnings in excess of normal	0	30,000

An investor would be willing to pay £600,000 to buy Company A because Company A earns the normal 20% return which justifies the fair market value of its tangible assets. Although Company B has the same net tangible assets, the investor would be willing to pay more for Company B than for Company A because Company B has a record of superior earnings.

The following are several methods which a prospective purchaser uses in estimating a value of goodwill.

1. *Negotiated price:* negotiated agreement between buyer and seller may be reached on the amount of goodwill. In the previous example it may be agreed that the fair market value of net identifiable assets is £600,000 and that the total purchase price for Company B will be £720,000. Thus providing £120,000 payment for goodwill.

2. *Multiple of earnings in excess normal earnings:* goodwill may be determined as a multiple of the earnings in excess of normal earnings. Referring to the previous example, a prospective buyer might be willing to pay for Company B three times the amount by which average earnings exceed normal earnings, indicating a value of £90,000 for goodwill. Therefore, the purchase price of Company B will be £690,000.

3. *Goodwill may be estimated by capitalizing the amount by which average earnings exceed normal earnings.* Capitalizing of earnings means dividing these earnings by the investor's required rate of return. In the previous example, if the prospective buyer decided to capitalize the £30,000 average earnings in excess of normal earnings for Company B at a rate of 20%, the value of goodwill will be £150,000 (£30,000 divided by 20%). Therefore, the purchase price of the business would be £750,000.

4. *Present value estimation of goodwill:* goodwill can be estimated by determining the present value of the future excess earnings purchased. In the previous example, if the expected earnings in excess of normal will continue to be £30,000 for the coming five years, then goodwill will be calculated as follows:

$$30,000 \times IF\ (n,i) \quad n=5 \text{ years}, \ i=20\%$$
$$30,000 \times 2.9906 = £89,718$$

Therefore the purchase price of the business would be £689,718.

It is evident that various approaches may be employed to estimate the value of goodwill and none of these provides the same results. Hence, a creative accountant will find it easy to adopt the approach which satisfies the company's need.

Amortization of Goodwill

Once goodwill has been recognized in the accounts, the next question is: which is the proper accounting method to use?

Three basic accounting methods may be suggested:

1. In the United Kingdom SSAP 22 provides that, *in case of acquisition, goodwill should be eliminated against reserves.* The SSAP does not require disclosure of how values are allocated to the net assets acquired nor the amount of any provision for any future variation costs. ED 47 is to make amortization from post acquisition profits mandatory. The Draft also allows for writing off goodwill over a period of time. However, in the United States, *Accounting Research Study No. 10* indicates that goodwill should be written off

immediately to stockholder's equity. The argument for this approach takes the position that goodwill cannot be sold without selling the business. In addition, ARS No. 10 notes that the accounting treatment for purchased goodwill and home-grown goodwill should be consistent. Goodwill grown internally is immediately written off and does not appear on the balance sheet. The same treatment should be accorded to the purchased goodwill. Furthermore, it is argued that amortization of purchased goodwill leads to double bundling because profit will be reduced by amortization as well as by internal expenditure made to maintain the value of assets. More importantly, determination of the period over which future benefits are to be received is too subjective.

2. *APB Opinion* No. 17 takes the position that *goodwill should be written off over its useful life*. The useful life should not exceed 40 years. The proponents of this approach argue that it provides better matching of costs and revenues.

3. Some accountants believe that *goodwill can have an identifiable life and should be maintained as an asset until a decline in value occurs*. They argue that inasmuch as internal goodwill is being written off to maintain the purchased goodwill, some forms of goodwill should always be assets. Furthermore, without clear evidence that a decline in goodwill value has occurred, it is arbitrary to write off goodwill and this leads to profit distortion.

The above argument showed that treatment of goodwill after recognition has a major effect on the profit and loss account, balance sheet and some key financial ratios. If it is in the interest of the company to improve the gearing ratios without affecting or reducing the reported profit, the company will adopt the third approach. If the company is looking for improving efficiency ratios, it would choose the first approach. If the company chooses to smooth its reported profit to avoid any unexpected uncertainty, it would be more efficient to amortize goodwill over its useful life. Thus, one should expect management to adopt the approach which satisfies its needs.

Tonkin (1991) in the *Survey of UK Published Accounts* noticed that no significant change took place after the issuance of ED 47. Companies still write off goodwill against reserves in the year of acquisition.

The Results of the Analysis of the European Sample Surveyed

An attempt has been made to investigate types of intangible assets reported by some companies operating in Britain, Germany, France and Holland. To serve this purpose, 25 companies from each country has been surveyed and the results are analyzed and disclosed in Table 8.1.

Table 8.1. The analysis of types of intangible assets reported by British, German, French and Dutch companies.

	British companies		German companies		French companies		Dutch companies	
	(No)	(%)	(No)	(%)	(No)	(%)	(No)	(%)
Goodwill	15	60	10	40	20	80	14	56
Franchise, industrial and similar rights			9	45			1	4
Advance payments							5	20
Patents			5	20	3	12	1	4
Brand	3	12						
Costs of issued shares					1	4		
Copyrights					1	4		
License fees			1	4			1	4
Research and development	1	4	1	4	3	12	3	12
Trademarks and trade Names	1	4	2	8	1	4	3	12
Software			6	24	2	8	1	4
Publishing rights					2	8	2	8
Development cost					1	4		
Lease right					2	4		
Preliminary expenses					1	4		

It obvious from Table 8.1 that most of the surveyed companies disclosed information on the treatment of goodwill. However, it is important to see how these companies accounted for the excess of cost over net assets of the acquired company. The result of the analysis is shown in Table 8.2.

Although there is variation in reporting the excess of cost over the net assets of the acquired company, it is clear that most of the surveyed French and Dutch companies debited/credited the excess to the stockholders' equity of the balance sheet and amortize over various periods of time (the period of time varies between 5–40 years). Hence, the outcome of this analysis may support Tonkin's (1991) opinion in the *Survey of UK Published Accounts* in which he believed that there is a growing evidence that capitalizing of goodwill is becoming more widespread in European countries other than the United Kingdom.

OPERATING OR FINANCE LEASE

A lease is a contractual document between the owner of the property (lessor) and the user of the property (lessee) that conveys to the lessee the right to use a

Table 8.2. Analysis of the treatment of excess cost over net assets of acquired companies.

	British companies (No)	British companies (%)	German companies (No)	German companies (%)	French companies (No)	French companies (%)	Dutch companies (No)	Dutch companies (%)
Reported separately as goodwill and amortized against retained earnings			6	24	1	4	1	4
Reported separately as goodwill and amortized against other revenue reserves			4	16				
Reported as an intangible asset and amortized over its economic life			5	20	2	8		
Written off directly to reserves	10	40	10	40	19	76	17	68
No information given	10	40	5	20	3	12	7	28

specific property owned by the lessor for a specific period of time in return for stipulated rent payments. The nature and the time period of leases range from very simple short-term rentals (the daily use of rental cars) to the complex multi-year contracts (a store leasing its retail premises).

The main motive to use the lease is derived from the fact that leasing in a certain manner leads to minor claims, it does not add debt on the balance sheet, and it does not affect financial ratios, hence it may add to the borrowing capacity. Certain types of lease arrangements need not be capitalized on the balance sheet. The liability section is frequently relieved from large future lease commitments that, if recorded, would adversely affect the debt/equity ratio. The reluctance to record lease obligations as liabilities may be one of the primary reasons behind the lessee's resistance and circumvention of reporting capitalized lease.

In 1964, *APB Opinion* No. 5 *Lease Accounting* and in 1966 *APB Opinion* No. 7 *Lessor Accounting* required that instalment purchase lease should be capitalized as any fixed assets purchased with a related obligation. However, the criteria set to distinguish capitalized and non-capitalized leases was circumvented by lessees because it increased the amount of their reported short-term and long-term debt, it increased the value of long-life assets and lowered income early in the life of the lease therefore lowering retained earnings. Thus, many companies believe that capital leases will have a significant impact on their financial position as their debt to total equity ratio increases and rate of return on total assets decreases. Consequently, the business community resists capitalizing leases.

However, *APB Opinion* Nos 5 and 7 did not require systematic classification of accounting for lease in the accounts of the lessor and the lessee. In 1972 and 1973, *APB Opinion* No. 31 on lease accounting was issued, but it did little to eliminate the inconsistencies in lease accounting practice.

In fact, it is difficult to reach an agreement on an appropriate accounting treatment for leases. Those who advocate no capitalization of any leased assets propose that since the lessee does not have ownership of the property, capitalization is considered inappropriate. Furthermore, a lease is an executory contract requiring continuing performance by both parties. Because executory contracts (such as commitments and employment contracts) are not usually capitalized, this view contends that leases also should not be capitalized. On the other hand, there are many other views which ask for capitalization after meeting specific conditions. One of those views defended capitalization of those leases similar to instalment purchase. This view contended that accountants should report transactions in accordance with their economic substance; therefore, if instalment purchases are capitalized, so also should leases that have the same characteristics as instalment sales. Another view defended the capitalization of all long-term assets. Under this view, the only requirement for capitalization is the long-term right to use the property. Often referred to as the property rights view, it could lead to the capitalization of all long-term leases. (*Accounting Research Study* No. 4 advocated this approach.) A final view suggests the capitalization of firm leases where the penalty for non–performance is substantial. Firm means that it is unlikely that performance under the lease can be avoided without a severe penalty. (Ijiri (1980) supported this view.)

In 1976 the FASB issued Statement No. 13 *Accounting for Lease* which replaced all previous official pronouncements on lease accounting. The FASB distinguished between operating the lease (non–capitalized lease) and capital lease (capitalized lease) by providing four criteria to classify and account for the arrangement as capital lease.

1. The lessor transfers ownership of the property to the lessee.

2. The lease contains a bargain purchase option.

3. The lease term is equal to 75% or more of the estimated economic life of the leased property.

4. The present value of the minimum lease payments (excluding executory costs) equals or exceeds 90% of the fair value of the leased property.

Leases that do not meet any of the four criteria above are classified and accounted for as an operating lease. On the other hand, in the United Kingdom SSAP 21 distinguished between finance and operating lease:

A finance lease is a lease that transfers substantially all the risks and rewards of ownership of an asset to the lessee. (Para. 15)

An operating lease is a lease other than finance lease. (Para. 17)

According to SSAP 21 a lease is considered a finance lease if at the start of the lease the present value of the minimum lease payments amounts to substantially all (normally 90% or more) of the fair value of the leased assets. The present value should be calculated by using the interest rate implicit in the lease.

According to *Accountancy Age* (July 1992) the ASB is expected to issue a proposal 'The Elements of Financial Statements and the Recognition of items in Financial Statements' which will define assets and liabilities (see chapter seven). *Accountancy Age* believes that the definition of assets and liabilities, and when to report them in the accounts, will make it difficult to distinguish between operating and finance lease where the former is not now reported on the balance sheet.

FASB Interpretation No. 19 (1976c) laid down that lease provision requiring the lessee to make up a residual value deficiency that is attributable to damage, extraordinary wear and tear, or excessive usage is not included in the minimum lease payments. Such costs are similar to contingent rentals in that the amount is not determinable at the inception of the lease. Like contingent rentals, such costs are recognized as period costs when incurred. However, the discount rate should be used by the lessee to compute the present value of the minimum lease payments. The lessee should use the incremental borrowing rate defined by *FASB Statement* No. 29 (1979a) Para. 5(1) as

> the rate that, at the inception of the lease, the lessee would incur to borrow the funds necessary to buy the leased assets on a secured loan with payment terms similar to the payment schedule called for in the lease'

In practice the lessee frequently does not know the implicit rate, because the lessee may not capitalize the leased property at more than its fair value, and the lessee is prevented from using an excessively low interest rate.

Undoubtedly, it is easy to manipulate the criterion and to report the lease as an operating lease and therefore drive the loans and the additional expenses off the financial statements.

In all events, prior to the issuance of FASB 13, the criteria defining capital lease were much narrower. As a result, a great number of long-term leases were accounted for as operating leases by the lessee. Operating leases are often considered to be off-balance sheet financing, because the obligation for the future lease payment does not appear as a liability in the balance sheet of the lessee. As a result of the criteria set forth in FASB 13, the number of lease contracts qualifying as operating lease has been generally reduced. Even though the accounting for long-term lease contracts and capital leases significantly improves the usefulness of the balance sheet in evaluating the resources and the obligations of those companies, which lease a substantial portion of their productive units, accounting for leasing is not without its own problems. Dieter (1979) argued that the actual results of FASB 13 concerning its objectives and assertion of *less susceptibility to varied interpretations* have not been reached. There are significant numbers of long-term leases that meet the criteria of a capital lease and continued to be accounted for as operating leases. In 1981 Abdel-Khalik indicated in his study that management behaviour did not change as a result of FASB 13. For example, many companies restructure their leases to avoid capitalization; others increase their purchase of assets instead of leasing; and thus, faced with capitalization, postpone their debt offering an issue stock instead. However, it is interesting to note that the study found no significant effect on the stock or bond prices as a result of the capitalization of lease. Jones (1989) demonstrated that quoted leasing companies have not received a favourable rating from the stock market over the past 18 months (the raise in interest rate levels and economic fluctuations suggests the opposite).

Owens (1984) argued that FASB 13 distinguished differences between operating and finance lease by applying mathematical proportion to the lessor's capital outlay which is paid for by the lessee during the initial irrevocable hiring period. The fact that the issue is so clearly defined has led to leasing schemes being divided to enable lessees to side step the requirement to capitalize the assets in their accounts. Owens said that such an approach inevitably suffers from the shortcoming that it provides those who wish to dodge the matter, the opportunity to do so with certainty.

Thus, despite the attention the accounting profession has given to lease accounting, uniformity of treatment has not been achieved and the assertion of lease susceptibility to avoid interaction has not been reached. As of late 1979, the FASB had amended Statement No. 13 seven times, has issued six interpretations and has made additional amendments and interpretation in Exposure Drafts of development stages. This puts lease accounting in the highest position among the seemingly insoluble and frustrating problem areas of the accounting profession. Carr (1985) stated that standards as they have been adopted in the United States and the United Kingdom give rise to such significant inconsistencies that all too often its interpretation is treated as more important than understanding the commerciality of a transaction. Carr indicated that FASB (13) was published in November 1976, and has been generally accepted, and as one would expect, it is far more specific than SSAP 21 and it identifies a number of tests that must be met for certain classifications to be made. Clause 17 of FASB (13) specifically permits the use of the residual profit with respect to sale type leases, while SSAP 21 leaves the issue in the open, and consequently much discussion can be anticipated. Stevens and Waterhouse (1986) claimed that

SSAP 21 is not looking to apply arithmetical certainty, but more important it is looking to the underlying economic attributes of the transaction. They believe that there is nothing magical about the 90% parameter. If this fundamental test is applied properly, it is unnecessary and inefficient to go to great lengths to structure deals so that the present value of the minimum lease payment amounts to 89.5% of the fair value of the leased assets rather than the 90% figure quoted in SSAP 21, thereby arguing that the transaction is off-balance sheet to the lessee. Stevens and Waterhouse proceeded to say that the most crucial test as to whether a lease is a finance or operating lease is the question whether or not it transfers substantially all risks and rewards of ownership of the asset to the lessee. Normally the question can be answered without this test. It is usually clear from the intention of the parties as to who bears risk or rewards. In spite of that, Taylor and Turley (1985a) contended that although accounting for lease has appeared to be a controversial topic, the accounting standard set to treat it does not provide a solution for the controversy. On the contrary, Holgate (1984) described the step towards publishing SSAP 21 as 'a bold step'. Sykes (1976) has tended to report a substantial proportion of lessees because of the advantage of off-balance sheet financing. In the same manner, Percy and Green (1982) found evidence on the accounting practice, in the *Survey of UK Published Accounts* (1981–1982), which confirms that controversial practices on the accounting has reflected the legal character of the leasing transaction. The vast majority of the lessees have taken lease rentals as expenses to income statement.

Rutteman and Daley (1985), in the *Survey of UK Published Accounts* (1984–1985), found that the general level of disclosure on leases was very poor. Eighty-nine per cent of the surveyed companies indulged in leasing activities. The proportion using hire purchase finance was only 4%. The survey reflects that the basic premise in SSAP 21, that of capitalizing finance lease, has already gained some acceptability by some lessees. However, they believe that it is not possible to see the true extent yet because disclosure is not sufficient to distinguish between the finance lease not capitalized and the operating lease. Tonkin (1987), in the *Survey of UK Published Accounts* (1986–1987), found that the disclosure on income recognition policy by lessors had been increased marginally. Hence, the examples he provided showed that this area of accounting practice is one in which there is no great consistency. He also found that there was a trend of increasing disclosure of lease capitalization and commitments. He built up his conclusion on the grounds that only 13% in the (1982–1983) survey of the 300 sample companies showed any of their lease agreements as capitalization, while the (1986–1987) survey showed that 41% disclosed information on lease capitalization. Tonkin claimed that this represents a substantial change in both measurement and disclosure practice.

The survey of *UK Published Accounts* (1987–1988), (1989–1990) and (1990–1991) demonstrated that the trends of the increasing disclosure of lease capitalization are continued. However, after considering the accounting for lease in theory and practice the question to be raised is 'do the FASB (13) and SSAP 21 solve the problem of off-balance sheet financing associated with lease accounting?'

SALE AND LEASE BACK SCHEMES

One of the most popular methods employed to obtain cash is the use of the sale and lease back method. This method dominates a range of off-balance sheet financing. Generally, this method is related to a company's freehold properties. To realize capital gains and raise cash to be invested in the business, the company sells its property to an institutional investor. The purchaser guarantees to lease the property back to its former owner.

The advantage to the selling company is to get a large amount of cash and to reclassify the assets from freehold to leasehold. In addition, in case the selling company has financed its freehold property by creditors, this scheme reduces the company's borrowings and interest charges and brings down gearing ratios. Hence the company's rentals are included in the operating costs.

Ironically, if the scheme did not use the cash received from the sale of the freehold to repay creditors, then the sale and lease back device cannot be considered as off-balance sheet financing.

RESEARCH AND DEVELOPMENT ARRANGEMENT

An interesting case, which might be adopted in practice, is the financing of research and development costs through innovative financing arrangements. To illustrate, suppose that a company needs £10 million to continue work on a specific project. A limited partnership is created to raise the required £10 million. The limited partnership is granted the right to receive the royalties of the future use of the product under research. In this case, the accounting question is how should the company account for these arrangements? One view is that the limited partners simply lend money to the company, which subsequently uses it to finance its research and development activities. If such a view is adopted, research and development is reported as an expense on the company's books along with liabilities for the loan. On the other hand, others argue that the research and development activities are those of the limited partnership. In this case, the company reports neither the research and development expense nor the related liabilities, but instead it provides footnote disclosure of the agreement. From the perspective of the company, the accounting treatment makes a significant difference. In one situation, an expense and liability are reported; in the other, only a footnote is presented. In the UK, SSAP 13 *Accounting for Research and Development* does not address this case of off-balance sheet financing. In the US, FASB No. 68 *Research and Development Arrangements* has taken the position that, to the extent that an enterprise is obliged to pay other parties monies received, a liability and related changes to research and development expense should be estimated and recorded. For instance, if the company, in the above mentioned example, guarantees payment to the limited partnership, irrespective of the success of the project, the expense and related liability must be reported in the books of the company. On the other hand, in the above example, if the risk associated with the research and development activities is assumed by the limited partnership, then the debt and related expenses need not be reported on the company's books.

ACCOUNTING FOR EXPLORATION AND DEVELOPMENT COSTS IN THE OIL AND GAS INDUSTRY

The exploration and development costs of oil and gas companies are substantial in amount. There have been two methods used by oil and gas companies to account for cost incurred in the exploration, development and production of crude oil and natural gas, the successful efforts method and the full cost method.

Under the *successful efforts method*, only the cost of successful drilling efforts are capitalized and subsequently charged against the revenue of the producing wells. Costs in connection with non-producing wells are considered to be expenses of the period in which they are incurred.

Under the *full cost method*, the cost of both successful and unsuccessful drilling efforts are capitalized and amortized against the subsequent petroleum production. This method creates a smoothing effect for the income stream generated by production and may yield significantly different periodic accounts from the successful efforts method.

Those who support the full cost method argue that a small proportion of exploration and drilling activities will bear positive results. However, unsuccessful activities should be viewed in the context of the entire exploration effort and, therefore, all costs related to the overall effort should be matched with the revenue that is generated from the successful well.

Those who support the successful effort method argue that exploration activities in one geographical area often bear little relation to efforts in a geographical area that may be quite different. Consequently, it is not theoretically correct to match the cost of unsuccessful wells with revenues of successful wells in other locations. The choice between those two methods provides an opportunity for creative accounting.

Letchet and Norton (1987), in the *Survey of UK Published Accounts* (1986–1987), investigated the approaches companies adopt to capitalize their costs. They found that large more established companies generally adopted the successful efforts basis, whereas smaller companies, particularly those with limited production, tended to favour the full cost approach. It has to be pointed out that when a company faces a significant drop in the market price of the principal commodity sold by the company to the extent that it becomes difficult to recover cost previously capitalized, the company deals with the issue by adopting what is called a 'ceiling test'. This represents an estimate of future income to be generated from proved resources and hence represents the ceiling for the book value of capitalized costs of oil and gas assets at any particular time. The SEC in the United States requires full cost companies to perform ceiling tests. Successful effort companies are not required to perform ceiling tests. In the United Kingdom, there is no formal requirement to undertake the ceiling test. However, the *Survey of UK Published Accounts* (1986–1987) found that UK companies performed the ceiling test in a variety of different ways. Most companies discounted net future cash flows in their ceiling test calculation. In general, the discount rate was not disclosed, but, when reported, the evidence indicated that many companies used the 10% discount rate required by the SEC. A further disclosure requirement by FASB No. 69 is the detailed disclosure of proved reserve quantities and standardized net cash flows based upon existing economic and operating conditions. As for the SEC rules for full cost companies, the value must be based upon year end prices and all future cash flows are discounted at 10% per year. This is not required in the United Kingdom. However, in the *Survey of UK Published Accounts* (1986–1987) Letchet and Norton (1987) found some instances where it was adopted. The Survey indicated that there was no consensus within the industry on writing down for permanent diminution in the carrying value of oil and gas assets in the accounts. Letchet and Norton concluded that there was a wide variety of practices adopted in the recognition and disclosure of the implications of a significant fall in the price of crude oil. Tonkin and Robertson (1991) in the *Survey of UK Published Accounts* noticed a variety of accounting treatments for what they called 'Extractive industry exploration costs'. In the survey conducted, some capitalize all exploration expenditures, while others capitalize exploration expenditures related to new exploration areas. Tonkin and Robertson detected that in its 1989 annual report British Petroleum only capitalized the exploration costs associated with successful efforts and reported this as intangible assets. When an exploitable reserve is determined exploration costs are classified as tangible fixed assets. However, they also found, in Shell's 1989 annual report, that exploration costs were charged against income whilst drilling costs were capitalized as a tangible asset.

ACCOUNTING FOR BRANDS

According to ED (52), the term *brand* is generally used to mean a conjunction of characteristics which operate in combination, and offer the expectation of a stream of future benefits exceeding in aggregate what the constituent items could produce separately or without brand. In general, brands are classified into acquired and home-grown brands. ED 52 *Accounting for Intangible Fixed Assets* permits capitalizing the value of acquired brands by deeming brands to be part of the goodwill, which is to be capitalized and amortized in accordance with ED 47 *Accounting for Goodwill*. ED 52 is justified on the grounds that it is difficult to distinguish brands from goodwill and even to see them separately sold. They are also valued in an identical manner.

Acquired Brands

A company generally acquires a brand name together with the rest of an entity's assets in a business acquisition (referred to as a business combination), although there could be cases where brand names alone are acquired. It has been a normal practice not to record the brand names separately as an asset on the balance sheet, but rather to include them in the overall value of the goodwill arising on the acquisition. This is then treated in accordance with the accounting requirements for goodwill.

Advantages of Reporting Brands on the Balance Sheet

Under the present accounting requirements, a company which acquires another company at a high premium over the value of its net tangible assets (i.e. paying for goodwill) is likely to see its consolidated reserves fall dramatically. Future reported profits (and hence its price/earnings ratio) could also be adversely affected for a number of years. Hence, it is argued that by reporting brands on the balance sheet the problem created by writing-off goodwill can be partially eliminated. Another advantage is that, by capitalizing separately the brand names acquired, a company is showing more of its valuable assets in its accounts, at the same time helping readers to assess the true effects of the acquisition. This is especially appropriate in cases where the value of the brands represents a significant portion of the purchase price.

A better assessment of a brand's continued contribution to a company's performance is also permitted. The acquired brand name will either be amortized over its useful life or, if a finite useful life cannot be identified, will be carried at cost until a provision for permanent diminution in value is needed. If re-valuation of a brand name becomes an accepted practice, a reader of accounts will be able to assess the brand's continuing contribution to the company's operations by following the movements in the value of the brand over the years.

On the other hand, there are also drawbacks to the capitalization of brands. Valuing acquired brands is very difficult. Although everyone knows that a good brand name is valuable, it is quite difficult to put a precise value on a brand acquired with the rest of a business.

The subsequent accounting treatment of capitalized brands can also cause problems. The amortization charge relating to a brand name (if the brand has a finite useful life) or any provision for permanent diminution in value will adversely affect the reported profits of future years. Yet, companies can still get around this problem by choosing not to amortize the reported brand.

Home-grown Brands

The value of home-grown brands is recognized as a traditional brand. This has shown consistency in the recognition and treatment between acquired and home-grown brands by attributing a value to the importance of home-grown brands.

Capitalizing both the acquired and the home-grown brands would not only reveal more of the assets a company presently hides from view, by showing the total worth of the concern's assets, it would also have a favourable effect on a firm's ability to raise finance and help to fight off the threat of any potential predators, that is, by the increase in gearing ratio.

As was the case with capitalizing acquired brands, there are disadvantages to capitalizing home-grown brands. Their valuation is more difficult than that of the acquired brands, because no market transaction has taken place to support the value of the tangible assets.

Another problem is that, by showing assets which were not previously reported on the balance sheet, the ratio between reported profits (which would not be affected by the new capitalization policy) and total assets will decrease. This could wrongly be interpreted as a weakening in the company's performance. This argument also applies for acquired brand names, although it is more significant if both acquired and home-grown brands are capitalized.

Apart from the advantages and disadvantages of capitalizing brand names, there are also a number of practical considerations, for example, the nature and the quality of brand names. In some cases, the brand name is so closely related to the product itself that it is virtually impossible to place a separated value on the brand alone. The quality of the brand also has an effect not only on its value but also on its expected useful life. The shorter the useful life, the higher the amortization charge against profits and consequently the lower the reported profits.

The first method involves determining the level of earnings sustainable by the brands and establishing a multiple reflecting current market transactions, prospective interest and inflation rate. The earnings attributable to a branded product could be multiplied by a factor which would be estimated after taking into account the considerations: durability, market sector and so on. This method would attempt to predict what a third party might pay to acquire the brand name. It has the advantage of being highly subjective and of taking into account the whole earnings attributable to the brand name (Coopers & Lybrand Deloitte, 1989).

Another method could be based on a *multiple* of notional royalties that could be received from the use of the brands. The factors that have to be considered are (Coopers & Lybrand Deloitte, 1989):

1. The sales that a third party could generate through using the name.

2. The nature of the licence. For instance, would it be an exclusive licence and would it include the benefit of future research and development?

3. How could the royalty be expressed? If it was expressed as a percentage of sales, what percentage would be 'normal' for the industry?

4. What 'multiple' should be used to arrive at a capitalized value for the royalty?'

These two methods contain elements of subjectivity that will have to be carefully assessed by the company and agreed with the auditors.

Independent valuation could be an attractive approach because it adds to the credibility and objectivity of the figure. However, it is difficult to find experts in this field and this involves added costs to the company.

Another practical problem is the subsequent accounting treatment of brand names. Once a company has capitalized its brand names, it will have to assess whether they have a finite useful life. If this is the case, the brands will have to be amortized over that period. On the other hand, if no finite useful life can be identified the brands will not be systematically amortized, but a provision will be needed as soon as permanent diminution in value becomes evident. In this case guide-lines need to be developed as to what actually constitutes a permanent decline in value.

Actually, part of the attraction in capitalizing separable intangibles is the absence of an accounting standard requiring amortization. This gives birth to creative accounting. For example, the capitalization of the name *The Independent* in the Newspaper Publishing Plc accounts left the company with net assets, at 26 September 1987, of £14 million instead of a £4.7 million deficit. Likewise, Milne (1989) showed that after Rank Hovis MacDougall capitalized their brands the balance sheet was improved and their borrowing appeared to be in a proper perspective. The gearings fall from 42 to 13% and the problem of writing-off goodwill eased. This approach assists capital raising for the company.

In 1991 Tonkin and Robertson noted in the *Survey of UK Published Accounts* that a variety of treatments have been used, by the surveyed companies, to account for brands and intangible assets. They attributed this variation to the lack of theoretical model or accounting treatment to suit the conditions of every company.

REVIEW QUESTIONS

1. What are the major problems related to accounting for intangibles?

2. It has been argued that, to comply with the conservatism convention, all intangible assets should be written off immediately after acquisition. Discuss the arguments which support the capitalization of intangible assets.

3. Explain the different methods of measuring goodwill and their effect on the profit and loss account and balance sheet.

4. In January 1993, LWS Inc. received an offer from an investment group to acquire 50% interest in LWS for £10,000,000. The book value of LWS' net tangible assets at the date of the offer was £15,000,000 but was considered to be worth £18,000,000. The directors of LWS were pleased to have such an offer but turned it down.
   Business continued to be good for LWS and in June 1993, the directors asked the bank for £7,500,000 loan to acquire new facilities. They have been told by the bank that their net assets were not large enough to warrant such a loan.
   LWS' directors are looking for means to justify the loan and they ask you to increase the value of net assets based on the investors' group offer. Show how this can be done.

5. 'Although the measurement of acquisition price of intangible assets looks straightforward, their application is subjective and gives scope for creative accounting.' State any possible scheme(s) of creative accounting related to acquisition of intangible assets and its/their effect on the profit and loss account and balance sheet.

6. Show the effects of amortization of intangibles on the profit and loss account, balance sheet, and some key financial ratios.

7. From the lessor's point of view, leases are classified as operating, direct

financing, or sale type leases. What are the major differences in the lessor's objections for engaging in a lease transaction for each classification?

8. Show the extent to which SSAP 21 succeeded in combating the off-balance sheet financing problem associated with accounting for leases.

9. John White Inc. has signed a contract to maintain a ship channel. In order to perform the required service, he must either rent, lease or buy a dredging vessel. John White's management is very concerned about its financial position because the covenant is an existing bond contract, which asks for maintaining a certain level of gearing ratios. Discuss the effects on the company's gearing ratios of each of the following courses of action:

   (a) renting the vessel on a monthly basis;

   (b) purchasing the vessel with a long term mortgage note;

   (c) purchasing the assets by issuing ordinary shares whose proceeds will be used to purchase the vessel for cash;

   (d) acquiring the asset through a capital lease.

10. Capitalization of brands partially solves the problem of immediate write off of goodwill and improves gearing ratios. Discuss.

CHAPTER 9

Accounting for Long-term Liabilities

NATURE OF LONG-TERM DEBT

Long-term debt consists of present obligations, arising out of past transactions, that are not payable within the operating cycle of the business or within a year. The 1991 discussion paper issued by ASB proposes the contract maturity to distinguish between short-term and long-term borrowing. Mortgages payable, bonds payable, lease obligations, pension obligation, long-term note payable, and long-term contracts for purchase of assets are examples of long-term liabilities. Long-term debt is usually used by companies as a means to finance growth and increase earnings available to shareholders.

Long-term creditors have no influence on management and receive a specific amount of money whether the firm maintains gains or losses. In general, long-term debts are subject to covenants to protect lenders. In many cases, they are the loan instalment or contract held by a trustee, who is usually a bank, or a trust company, who acts as an independent third party to protect the interests of the lender and the borrower.

MORTGAGE PAYABLE

This is a promissory note secured by a document called a mortgage. It pledges title to specific assets as collateral for the loan. If the borrower defaults on the note, the borrower may foreclose upon the assets.

Mortgages may be payable in full at the maturity date or in instalments over the life of the loan. If payable in full at the maturity date, it should then be shown as long-term liabilities in the years prior to this date. On the other hand, if it is payable in instalments, the current instalment due should be shown as current liabilities with the rest shown as long-term liabilities. Manipulation is likely to occur in classifying the instalment to be paid. This will affect liquidity and gearing ratios.

BONDS PAYABLE

A bond arises from a contract known as an indenture and represents a promise to pay a sum of money at a designated maturity date plus periodic interest at a specific rate on the face value.

In accounting for bonds, the issuer records the cash amount received for a bond, as the value of liability (the maturity amount plus or minus any premium or discount). The difference between the cash received on the sale of the bond and the maturity value represents the premium or the discount on bonds. Bond discount or premium affects the reported interest expense in the profit and loss account and the balance sheet liability amount.

To record and report the effects in accordance with the matching principle, bond discount or premiums must be amortized as an interest expense over the useful life of the bond. In general two amortization methods are employed.

1. Straight-Line Amortization

Under this method, equal amounts of discount or premium are amortized each period over the period the bonds are outstanding.

This issue has been considered by *APB Opinion* No. 21 when it stated:

> the difference between the present value and the face amount should be treated as discount or premium and amortized as interest expense over the life of the bond in such a way as to result in a constant rate of interest when applied to the amount outstanding at the beginning of any given period. This is the interest method.... However, other methods of amortization may be used if the results obtained are not materially different from those which would result from the interest method.

2. Present (Interest) Value Method

This method is based on the concept of annuity because the constant amount of cash interest for each period is viewed as rent and periodic interest expense is computed by applying a constant rate to the periodic book value of the bonds. The 1991 discussion paper issued by ASB favours this approach to allocate the cost associated with liabilities. Therefore, bond discount or premium amortization can be allocated as below:

$$\text{Straight-line method} = \frac{\text{Bond discount or premium}}{\text{No of interest periods}}$$

$$\text{Interest value method} = \begin{bmatrix} \text{Book} \times \text{Effective} \\ \text{value} \quad \text{interest} \\ \text{of the} \quad \text{rate} \\ \text{bonds} \end{bmatrix} - \begin{bmatrix} \text{Face} \times \text{Stated} \\ \text{value} \quad \text{interest} \\ \text{of} \quad \text{rate} \\ \text{bonds} \end{bmatrix}$$

To illustrate the effect of each of the above methods on the profit and loss account and the balance sheet the following example is used:

Assume on 1 January 1992 X Inc. sells £500,000, 5-year, 10% bonds at £463,195 with interest payable on 1 July and 1 January. The sale on discount resulted in an effective interest rate of 12%. At 1 January 1992, bonds payable and discount on bonds will be presented on the balance sheet as follows:

Bonds payable	£500,000
Less discount on bonds payable	36,805
	£463,195

The £463,195 represents the book value of the bond.

The issuance of bond below the face value causes the total cost of borrowing to differ from the bond interest paid. That is, X Inc. must pay off not only the stated rate of interest over the term of the bonds but also the face value at maturity. Therefore, the difference between the issuance price and the face value of the bond (£36,805) is an additional cost of borrowing that should be recorded as bond interest expense over the life of the bonds.

To amortize the £36,805 discount using the straight-line method, this amount should be divided by the useful life of the bond.

$$\frac{£36,805}{10\star} = £3,680.5$$

*5 years semiannually

The £3,680.5 will be charged in an identical manner. By using the interest method, amortization expense for the first six months will be:

$$(£463,195 \times 6\%) - (£500,000 \times 5\%) = £2,791$$

For the second half of the year, amortization expense will be:

$$[(463,195 + 2,791) \times 6\%] - (£500,000 \times 5\%) = £2,959$$

Therefore, amortization expense for the year 1992 under the straight-line method will be equal to £3,680.5 × 2 = £7,361. On the other hand, amortization expense under the interest method will be £2,791 + £2,959 = £5,750.

The effects of the use of each of the above approaches on the profit and loss account and the balance sheet of X Inc. will be as follows:

	Straight-line method	Interest method
Interest expense for 1992	£7,361	£5,750
Reported bonds payable on the balance	£470,556	£468,945

Thus the choice between the straight-line and interest methods will affect profitability and gearing ratios.

CONVERTIBLE BONDS PAYABLE

Convertible bonds represent a popular form of financing, especially during periods when ordinary shares' prices are rising. The conversion gives bond-holders the opportunity to benefit from the rise in the market price of the ordinary shares while still maintaining their status as creditors rather than shareholders. As a result of this expected gain, convertible bonds generally carry a lower interest rate than non-convertible bonds. Bonds are converted into ordinary shares by using a conversion ratio. The market value of the ordinary share represents the share value of the bond. For example, suppose that the current rate of interest on a long-term bond is 8% and that the market value of the ordinary share of ABC Company is £5. Instead of issuing 8% bonds payable ABC might issue 5% convertible bonds with a conversion ratio of 150 to 1. At the issuance date the market value of each convertible bond would be only £750 (150 × £5). If the value of the ordinary share rises to £7 (conversion price), the share value of each convertible bond will rise to £1,050 (£50 above the face value of the bond on the assumption that the face value of each bond is £1,000).

There is some confusion on how to report conversion bonds payable. IASC issued E 40 *Financial Instruments* as part of a joint project with the Canadian Institute of Chartered Accounts to develop recognition, measurement and disclosure standards for financial instruments. E 40 defined a financial instrument as any contract that gives rise to both a financial asset of one enterprise and financial liability or equity to instrument of another enterprise. A financial asset is a contractual right to exchange a financial instrument with another enterprise under conditions that are favourable. A financial liability is a contractual obligation to exchange a financial instrument with another enterprise under unfavourable conditions. Hence the main thrust of the Draft is that, if the rewards or risks associated with financial asset instrument and liabilities are assumed and measured, they should be reported on the balance sheet. The proposed Draft is similar to ED 49. However, under E 40 the proceeds from convertible bonds represent financial liability and equity instruments. Following from E 40, the ASB issued a lengthy discussion paper *Accounting for Capital Instruments*. One of the main issues addressed by the paper is how to determine whether or not a capital instrument should be classified as a liability or as an equity. The paper suggested that all economic instruments which contain an obligation to transfer economic benefits should be classified as liabilities. In this case, convertible debts contain an obligation to make payments. Hence, they should be classified as liabilities.

In the 1990 annual report, Boots Company plc treated *convertible capital bonds* as quasi-equity. They justified their treatment on the grounds that the 'bonds are convertible at any time into redeemable preference shares of Boots Finance Ltd., which in turn are immediately exchangeable to ordinary shares of the Boots Company PLC at 335 pence per share'.

DEEPLY DISCOUNTED OR ZERO COUPON BONDS

In 1982, the Chancellor of the Exchequer announced that companies could issue zero coupon bonds and deeply discounted bonds. These are loans made to companies by investors at a very low interest or even zero rate. To compensate for this, the bonds are issued at a large discount to their face value, which is the amount that a company will have to pay to redeem them at some future time. The attractiveness of lower or zero coupon bonds may be derived from the tax treatment and the front loading problem associated with the conventional bonds (they shift the costs to the end of the bond's life). Schaefer (1985) believed that tax rules provide the basis for a potentially interesting financing opportunity. The advantage to the company is the timing difference between the two; the tax deduction is allocated over the useful life of the bond, whereas tax is payable only on redemption or sale. In effect, tax authorities provide companies with an interest free loan equal to the amount of tax payable. Hills (1984) argued that the main difficulty with the conventional bonds is the *front loading* problem (interest burden). During times of inflation, the real interest burden is greater at the start of the bond's life. This results in cash flow problems.

Among the applications of Technical Release 677, ICAEW (1987), *Accounting for Complex Capital Issues* is the treatment of deep interest bonds, including zero coupon bonds. The Technical Release sets out six general principles and the appendix sets out examples of how the principles apply to seven instruments found in current practice. The chief principle is that interest costs, whether explicit or hidden, should be treated as such and charged against income. This approach will result in the income statement bearing a charge for the market rate of interest. In considering the zero coupon example, the principle gives clear guidance that the discounted issue price is in the nature of interest and should be charged to the income statement on an appropriate basis. The actuarial method is the most accurate method to be used where the amounts involved are material which result in constant percentage of the capital plus rolled-up interest from time to time.

The *Companies Act (1985)* permits the discount on the issue of debentures to be written off to the share premium account. The Technical Release leaves it open to the company to transfer the amount of the discount from the income statement to the share premium account. Holgate (1988) claimed that many companies already deal with the interest cost inherent in deep discounted bonds in the way advocated by the Release. On the other hand, the Technical Release is not clear about the presentation of deep discounted bonds. There are two ways to present deep discounted bonds on the balance sheet; net and gross methods.

In fact, neither of the two methods is considered correct or perfect. Sch. 4 para. 5 of *Companies Act 1985* does not allow assets and liabilities to be set off against each other. Therefore it might be useful to include the gross amount in the balance sheet. Sch. 4 para. 24 allows the discount to be shown as an asset. Thus, where the terms of the loan are such that the liability is not required to be presented gross, it is preferable to show the borrowing net of unamortized discount in the balance sheet.

Holgate (1988) believed that there are two principal defects with the gross method. By reporting the gross amount as long-term debts instead of net, the company's gearing is overstated. The second defect is that the gross method creates a very dubious asset. It is not a receivable, it is not a repayment, it is not a fixed asset. Indeed, it is really difficult to know what it is.

To illustrate, suppose a company issues £100 face value bonds which is the amount that it promises to pay after five years. No interest is payable on the bond during this period of time. Assuming that the current interest rate payable on a bond of a similar maturity and risk is 10%, the company will be able to sell the bond at £100 × IF 10%,5, (£100 × 0.62) = £62. The question raised here is should the company record liabilities at £100 or at £62, or should the liability be recorded as £100 and the difference of £38 be recorded as a prepayment of interest to be amortized over the bond's life? Even though the presentation of the amount is the same, the financial structure of the company's capital looks quite different. The availability of different approaches provides an opportunity for window dressing. However, while the case for the zero coupon bond is a straightforward example, a creative accountant may use the company's long-term financial arrangements as a vehicle for misrepresentation and accounting standard avoidance. For example, if a company has long-term liabilities which had been issued many years ago at a fixed interest rate and this rate is materially lower than the current market rate, the market value of the loan is lower than its face value. The creative accountant may suggest the revaluation of the loan in the balance sheet to reduce it to its market value. This approach might have the support of finance theory and corresponds to economic reality. Moreover, the creative accountant may argue, he might obtain the same results as revaluing downward if he was to buy back the loans in the market.

Worth and Derwent (1990), in the *Survey of UK Published Accounts* (1989–1990) reported many cases of companies involved in the use of deeply discounted bonds. In one of these cases, the amount of discount charged during the year was disclosed but the company failed to explain the accounting policy adopted. Another case reflected that the discount is written off over the term of the bond in a straight-line basis. Worth and Derwent concluded that the majority of the companies, which had issued deeply discounted bonds, have used the net method. However, they reported that a company, Redland plc, which employed the gross method in their 1987 accounts, reported in notes to the accounts information on their loans and overdrafts. They showed that a subsidiary had issued £60,000 million zero coupon notes in 1982. They had reported only £36.3 million.

IN-SUBSTANCE (OR ECONOMIC) DEFEASANCE

Defeasance is a form of extinguishment (the payment of debt recorded). If the bond or any other form of debt security is held until maturity, the accounting for it is easy. In this situation, no gains or losses occur since the net book value of the debt will be equal to the amount of cash needed to pay the retired debt. At the date upon which the long-term liability is matured, any premium or discount will be fully amortized. Consequently, the book value will be equal to the maturity value of the debt. Thus, no gain or loss exists. Hence, one may ask what will be the case if a firm repurchases the debt directly from the market? However, the shortcoming of this approach is that only a portion of the outstanding debt issue can be purchased. If a company purchases a substantial amount of the outstanding debt, this will result in an increase in the bond's market price, making the purchase more expensive. In addition, bondholders might not desire to sell their investments. Moreover, the gain on repurchase is taxed immediately. In the case where the repurchased debt is used to finance specific assets, the gain can be used to reduce the carrying value of the related assets, and for that gain to be allocated on the useful life of assets invested.

However, accountants face problems when the debt is extinguished prior to maturity. One type of extinguishment is the *in-substance (or economic) defeasance*. This is an arrangement whereby a company provides for future repayments of one or more of its long-term issues by placing purchased securities in an irrevocable trust, the principal and interest of which are pledged to pay off the principal and interest of its own debt securities as they mature. However, the company is not legally released from being the primary debtor under the debt that is still outstanding. In some cases, debt holders are not even aware of the transaction and continue to look to the company for repayments.

Be that as it may, one may ask why companies adopt an in-substance defeasance scheme? There are several reasons for such schemes. First, the debt is removed from the balance sheet without actually being repurchased (off-balance sheet financing). In some cases, actual repurchase causes problems because (a) it may be costly if a high call premium is required to be paid, or (b) much of the debt may be publicly held and may therefore be difficult to buy back in large quantities. Second, because the cost of the purchased securities is usually less than the carrying value of the company's debt (as interest rates rise, the fair value of the outstanding debt falls below the carrying value), the company records a gain in its profit and loss account. If the company repurchases the debt the gain is taxable immediately. With an in-substance defeasance scheme the debt is not legally retired and therefore the gain does not represent an immediate tax liability. For example, suppose a company has £3,500 worth of 5% bonds outstanding, due in 10 years. Suppose also that the current yield on 10-year treasury bonds is 10%. Now the company can buy £3,500 of 10% treasury obligation for £3,000. If these treasury bonds are placed in an irrevocable trust, used entirely to pay off the corporate debt, the debt is removed from the books. This occurs despite the fact that the debt is not actually retired. The effect of in-substance defeasance on the financial statements is as follows:

Balance sheet before defeasance

Assets	£5,000
Cash	£10,000
Other assets	£15,000
Liabilities and equities	
Current liability	£3,000
Long-term liability	£3,500
Equity (500 shares)	£8,500
	£15,000

Profit and Loss account before defeasance

Revenue	£5,000
Expenses	£4,500
Income	£500
EPS	£1

Balance sheet after defeasance

Assets	
Cash	£2,000
Other assets	£10,000
	£12,000
Liabilities and equities	
Current liability	£3,000
Equity	£9,000
	£12,000

Profit and Loss account after defeasance

Revenue	£5,000
Expenses	£4,500
Margin	£500
Gain	£500
Income	£1,000
E PS	£2

It can be noted that the financial position of the company is improved. Earnings per share ratio, the debt/equity ratio, and the return on total assets ratio all are improved. The important advantage is that the company is allowed to report the gain. The gain is not taxed until the maturity date of the debt.

In fact, in-substance defeasance techniques are adopted to set aside sufficient risk-free investment, to refund all interest and principal payments on the company's long-term debt. In this situation, not only the balance sheet but also the difference between the carrying value of the long-term debt and the value of free risk investment is reported as a gain in the profit and loss account.

However, in substance defeasance can be classified into *legal and covenant defeasance*. The legal defeasance transactions are specifically covered by the original bond indenture when the bond is sold. After placing riskless assets in an irrevocable trust, the issuer is released from any subsequent obligations under the indenture, and the trust becomes the primary debtor of the debt. Similarly, covenant defeasance is covered specifically in the bond indenture. The riskless assets are also placed in a trust and the issuer is able to remove the original debt from its books and is released from all covenant restrictions under the indenture. Nevertheless, unlike the legal defeasance, the issuer remains the primary debtor on debt.

In-substance defeasance can be carried out by using the trust techniques mentioned or an assumption approach. The assumption approach does not require the use of a trust. Instead, the trustee transfers a specified amount of cash to a third party investor, who assumes the outstanding debt obligation of the issuer. In this case, the defeased debt does not have to be matched by the required risk-free securities or government obligations because there are no restrictions on the investors' use of the funds received. The transaction is usually secured by a guarantee or letter of credit covering the payments to be paid by the third party, to ensure that any future payments by the issuer are remote.

However, this issue was considered by the FASB issued Statement No. 76 *Extinguishment of Debt* as its prescription for accounting for in-substance defeasance transactions. To be considered a debt extinguishment (removal from the balance sheet), the FASB ruled, the debtor must place (1) cash, or (2) risk-free securities in an irrevocable trust to be used solely for satisfying the interest and principal of debt, and the possibility that the debtor will be required to make any future payments with respect to the debt must be remote. Because of the difference in interest rates in different world financing markets, it is possible for a company to borrow at one interest rate and concurrently invest in essentially risk-free assets that yield a higher rate. Immediately placing such assets in an irrevocable trust effects what is referred to as *instantaneous in-substance defeasance*. The profession does not permit extinguishment of debt through instantaneous defeasance. FASB No. 76 applies only to in-substance defeasance of a previously outstanding debt, not to newly issued debts. Instantaneous defeasance is accounted for as borrowing and investment, not as an extinguishment (FASB Technical Bulletin No. 84–4 *In-Substance Defeasance of Debt*). Also, the FASB ruled, in FASB (76), that only the trust method is acceptable and the assumption defeasance techniques are not acceptable.

This standard is controversial and has been subjected to criticisms. Opponents of the statement believe that a gain or loss recognition should be extended to situations where the debtor is not legally released from being the primary debtor under the debt. They contend that the

> setting aside of assets in trust does not, in and of itself, constitute either the disposition of assets with potential gain or loss recognition or the satisfaction of a liability with potential gain or loss recognition. (FASB No. 76).

In other words, while committing the assets to a single purpose might ensure that the debt is serviced in a timely fashion, this event alone merely matches up cash flows. It does not satisfy, eliminate or extinguish the obligation. For the debt to be satisfied, the creditor must be satisfied. This is not the case in an in-substance defeasance. On the other hand, the proponents of the statement believe that the effect of an in-substance defeasance is essentially the same as a cash settlement. They also believe that the liability should be removed from the balance sheet because placing sufficient risk-free assets irrevocably in trust ensures that the possibility of the debtor having to make additional future payments is remote.

The motive to extinguish debt arises for many reasons. As noted in the above illustrated example, the extinguishment of debt improves specific balance sheet indicators, such as debt-to-equity ratio. This enables the company to increase its borrowing capacity and to secure new borrowing at lower interest rates. On the other hand, in-substance defeasance still plays an important role as an efficient financing tool since it avoids all the direct purchase of debt disadvantages. The in-substance defeasance is not subject to tax and the trust is not recognized as changing the issuer's position. A company which had purchased risk-free securities is taxed on the securities income. In case the company has sold the government securities at discount, the capital gains are incurred on the debt only when they mature. Likewise, covenant defeasance is dealt with as a non taxed event. Hence, under the assumption type of in-substance defeasance, the issuer cannot deduct interest on the debt because third party investors have assured this expense.

By adopting defeasance, an entire debt issue may be extinguished in a single transaction without bearing the consequences associated with repurchase of debt in the open market where the bondholders may not be willing to sell. In addition adopting defeasance does not require the issuance of common stock, and this will not result in dilution in earnings per share. Furthermore, defeasance arrangements do not contradict the loan agreements on indenture covenants which prohibit the repurchase or retirement of debt. Yet, defeasance is associated with several risks. Government securities are considered a risk-free investment and, as a result of this, they are more expensive than the comparable corporate debt. In addition, the issue of legal status after the use of in-substance defeasance does not change because liability and financial covenants remain intact. Another risk arises from the abstracted and contradictory laws guiding the issuer and the trustee, the main problem being the impact of bankruptcy on the rights of obligation of bondholder and creditors. For instance, can other creditors claims in a bankruptcy be satisfied with the use of the trust assets?

Despite this, it seems that FASB (76) established a new financial means for accountants and managers. According to Chaney (1985) after the release of FASB (76) there was a dramatic increase in in-substance defeasance proposals. Hence, he considered defeasance as 'nothing more than balance sheet cosmetics for hiding poor operating performance'. He concluded that in-substance defeasance will be used as a smoke screen to hide poor earnings performance. However, Chaney believes that the defeasance approach can be used for sound economic reasons, such as solving the problems associated with the direct repurchase of debt.

Indeed, as far as off-balance sheet criteria are concerned, in-substance defeasance meets the criteria. The liabilities are taken off the balance sheet and the company enjoys the improvement in its debt-to-equity, return on assets and earnings per share ratios. In addition, the gain is not taxed until the securities are matured. However, Brindle (1986) reported some examples of UK companies using in-substance defeasance in *A Survey of UK Published Accounts* (1985–1986) under a chapter entitled 'Off-balance sheet financing'. He reported that a company included in its trust deed for the issue of debenture stock an option of substitution which might be construed as an intention to apply defeasance procedures if they were exercised.

BORROWING ACROSS THE END OF THE YEAR

One of the techniques a creative accountant may apply to improve the ratios of available cash to liabilities is borrowing across the end of the year. For example, suppose that before the end of the accounting period, Company X and Company Y have an identical balance sheet of cash, receivables, and payables; £1,000; £2,000; and £4,000 respectively. Company Y has borrowed £2,500 for the purpose of window dressing its balance sheet at the end of the year. Both companies have £(1,000) of working capital. If one looks at the relevant financial ratios which are used by financial analysts to get a quick insight into the financial position of the company, it will be clear that Company X has, at the balance sheet date, £1,000 of its £4,000 debts in cash (25% of its debt). On the other hand, Company Y has £3,500 cash with which to pay its £6,500 of debt (54% of its total debt). Also its liquidity position, based on its financial ratios, looks much better. It can pay 85% of its debts, while Company X can only pay 75% of its debts. Even though the two companies have the same shortfalls in working capital, Company Y seems to have a less pressing problem. This effect can be made to look even better if the assets and liabilities reflected in the shortfall position can be netted off against each other. In general, this is not allowed by company law and can only be done when a legal right of a set-off exists.

REVIEW QUESTIONS

1. Under what conditions should short-term obligations be classified as a long-term debt? State the effect of classification on some key financial ratios.

2. It could be argued that the appropriate method of amortizing premium or discount on the issuance of bonds is the effective interest rate.
   (a) What is the effective interest method of amortization and how is it different from and similar to the straight-line method of amortization?
   (b) How is amortization computed by using the effective interest method and why and how do amounts attained by using this method differ from accounts computed by using the straight-line method.
   (c) Show the effect of the use of each approach on some key financial ratios.

3. Judi Books has a 10-year bond issue with the following disclosure on its 31 December 1992, balance sheet and notes:

   Long-term liabilities
   Bonds payable (Note 5)   £950,000

   Note 5: The company issues £1,000,000 worth of 16% bonds on 1 July 1992 for an effective yield of 18%. There were no charges to profit for 1992 because the first interest payment is scheduled for 1 July 1993.
   (a) Indicate the effect of Judi's approach on the profit and loss account and the balance sheet;
   (b) Suggest an alternative approach to that of Judi's and compare it with the disclosed one.

4. In April 1992, AC Colours Company issued 10-year bonds having a par value of £7,500,000 at a significant discount. The company has 31 Decem-

ber year end and pays interest on the bonds on 1 March and 1 September of each year. The president of the company is concerned about the current year's reported profit and requests an analysis of the impact the following accounting alternatives will have on the reported profit.
(a) Immediate write off of discount;
(b) Amortization of discount by using the effective method;
(c) Amortization of discount by using the straight-line method.

5. Accountants face problems in accounting for the termination of bonds before maturity date. State the main problems they may face and suggest solutions.

6. Explain what is meant by deeply discounted and zero coupon bonds. Show the attractions of these types of bonds and how they may present an opportunity for creative accounting.

7. On 30 June 1992, Steve Robinson Company issued £500,000 face value bonds which is the amount that the company promises to pay after 10 years. No interest is payable on the bonds during this period of time. Assume that the current interest rate payable on a bond of a similar maturity and risk is 12%. The company is planning to sell the bonds for £160,000. Robinson is confused about how to report the deeply discounted bond but he wishes to keep his gearing ratios at a minimum.
(a) Suggest to Mr. Robinson efficient methods that can be used to report the deeply discounted bonds.
(b) Explain to him the effect of each of the suggested approaches on the gearing ratios.

8. EFG Company disclosed the following profit and loss account and balance sheet:

Profit and Loss Account

Revenue	£50,000
Expenses	35,000
Profit	£15,000

Balance sheet

Cash	£20,000
Other assets	25,000
	£45,000
Current liabilities	£15,000
Long-term liabilities	10,000
Ordinary shares (£1 each)	20,000
	£45,000

The company has £10,000 worth of 10% bonds outstanding and due in 5 years. The current yield on 5-year treasury bonds is 20%. The company bought £10,000 of 20% treasury obligations for £8,000 and placed them in an irrevocable trust used entirely to pay off the corporate bond.

Show the effect of the in-substance defeasance on the profit and loss account and balance sheet, and earning per share ratio.

9. TW Company has the following balance sheet before disclosing it to the users:

	(£)		(£)
Cash	5,000	Current liabilities	30,000
Debtors	3,000	Long-term liabilities	5,000
Stock	7,000	Ordinary shares	
Fixed assets	35,000	(£1 each)	15,000
	50,000		50,000

The company's manager noticed that his company has a poor liquidity ratio. He asks you to suggest means to improve his liquidity ratios.

10. Before the end of the accounting year, the manager of XYZ realized that his company has a high level of stock which will affect his acid test ratio. The company financed its stock by long-term debt. The manager seeks your advice on means that can reduce both stock levels and reported liabilities on the balance sheet.

CHAPTER 10

Accounting for Shareholders' Contributed Capital (Equity)

INTRODUCTION

Equity is the third major balance sheet item, the others being assets and liabilities. The amount of money assigned to equity on the balance sheet is equal to net assets (Total assets − Total liabilities). It indicates the amount of assets of an entity financed by the shareholders. FASB (1980) in its conceptual framework defined equity as 'a money amount which represents the residual claim of owners in the assets of the entity'.

It is important to classify contributed capital in order to evaluate the sources of the entity's assets. A specific percentage of the contributed capital may come from the sale of ordinary shares, preferred shares, and other sources (operations). Thus, the classification helps in evaluating the financial position of an entity.

ORDINARY SHARES (COMMON STOCKS)

An ordinary share represents the basic issue of shares which possess the basic rights of ownership including the right to vote. It represents the residual element of ownership in a corporation.

PREFERRED SHARES (PREFERRED STOCKS)

A preferred share is a class of capital share usually having preferences as to dividends and in the distribution of assets in the event of liquidation. The preference in privileges may relate to the following:

1. Dividend;
   (a) Cumulative
   (b) Non–cumulative

155

(c) Fully participative
(d) Partially participative

2. Assets

3. Redemption

4. Convertibility.

A preferred share is usually a par value share, in which case the dividend preference is expressed as a percentage. For example, 10% preferred shares would carry a dividend preference of 10% of the par value of each share.

Debt Characteristics of Preferred Shares

With the rights and combination of features such as fixed return, convertible and redeemable, preferred shares perhaps more abut to creditors than to owners. However, preferred shares generally have no maturity date, but the preferred shareholder's relationship with the entity may be terminated if the entity exercises its call privilege. Despite these characteristics, preferred shares are reported in the shareholders' equity section of the balance sheet.

In 1979, the SEC issued a rule preventing companies from combining preferred shares with ordinary shares on the balance sheet. Amounts should be separately presented for redeemable preferred shares, non-redeemable preferred shares, and ordinary shares. The amounts applicable to these three categories of equity items cannot be totalled or combined for SEC reporting purposes. The general heading 'Shareholder's Equity' should not include redeemable preferred shares. According to the SEC such shares involved a commitment to use future resources of a company to redeem the issue, giving the holder a claim against prospective cash flow and thus a status different from that of holders of equity securities that represent permanent capital investment. In the United Kingdom, TR 603 considered the issuance of preferred shares in subsidiaries as a scheme of window dressing. According to this release, a subsidiary company may issue to a third party preferred shares which carry a divided rate related to the interest rate and related to a mandatory future redemption. Hence, the dividend rate is equivalent to the interest charged on loan finance. The preferred shares are usually presented in the shareholders' equity section of the balance sheet. This scheme improves the gearing ratios of the company.

On the other hand, one of the requirements of E 40 (see Chapter 9) is that, when a financial instrument requires the issuer to deliver cash or any other financial assets to the holder, it should be classified as a liability regardless of legal form. Hence, if E 40 is to be applied, redeemable preferred shares should be classified as liabilities.

In the analysis of the annual report of 25 European companies, two German companies, six French and seven Dutch companies reported preferred shares as part of the stockholders' equity of the balance sheet.

ACCOUNTING FOR THE ISSUANCE OF SHARES

a. Subscriptions

In most cases, shares are issued and sold for cash. In this case, the capital share is credited for the par value of the shares times the number of shares issued, and the excess over par is credited to a descriptively named contributed capital account to record the source in detail. However, in some cases, shares may be sold on a subscription basis. In this case, prospective shareholders may sign a contract to purchase a specific number of shares with payment to be made at one or more specified dates in the future. Such a contract is known as a share subscription. An asset 'subscription receivable' is recorded at the time the share is offered, and subscribers have a legal obligation to the corporation. Any premium should be recorded when the subscription is received rather than later when cash is collected. Subscription receivable is classified as a current asset if the company expects a current collection. If it is not current, it is a long-term asset.

Controversy exists concerning the presentation of the subscription receivable. Subscription receivable cannot be considered as a realizable asset and by adopting the above mentioned approach, the company will improve its liquidity as well as gearing ratios. Hence, some accountants offset subscription receivable against capital stock subscribed reported in the shareholders' equity section of the balance sheet.

b. Special Sale of Shares

Another problem that may face accountants in accounting for the issuance of shares is the non-cash sale of shares: when a company issues shares as payment for assets or services, the question of share value for accounting purposes arises. This problem is dealt with by *APB Opinion* No. 29 *Accounting for Non-monetary Transactions* which provides the following approaches to determine the value of shares:

1. The fair market value of the shares issued or the fair market value of the assets or services whichever is more clearly determinable. If both are readily determinable and the transaction is the result of an arms' length exchange, there will probably be little difference in their fair market value. It should not matter which value is regarded as their fair market value. If the fair market

value of the stock being issued and property in service being received are not readily determinable then;

2. an appraised value of assets on services received is used; or

3. the valuation of assets or services is to be estimated by the board of directors.

In this case, the same asset or service could be reported on the balance sheet of different values by different companies.

c. Lump Sum Sale of Shares

A company may sell two or more classes of securities for one lump sum. This situation presents an accounting problem. In this case, the proceeds must be allocated among the classes of securities sold on some logical basis. The methods available for accounts are:

1. *The proportion approach* where the lump sum received is allocated proportionally among the classes of shares sold on the basis of relative market value of each security.

2. *The incremental approach* where the market value of one security is used as a basis for that security and the remainder of the lump sum is allocated to the classes of security.

If the market value or other sound basis for determining relative values is available for each class of securities, the lump sum received is best allocated between the classes of securities on a proportional basis. In situations where the market value of all classes of securities is not determinable, the incremental method may be employed. If no fair market value is determinable for any of the classes of shares involved in a lump sum exchange, the allocation may have to be arbitrary.

Thus, each of the above discussed methods is a different shareholder's equity structure.

UNREALIZED CAPITAL DECREMENT (DEBIT BALANCE)

Unrealized Capital Decrement is a contra (negative) account in the shareholders' equity section of the balance sheet. It arises when assets are written down under specific circumstances. The write down may be reported on the balance sheet in either of two ways:

1. To report the write down as a reduction in the current year's profit. The use of lower of cost or market approach to evaluate short-term investment and stock justifies the use of this approach. Another example which justifies the use of this approach is the write down of an operational asset due to a diminution of going value such as the write down of an idle plant. A further example is the recognition of loss due to discontinuation of a segment of a business.

2. The write down should be charged to the shareholders' equity section of the balance sheet. *FASB* No. 12 *Accounting for Certain Marketable Securities* (1975d) requires recording unrealized decrement on long-term investment as a contra account to the shareholders' equity.

It could be noticed that each of the above discussed approaches has a different impact on some profitability and gearing ratios.

UNREALIZED CAPITAL INCREMENT

This arises when assets are written up from cost. Because of compliance with the cost principle and the concept of conservatism, assets are rarely written up from cost to market value (in the United Kingdom this often seems to happen with lands and buildings). An example of such write up is the discovery of natural resources. An upward adjustment requires an offsetting of credit to either revenue or unrealized capital increment. If the discovery value is not reported in the current profit and loss account as gain or revenue, it may be reported as an increment in shareholders' equity.

There are a number of unresolved issues such as measurement of market value, classification of credit and adequate disclosure.

REPURCHASE BY A COMPANY OF ITS OWN SHARES

Partial liquidation of a company may occur when a specific class of stock is called and redeemed. This will result in a decrease in invested capital. An example of this is the purchase of outstanding shares of a company. If the company does not retire these shares formally but instead holds them for later reissue, the shares are referred to as *treasury stocks*. A corporation may require shares of its own stock to be available for stock option plans, for bonuses, for use in mergers and acquisitions or for other legitimate business purposes. The acquisition of treasury stock represents a purchase of the ownership interest of

certain stockholders. The purchased shares are not considered to be an asset
because, in theory, a company cannot purchase an ownership interest in itself.
However, *APB Opinion* No. 6 failed to give an objective approach on how the
treasury stock should be classified in the balance sheet. The opinion says:

> When a corporation's stock is acquired for purposes other than retirement (formal
> or constructive) or when ultimate disposition has not yet been decided, the cost of
> acquired stock may be shown separately as a deduction from the total capital
> stock, capital surplus, and retained earnings, or may be accorded the accounting
> treatment appropriate for retired stock, or in some circumstances may be shown
> as an asset.

However, the choice encourages creativity. In some cases, treasury shares
represent a reduction in stockholders' equity. In other cases, where treasury
stock is considered an asset, the justification is that such shares were purchased to
be made available for the purpose of fulfilling stock option or incentive
programmes for corporate officers or employees. Thus, the purchase of the
stock is viewed as the acquisition of an asset to be used in satisfying the
corporation's liability under the programme. In its 1984 balance sheet, General
Motors Corporation reported treasury stock as a separate asset item entitled
Common Stock Held for the Incentive Program. At 31 December 1984, 2,053,560
shares of GM's common stock at a cost of $144,200,000 were included among
the long-term assets between 'Investments' and 'Property'. The justification for
classifying these shares as assets is that they will be used to liquidate a specific
liability that appears on the balance sheet.

In the United Kingdom, after the *1981 Companies Act*, corporate treasurers
have the opportunity to buy back their outstanding shares. Section 46–62 of the
1981 Companies Act allows the company to purchase its outstanding shares and it
became fully operative in June 1982. Specific requirements should be met before
the repurchase is allowed. The most important one is that the purchase has to be
made only out of distributable profits (or the proceeds of the fresh issue);
shareholders' prior approval is required and the shares must be cancelled
(although this does not reduce authorized share capital). The *1985 Companies
Act* specifies that only fully paid shares can be purchased. Yet, Smith (1992)
reported that Maxwell used to purchase shares in Maxwell Communication
Corporation (MCC) and Mirror Group Newspapers (MGN) to support their
prices. His act had never been disclosed to the public in accordance to the
Companies Act and Stock Exchange requirements. Smith believes that this
misled investors about the reasons for the rise in share prices.

In accounting for treasury stock two acceptable methods are used, namely the
cost method and the par value method. The cost method results in debiting the
treasury stock account for the reacquisition cost and in reporting this account as
a reduction from the total paid in capital and the retained earnings on the

balance sheet. The par value method records all transactions in treasury shares at the par value of the shares and reports the treasury stock as a deduction from the balance of the capital stock account. It seems that each approach is appropriate for different circumstances. If shares are acquired by purchase with the express purpose of reselling to employees, or other special groups, the cost method is relevant. If the objective of the acquisition is to purchase the shares of dissident shareholders or to affect the eventual retirement of certain classes of stock, the par value approach should apply, even though these shares might be resold at a later date. Thus, if eventual collection is the objective, the par value approach is obviously appropriate. No matter which method is appropriate, the choice between the cost method and the par value method keeps the door open to the creative accountant not to treat similar situations uniformly. The 1984 edition of *Accounting Trends and Techniques* indicates that of its selected list of 600 companies, treasury stock was accounted for at cost by 358 companies and at par value by 38 companies. Nevertheless, UK companies are less likely to repurchase their shares than US companies. UK regulations do not contain the US concept of *treasury stocks* available for reissue. (In the United Kingdom, repurchased stock has to be cancelled.) In addition, the US regulations have few restrictions as is exemplified by the practice of *green mail*, where a possible predator is effectively bought off by a repurchase of his block of shares at a large premium over market price. However, this subject is relatively new in UK corporate finance and in time familiarity may help foster it as a conventional option to be considered by those with corporate finance responsibilities.

The Results of the Analysis of the European Sample Surveyed

A attempt has been made to find out whether the European companies surveyed reported treasury stock. The result of this analysis is shown in Table 10.1.

Table 10.1 indicates that some of the European companies surveyed (particularly the German and the French) have experience with treasury stock. However, treasury stock seems unpopular in Britain and Holland. However, what attracts one's attention is the method followed by the French company Moet Hennessy Louis Vuitton (LVMH), which reported treasury stock as part of its current assets.

REVIEW QUESTIONS

1. In what ways may preferred shares be more like debt security than equity security. How should preferred shares be classified on the balance sheet? Show the effect of this classification on the gearing ratios.

Table 10.1. Analysis of companies disclosure of treasury stocks

	British companies (No)	British companies (%)	German companies (No)	German companies (%)	French companies (No)	French companies (%)	Dutch companies (No)	Dutch companies (%)
Number of companies reported treasury stocks in the stockholders' equity section of the balance sheet			5	20	6	24	1	4
Number of companies reported treasury stocks in the assets section of the balance sheet					1	4		
Value used to report treasury stock								
At the issue price			1	4	1	4		
At market price			2	4	1	4		
No information provided			2	8	3	8	1	4

2. When might the Share Subscription Receivable account be classified as:
   (a) a current asset,
   (b) a non-current asset,
   (c) a deduction in the shareholders' equity?
   Show the effect of each of the above classifications on liquidity and gearing ratios.

3. Explain the difference between the proportional and incremental methods of allocating proceeds of lump sum sales of share capital. Show the effect of the use of each approach on the capital structure.

4. What are the different bases for share valuation when assets other than cash are received for issued shares?

5. In what circumstances does a corporation purchase its own shares?

6. Distinguish between the cost method and the par value method of accounting for treasury stock.

7. How is the shareholder's equity affected by using the cost method instead of the par value method for treasury share purchase.

8. What is the difference between unrealized capital increment and unrealized capital decrement? Explain how they present a major problem to accountants and suggest some solutions.

9. Prepare a counter argument to the following statement: 'Treasury stock is purchased at a fair market price. It can be sold for value or reissued for services performed. It has the attributes of an asset and should therefore be reported as an asset on the balance sheet.'

10. Autopack Inc. disclosed the following line item on its preliminary profit and loss account:

    Extraordinary Item: Gain on receipt of donation of property locations from the City Council, £150,000.

    What impact on total assets and total owners' equity can such a classification have? Explain the correct accounting treatment for such a transaction.

CHAPTER 11

Further Examples of Creative Accounting

INTRODUCTION

The purpose of this chapter is to examine some of the more recently identified examples of creative accounting.

NON-SUBSIDIARY DEPENDENT COMPANIES

Controlled non-subsidiaries were defined in TR 603 as a company (or other entity) that is set up in such a way that, although it is under the control of a company instrumental in its creation, the parent, it is not legally a subsidiary. Assets and liabilities are then transferred from the parent to the new subsidiary company with the intention that they should be excluded from consolidation. However, the Exposure Draft ED 42 defined the controlled non-subsidiary as:

> a company, trust or other vehicle which, though not fulfilling the Companies Act definition of a subsidiary, is directly or indirectly controlled by, and a source of benefits or risks for, the reporting enterprise or its subsidiaries that are in substance no different from those that would arise were the vehicle a subsidiary.

In this respect, the definition of a subsidiary is set out by section 736 of the *Companies Act 1985*. The Act states that:

> A company is deemed to be a subsidiary of another if (but only if)
> (a) that other either:
> (i) is a member of it and controls the composition of its board of directors, or
> (ii) holds more than half in nominal value of the equity share capital.

The definition contains two separate parts. If either of the two parts is met, this means that one company is a subsidiary of another. Thus, any company which does not meet either part of the definition is considered to be a controlled non-subsidiary.

However, it is easy to manipulate the first part of the definition because it is not difficult to ensure that the investing company does not have the power to appoint the majority of the board members. The second part of the definition depends on what is meant by equity share capital. The Act defined the equity share capital as a company's

> issued share capital excluding any part of the capital which, neither as respects dividends nor as respects capital, carries any right to participate beyond a specified amount in a distribution.

Companies can overcome this problem by establishing preference shares with fixed dividends which carry the right to participate beyond a certain amount in the dissolving of a company, and is therefore equity capital. It might be easy also to design shares that do not carry rights to participants beyond a specific amount in the winding up of the company. Yet, this does not have the right to the majority of income or the loss of a company by a way of large fixed dividends. Such a capital might have a greater share financially in the result of the company, but may not be classified as equity capital.

On the other hand, it is important to point out that many controlled non-subsidiary schemes may remain a subsidiary for taxation purposes. In this case, the controlled non-subsidiary company takes an advantage since any losses it maintains can be relieved against the income of the group companies. Hence, the definition of the subsidiary for tax purposes differs from that contained in the *Companies Act 1985* and depends on whether the investing company holds more than half of the other company's ordinary share capital. However, the *Income and Corporation Tax Act 1970* section 526 (5) defined the ordinary share capital as:

> in relation to a company, ... all the issued shares capital (by what ever name called) of the company, other than capital the holders whereof have a right to a dividend at a fixed rate, but have no other right to share in profits of the company.

Thus, implementing the non-subsidiary dependent schemes allowed the company to transfer assets and liabilities from the parent's balance sheet to the new non-subsidiary company with the intention that they be excluded from consolidated financial statements. In addition, the company takes the benefit of tax reliefs. This will positively affect the parent's gearing, working capital and return on capital employed ratios.

The opportunity for using this particular off-balance sheet financing scheme seems likely to be restricted given the provision of the *Companies Act 1989*. This Act has changed the definition of a subsidiary. According to the Acts all subsidiary *undertakings* are to be consolidated, including partnerships and unincorporated associations carrying on a trade or a business (with or without a view to profit).

The existing test of a subsidiary based on ownership of equity share capital is replaced by one based on voting rights. The Act states:

A parent company is one that holds a majority of the rights to vote at general meetings. Any rights held by a nominee on behalf of the parent are treated as held by the parent.

The Act goes on to say that subsidiaries should include undertakings where the parent;

1. Is a member and has the right to appoint or remove directors holding a majority of the voting rights.
2. Is a member and controls on its own a majority of voting rights pursuant to an agreement with other shareholders.
3. Has the right to exercise a dominant influence (including at least a right to direct the undertaking's operating and financial policies) by virtue of either provisions in its memorandum or articles or written contract (or control contract).
   Actually exercise a dominant influence over the undertaking or is managed on a unified basis with it.

The most common reason used by companies to justify non-consolidation is dissimilar activities. The highly geared company can benefit from such a scheme by improving its current and gearing ratios. CA 89 tried to tighten this scheme by requiring non-consolidation only when 'inclusion would be incompatible with obligation to give true and fair view'. In June 1990 the ASB issued Exposure Draft 50 *Consolidated Accounts* which identified the conditions under which an enterprise is to be considered as a subsidiary. The Draft also discussed the meaning of control and determine whether an enterprise is a subsidiary of another. ED 50 proposes that it should be only applied to banking and insurance subsidiaries of non-banking or insurance groups or vice versa. The scheme is expected to be tightened if ED 50 became a standard. It is these last two points that give rise to the suggestion that non-controlled subsidiaries may be limited as a means of OBSF in the future.

However, Brindle (1987) reported examples on non-consolidation of subsidiary companies in an off-balance sheet financing chapter in the *UK Survey of Published Accounts* of (1985–1986) and (1986–1987). In one of the examples, the company consolidated on a one line equity basis with additional informa-tion being provided by notes. The quality of the reported information is less than would be required if the subsidiary had been consolidated. The company reported minimum information on receivables and payables. In addition, the subsidiary company has negotiated a facility loan and interest equivalent to the consolidated turnover. An example on controlled non-subsidiary appears in the accounts of Marks and Spencer concerning a subsidiary of the group in charge of credit card operations that provided credit to customers. This subsidiary performs banking functions which are funded separately from the rest of the group. The subsidiary is not consolidated in the group's balance sheet, but the assets and liabilities are presented as a single item, *'Net Assets of Financial Activities'*. In 1987 the Burton Group was criticized for not consolidating the accounts of their finance house activities when their assets in the region were £500 million with debt of £400m. The financial gearing of the group was reported at 41%. If the group's financial activities were consolidated, the level of gearing would have exceeded 50%.

The annual report of Next Plc (1990) showed that the company did not consolidate the accounts of Club 24 'because its activity is significantly different from that of the group'. Non-consolidation improved the current ratio from 1.9 to 1.5 and the net borrowing to stockholders ratio from 115 to 37%.

OVERNIGHT SALE AND REPURCHASE OF ASSETS

At the end of the fiscal year before preparing the financial statements, a company may sell part of its assets to another company and agree to repurchase them in the following accounting period. This step might show the balance sheet in good shape and improve the efficiency ratios.

THE ABUSE OF ACQUISITION ACCOUNTING

A business combination takes place when two or more business organizations come together to form a single economic unit. Business combinations take many different forms. The combination of the business units is often achieved through fusions of different companies into a large single unit. Such a fusion is accomplished through mergers or acquisitions. A business combination is also achieved by acquisition of control by one company over the operations of another. Control of a corporate body is achieved through stock ownership or through interlocking directorships. Such control results in unified and integrated operations of a business enterprise while permitting component units to retain their separate corporate identity.

Ordinarily, the acquiring company takes over all assets and assumes all liabilities of the company to be absorbed. Upon transfers of assets and liabilities, the acquiring company makes payment for the acquisition with cash, securities of the acquiring companies, or both. Such payments are distributed to the shareholders of the company that is to be dissolved. In this respect, SSAP 23 provides guide-lines to account for acquisition and merger. It sets out various criteria to determine which method should be used. The principal criterion on which the standard is based is whether or not any material resources leave the combining companies: if they are not, either merger accounting or acquisition accounting may be used. The SSAP was prepared in the light of the so-called *'merger relief'* provision introduced by the *Companies Act 1981* sch. 131 and 133 and the *Companies Act 1985*. The Act gives relief from setting up a share premium account to a company issuing shares in respect of a takeover, provided they are issued under the arrangement whereby the holding company reached at least 90% of the consideration for the purchase of shares. In the remainder of this section this relief has been referred to as share premium relief rather than merger relief to avoid any confusion with merger accounting. The principal additional criteria in the SSAP 23 definition of a merger are that (a) the offeror must not hold 20% or more of the equity or the voting shares in the offerree prior to making the offer, and (b) at least 90% of consideration given by the offeror for the equity and any other voting shares must be in the form of equity and/or voting shares. Under acquisition accounting the results of the acquired companies are brought into the group account from the date of acquisition only. Fair values as at the date of acquisition are attributed to the underlying net assets acquired. Goodwill usually arises, being the difference between the aggregate of the fair values of the separate net assets and the value of consideration given. Accounting for goodwill is dealt with in SSAP 22, which provides that it should be eliminated against reserves immediately following the acquisition. On the other hand, under merger accounting, there is no requirement to revalue the assets at fair value and no goodwill arises. The accounts of the two combining companies are aggregated and presented as if the companies have always been combined. Thus, premerger figures are also restated on this aggregate basis.

Thus, it can be seen that although the terms *merger* and *acquisition* are often used synonymously to describe business combinations, each has a specific accounting treatment which significantly affects the reported income. However, the approach adopted in SSAP 23 can be contrasted with that adopted in the United States. Under the American Statement APB (16), merger accounting must be used if the combination meets specific criteria. The conditions are very stringent and most combinations other than straightforward share for share exchanges fail to meet at least one.

SSAP 23 requires acquiring companies to attribute fair values to the assets acquired. It is here where most of the criticisms of acquisition accounting are directed. Westwick (1986) demonstrated that it may happen that when acquirer X makes a bid for acquiree Y's shares that X's shares are quoted at a price a_1. By the time the bid is accepted, the share's price may change to a_2 and by the time the shares are actually exchanged, prices may change to a_3. The question that then arises is which price should be used for the fair value of the X's shares in determining the investment in Y for the purpose of acquisition accounting?

The value of assets acquired may also be different from their value in the original company. Reorganizing and integrating the business may also result in a reduction in the carrying value of assets and the creation of provision for reorganization costs. Hence, writing down the value of the net assets and increasing the value of goodwill will result in low future depreciation and high earnings growth. In addition, future return on capital appears stronger. Thus, fair value accounting and the creation of reorganization provisions are subjective areas.

Another difficulty associated with accounting for acquisitions and mergers is the treatment of goodwill. SSAP 23 recommends goodwill to be written off immediately after acquisition. Companies adopting acquisition rather than merger accounting are able to exploit the subjectivity underlying the attributed fair values of the assets acquired. The advantage occurs when a company attributes the lowest possible values to the net assets and the highest possible values to goodwill. According to SSAP 22, goodwill should be written off directly to reserves, the net assets with low values are subject to small future depreciation charges. However, the company might face a problem if reserves are not sufficient to bear heavy write offs. SSAP 22 permitted companies at the time of acquisitions to establish provisions for reorganization and rationalization costs and losses.

SSAP 22 does not require disclosure of how values are allocated to net assets acquired, nor of the amounts of any provisions for future transaction costs. Another possible benefit companies may secure from establishing reorganizational and rationalization provisions is that, to the extent that any such provision is found in later years to be excessive, it is quite legitimate to write it back to the income statement as an undisclosed adjustment and thus improve the earning figures.

Some companies feel quite happy with the contents of SSAP 22, since amortizing goodwill will depress future income and immediate write off of goodwill results in favourable impact on profit growth. However, writing off goodwill reduces the total in the equity section of the balance sheet which will affect gearing.

One attraction of merger accounting is that goodwill does not arise. Merger accounting also allows two companies' figures to be shown as if they had been together before the merger. This is generally criticized because it enables companies to create instant earnings and to distort holding company's profitability, since goodwill does not arise, merger accounting gets around the problem of having to write off goodwill, which could affect either profits or services of subsequent years. In this respect, Griffiths (1987) believed that the desire to avoid goodwill has been the main driving force behind the increase in the abuse of merger accounting rules. He went on to say that for that reason the debate about SSAP 23 is linked with the future of SSAP 22 which deals with goodwill.

A further incentive to use merger accounting is that under merger accounting the investment is recorded at its nominal value and assets and liabilities are not revalued, while under the acquisition accounting the investment by the holding company is recorded at its market value and the assets and liabilities of the acquired company are revalued to their fair values. The effect is that the acquisition accounting may increase the depreciation charges resulting from the increase in the revalued assets.

On the other hand, the treatment of intangible assets has become an important and controversial issue in recent years. In the past it was common to include brand names in the value of goodwill. Now there seems to be a strong incentive to separate them from goodwill figures. Unlike goodwill, brands and publishing titles are separable assets and may be identified and sold separately without disposing of the business as a whole. In this respect, SSAP 22 states that the identifiable intangibles should be valued and included as separable net assets, not omitted or merged into goodwill. According to Bryant (1989) some companies have opted for this method and others have not. In his opinion both the Companies Act and SSAP 22 support the separation of intangibles. The *Companies Act 1985* requires all fixed assets to be written off systematically over their useful life. SSAP 22 suggests that separable intangible assets should be amortized or eliminated from the accounts. Actually, part of the attraction in capitalizing separable intangibles is the absence of an accounting standard requiring amortization. This gives birth to creative accounting.

The ASB seems to respond to the above mentioned difficulties by publishing ED 47 *Accounting for Goodwill* and ED 48 *Accounting for Acquisition and Merger* (see the discussion on ED 47 in Chapter 8). ED 48 put more emphasis on the substance of the combination rather than the form. The Draft defined acquisition as 'the application of resources by an enterprise to obtain ownership or control of another enterprise or enterprises'. The Draft defined merger as 'the coming together of two or more enterprises for a mutual sharing of the risks and rewards of the combined enterprise. In a merger no party to the combination can be identified as acquiror or acquiree'. The draft stated that the combination should be treated as an acquisition except when, in the combination together with any related arrangements, all of the following apply:

1. none of the parties sees itself as acquiror or acquiree;

2. none of the parties dominates the management of the combined entity;

3. the equity shareholders of none of the parties have, or could have, disposed of a material part of their shareholding, directly or indirectly, for shares carrying significantly reduced rights as any other non-equity conditions;

4. no minority interest with more than 10% of the equity remain in any of the enterprises to which an offer is made;

5. none of the combining parties is more than 50% larger than any other entity which is a party to the combination unless special circumstances prevent the larger from dominating the other;

6. the share of the equity in the combination allocated to one or more parties does not depend on the post-combination performance of any of the businesses previously controlled by that party(ies).

The (1985–1986) *Survey of UK Published Accounts* showed that in practice some takeovers were accounted for as mergers, even where there was a substantial cash element in the consideration. These should not have been eligible under the SSAP 23 criteria. Wilkins (1987) concluded that, although SSAP 22 and SSAP 23 are issued to help in improving the levels of financial reporting, it is unlikely that they affect current practice. As mentioned earlier, where a business combination meets the criteria in SSAP 23, the combination may be accounted for by using the acquisition approach or the merger approach.

Wild (1987), in the *Survey of UK Published Accounts* (1986–1987), found most of the companies adopted merger accounting. He noticed two examples of companies meeting the merger criteria but using acquisition accounting. He found with acquisition accounting many companies adopting the immediate write off goodwill approach, but there was considerable divergence as to which reserves were used for this purpose. Some companies used revaluation reserves to write off goodwill (DTI outlawed this practice). Other companies have specified goodwill reserves. Although SSAP 22 encourages the immediate write off goodwill approach, it offers the option of amortization of positive goodwill over its economic life.

Wild found cases where other presentations have been adopted. A company has excluded the charge for profit on ordinary activities and has presented the charge as a separate line between the ordinary and extraordinary activities. He also found companies adopted different approaches to the life of goodwill. In this case, SSAP 23 might have misled the user of the accounts into thinking that they are comparable. In addition, in one case, the two treatments of goodwill have been adopted in one set of accounts. Wild believes that the issuance of

SSAP 22 and SSAP 23 have little effect on practice and in some cases the SSAPs cause more confusion rather than less. He said that:

> the explanatory foreword of SSAP states that the primary aim of SSAP is 'to narrow areas of differences and variety of accounting treatment of the matters with which they deal.'

He went on to say that 'it must be questionable whether either SSAP 22 or SSAP 23 meets this aim.' He concluded 'it is certainly questionable whether a SSAP which does not meet its stated aim should be left to give the misleading impression that uniformity is being achieved.'

The Results of the Analysis of the European Sample Surveyed

An attempt has been made to see what reasons European companies give for consolidation. The results of the analysis are reported in Tables 11.1 and 11.2.

Although the majority of the surveyed French companies provide the same reason for consolidation, the surveyed German and Dutch provide different reasons. However, since most of the surveyed British companies consolidated all their subsidiaries, one should expect little information on the reasons they disclosed for consolidation. Hence, it is difficult to say that the European companies surveyed are consistent in the way they consolidate their financial statements.

As was the case with reasons given by the surveyed companies for consolidation, various reasons are given for non-consolidation.

FOREIGN CURRENCY TRANSLATION

A main accounting difficulty which arises when a firm enters into a variety of business transactions, including exports of goods and services and foreign borrowing, is the translation of its financial statements. The translation of financial statements involves dealing with two main issues: the exchange rate at which various accounts are translated from one currency into another (translation method) and the subsequent treatment of gains or losses. In general, four approaches have been suggested for translation: current–non-current, monetary–non-monetary, temporal, and current rate method. The choice between these methods creates opportunities for creative accounting.

Another difficulty in the accounting for foreign currency is the treatment of gains or losses. Shark and Shamis (1979) demonstrated that gains or losses result from realized transactions, unrealized future transactions and the translation of

Table 11.1. Reasons given by the surveyed German, French and British companies for consolidation.

	British companies (No)	British companies (%)	German companies (No)	German companies (%)	French companies (No)	French companies (%)	Dutch companies (No)	Dutch companies (%)
Significant majority interest and directly or indirectly controlled	5	20	9	36	14	56	8	32
Participate directly or indirectly on a permanent basis with equal to or more than 50% or it can exercise control over subsidiary's operations			5	20	4	16	9	36
Subsidiaries the company has direct or indirect interest with durable nature and the company can exert influence on management even though interest may represent less than 50% of the issued capital			2	8	2	8	4	16
Subsidiaries who have a material effect on consolidated financial statements			2	8	2	8		
No reason given	20	80	7	28	3	12	4	16
	25	100	25	100	25	100	25	100

foreign currency balance sheets. In general, several options for dealing with the gains and losses are used. The first approach requires the gain or loss to be taken directly to the income statement. FASB (8) requires that the gain or losses be treated as an ordinary item in the period in which it occurs. Another approach contained in Chapter 12 of *Accounting Research Bulletin* 43 of the AICPA (1961) was the deferral of all unrealized gains and losses.

Other approaches deferred all gains and losses. The deferrals are put into a reserve account, which has the effect of eliminating the earnings impact of foreign exchange gains and losses. An attractive approach which also attempts to eliminate the earnings impact treats gains and losses as adjustments to the stockholders' equity. Another two approaches involve a deferral of gains and losses and refer to special ways of dealing primarily with losses arising from the translation of long-term debt. In one of these two approaches, the feeling is that foreign currency debt was entered into because of favourable interest rate

Table 11.2. Reasons given for excluding subsidiaries from consolidation.

	British companies (No)	British companies (%)	German companies (No)	German companies (%)	French companies (No)	French companies (%)	Dutch companies (No)	Dutch companies (%)
Dissimilar activities	1	4	2	8			1	4
Lack of control	1	4	1	4	9	36	9	36
Insignificant	3	12	12	48	4	16	7	28
Lack of operations and insignificant business volume/no major volume interest (the subsidiary should meet specific sales volume and capital in order to qualify for consolidation)			1	4	7	28	4	16
No material effect on consolidated financial statements			1	4	1	4		
No subsidiary excluded	18	72			4	16	4	16
No reason given	2	8	8	32				
	25	100	25	100	25	100	25	100

differentials. Therefore, the foreign exchange loss resulting from translation should be viewed as an adjustment of interest expense and therefore be written off over the life of the debt. The second approach relates the cost of the debt with the acquisition of an asset which is translated at the historical rate. As the exchange rate changes, only the debt changes in value. The resulting gain or loss would be considered as adjustment of the assets purchased and amortized over the life of the assets.

In 1983 SSAP 20 was issued. The standard is quite similar to FASB (52). When a statement is prepared for an individual company that has transactions determined in foreign currency, SSAP 20 provides for transactions into the domestic currency at the rate in effect on the transaction date or if the rates do not fluctuate significantly, an average rate may be used as an approximation for the period. Non-monetary items that have been translated and recorded should be carried in the firm's book at subsequent reporting or settlement date. Monetary assets should be translated at the balance sheet rate. The resulting foreign exchange gain or loss is recognized in current income.

In an attempt to see if companies are consistent in using accounting methods relating to the translation of balance items and items in the profit and loss account, the survey of UK published accounts has been used and the results reported in Tables 11.3 and 11.4.

Table 11.3. Translation methods used for balance sheet items.

Method	Year 1982–83 (%)	1983–84 (%)	1986–87 (%)	1988–89 (%)
Closing rate method	81	94	86	77
Temporal method	1	1	–	–
Monetary/non monetary	1	1	–	–
Current/non current	1	1	–	–
Others	–	–	2	8
Policy not disclosed	3	3	1	2
No evidence of foreign operations	13	–	11	13
	100	100	100	100

Table 11.4. Translation methods used for the profit and loss account.

Method	Year 1982–83 (%)	1983–84 (%)	1986–87 (%)	1988–89 (%)
Closing rate	48	55	33	35
Average Rate	24	27	40	37
Other methods	3	3	–	–
Not disclosed	12	15	15	16
No evidence of foreign operations	13	–	12	12
	100	100	100	100

Table 11.3 reveals some slight variation over time in the methods used to translate balance sheet items. If the same companies were being surveyed in different years, this may point to the possibility that companies tended to switch from one translation method to another. However, Tonkin (1991) in the *Survey of UK Published Accounts* noticed that the practice of translation methods relating to balance sheet items, used by the surveyed companies, has been stabilized on the closing rate method. The same thing can be seen in the surveyed French and the Dutch companies (see Table 11.5).

Like Table 11.3, Table 11.4 also reveals some variation over time in the translation methods used for profit and loss account items. The variation may be indicative of switching from one translation policy to another. However, Tonkin (1991) noticed in the *Survey of UK Published Accounts* (1990–1991) that there is an increasing trend towards the use of average rate for translating profit and loss items. This phenomenon is evident in the European Sample (see Table 11.6).

The Results of the Analysis of the European Sample Surveyed

An attempt has been made to see whether the European companies surveyed are consistent in their treatment of the translation of foreign currency. The results of the analysis are reported in Tables 11.5, 11.6, 11.7 and 11.8.

Table 11.5 reveals that most of the British, French and Dutch companies surveyed use the exchange rate at the balance sheet date to translate their balance sheet items. However, the surveyed German companies used different rates to different balance sheet items.

Table 11.6 shows that a reasonable proportion of the surveyed companies employed the average rate to translate the profit and loss account items. However, even in the use of the average rate the companies were not consistent. While some of the surveyed companies used the monthly rate to arrive at the average, others used the quarterly rate. On the other hand, an attempt has been

Table 11.5. Translation rate used for balance sheet items.

Method	British companies (No)	British companies (%)	German companies (No)	German companies (%)	French companies (No)	French companies (%)	Dutch companies (No)	Dutch companies (%)
Year end exchange rate	19	76	6	24	22	88	20	80
Average				2		8		
Different exchange rates used	2	8	11	4	1	4	5	20
Policy not disclosed or not clear	4	16	6	24	2	8		
	25	100	25	100	25	100	25	100

Table 11.6. Translation rate used for profit and loss accounts.

Rate	British companies (No)	British companies (%)	German companies (No)	German companies (%)	French companies (No)	French companies (%)	Dutch companies (No)	Dutch companies (%)
Rate at the time of the transaction	4	16	1	4			3	12
Closing rate	2	8	3	12	2	8	6	24
Average rate	13	52	12	48	17	68	11	44
Other methods					1	4		
Not disclosed/ not clear	6	24	9	36	5	20	5	20
	25	100	25	100	25	100	25	100

Table 11.7. Treatment of currency difference arising from the conversion of balance sheet items.

	British companies (No)	(%)	German companies (No)	(%)	French companies (No)	(%)	Dutch companies (No)	(%)
Taken to reserves	15	60	5	20	12	48	15	60
Differences from translation of fixed assets are included with the beginning balance, the acquisition, or the manufacturing cost, as well as accumulated depreciation			1	4				
Taken to the profit and loss account	4	16	5	20	6	24	7	28
Taken to the earnings	2	8	2	8	2	8	1	4
Not disclosed/ not Clear	4	16	12	48	5	20	2	8

Table 11.8. Treatment of currency difference arising from the conversion of profit and loss account items.

	British companies (No)	(%)	German companies (No)	(%)	French companies (No)	(%)	Dutch companies (No)	(%)
Taken to shareholder's equity/reserves	8	32	3	12	13	52	12	48
Taken to the profit & loss account	8	32	11	44	2	8	9	36
Taken to retained earnings	1	4			5	20	1	4
Not disclosed/ not clear	8	32	11	44	5	20	3	12

made to see how the European companies surveyed accounted for any exchange gains or losses resulting from translation. The outcome of the analysis is reported in Tables 11.7 and 11.8.

Table 11.7 illustrates that the European companies surveyed use different approaches to account for the difference in the currency translation. However, a sizeable number of the German companies surveyed either did not disclose how they treated the difference or they disclose it in an abstracted way. In general, the treatment of the difference which emerges from the translation of the balance sheet items lacks consistency among the European companies surveyed. Undoubtedly, this will affect figures in the profit and loss account as well as the balance sheet.

Similarly, Table 11.8 reveals that the European companies surveyed were inconsistent in accounting for the translation difference resulting from translating the profit and loss account.

EXTRAORDINARY ITEMS

These items are defined as material items of a character significantly different from the typical business activities of an entity which would not be expected to recur frequently and which would not be considered as recurring factors in any evaluation of the ordinary operating process of the business. *APB Opinion* No. (30) states that

> extraordinary items are events and transactions that distinguished by their unusual nature and by the infrequency of their occurrence.

On the other hand, SSAP 6 defined extraordinary items as:

> those items which derive from events or transactions outside the ordinary activities of the business and which are both material and expected not to recur frequently or regularly.

SSAP 6 indicated that what is extraordinary in one business will not necessarily be extraordinary in another. In December 1991 FRED 1 *The Structure of Financial Statements – Reporting of Financial Performance* issued by the ASB illustrates the difference between exceptional items and extraordinary items. Para. 49 states '*In view of extreme rarity of extraordinary items, no examples are provided. Items falling into the category of exceptional items as discussed in para 46, by definition, cannot be extraordinary*'. Para. 46 *states 'Examples of items which may include profit or loss on the sale of fixed assets and losses on the expropriation of assets'*. It seems that the statement tries to make extraordinary items extremely rare. However, the attempt made by the draft to distinguish between exceptional and extraordinary items complicate matters.

Unfortunately, it is often difficult to determine what is extraordinary because accountants have never clearly defined materiality nor the distinction between frequently and infrequently. Hence, firm guide-lines to follow in judging when an item is or is not material have not been established. The point is that as long as the definition of materiality is not sharply outlined, it will often be difficult to differentiate ordinary items from extraordinary items. In this respect, Bernstein (1970) reported on an article published in *Forbes Magazine* (issue of 15 May 1969) entitled 'The Dimensions Of American Business'. This was a statistical profile of the country's biggest corporations and contained information on net income as well as extraordinary charges and credits included therein. Out of about the 800 companies covered, 145 reported extraordinary gains and losses. In examining the financial reports of the 145 companies, they revealed 215 individual items of extraordinary gains and losses. On the basis of the extraordinary items included in the 145 reports and a number of interesting examples of reporting found in other published company reports, Bernstein raised a number of questions concerning what is materiality, what is extraordinary, when are sizeable gains and losses not extraordinary, how do we distinguish between extraordinary and unusual, or offsets and provisions for losses.

The study found that the practice of reporting extraordinary gains and losses reflected a complete lack of agreement on what constituted a material relationship between an extraordinary item and the income preceding it. Hence, the practice revealed that the lack of definition of the concept of materiality continues to result in a great variety of interpretations as to what is and what is not material. *Accountancy* (September 1987, p. 52) 'Reports and Accounts', revealed that the Midland Bank treated the debts of third world countries as an extraordinary item, while Barclays, Lloyds, and the National Westminster treated them as exceptional.

Another difficulty is that of deciding just what is meant by the word extraordinary. The *APB Opinion* No. (30) defined extraordinary items as material items 'of a character significantly different from the typical or customary business activities of the entity'. Linked with the concept of "'typical or customary" activity is the concept of "nonrecurrance"'. Bernstein found that there is ample room for doubt that the above characteristics of '"typical and customary activity" and "nonrecurrance" are sufficiently clear and definitive to constitute a workable definition of "extraordinary items".'

However, para. (22) of *APB Opinion* No. (9) stated that 'certain gains or losses, regardless of size, do not constitute extraordinary items'. Although there is opposition to the idea that size alone can cause an item to become extraordinary, Bernstein found that many corporations reported extraordinary items on the basis of size. He concluded that the *APB Opinion* needs to be stricter in this area and in another part of his study he claimed that this area is in need of clarification and reassessment.

One further problem mentioned by Bernstein is the distinction between extraordinary and unusual items. He believes that professional literature does not shed light on this distinction and that the reader of financial statements might get confused and consider these terms as synonymous.

More difficulties revealed in practice are the offsetting of extraordinary items and of providing reserves for future losses. Bernstein provided examples of offset of extraordinary items where an extraordinary gain is offset by the change of an equal provision for some sort of future contingency or loss.

Another problem deals with what is referred to as the 'big bath' approach. If companies see that a large loss is inevitable, then they write off as large an amount as possible on the understanding that investors do not make a great distinction between a small loss and large one. Future statements are thus relieved of these losses and provide the company with an earnings injection.

The company may use the category of extraordinary items to report costs to be excluded from the company's pretax income, and more importantly, from its earning per share record. This might be important because earnings per share is the main component in the price earnings ratio, which is used by the stock market as a key performance indicator.

Thus, the above discussion showed that the abuse of the undefined concept of materiality may result in creative accounting. This would result in better EPS before extraordinary items.

Hodgson (1986) in the *Survey of UK Published Accounts* (1985–1986) showed that there is considerable variation in how companies interpret SSAP 6. The Survey reported that the variations in treatment were largely from the adjustments arising from the *Finance Act 1984*. Despite the fact that SSAP 6 attempts to give a clear indication as to how profit on the disposal of investment property should be treated, there was still diversity of treatment. There was also disparity in the treatment of disposals of previously revalued assets.

The (1986–1987) *Survey of UK Published Accounts* shows that there has been a substantial move from extraordinary items accounting towards reserve accounting, particularly in the case of foreign currency differences, goodwill and intangibles, and profits and losses on the sale of fixed assets and other non-trading assets. In each of these cases, there is an accounting standard (SSAP 20, SSAP 22, SSAP 19) which requires some element of reserve accounting. It is assumed that the shift is a result of these standards.

Hodgson (1988), in the *Survey of UK Published Accounts* (1987–1988), indicated that accounting policies for extraordinary items were uncommon. He found that, while the standard distinguished between the reorganization cost of continuing business segments (exceptional costs), and costs incurred in the close of business segments (extraordinary costs) such a distinction can be rarely seen in practice. He concluded that different policies for dealing with extraordinary items indicate that major restructuring is widely considered to fall outside the strict criteria for extraordinary items laid down in SSAP 6.

Tonkin and Watson (1990), in the *Survey of UK Published Accounts* (1989–1990), reported that different companies interpreted the same transactions in different ways, showing inconsistency in distinguishing between exceptional and extraordinary items.

The Results of the Analysis of the European Sample Surveyed

The analysis of European companies showed that a sizeable number of the companies surveyed report extraordinary items (see Table 11.9). What attracts one's attention is that most of the British and Dutch companies surveyed reported extraordinary items. Yet, various reasons have been used by the surveyed companies to justify their reporting (see Table 11.9).

Table 11.9. European companies reported extraordinary items.

	British companies (No)	British companies (%)	German companies (No)	German companies (%)	French companies (No)	French companies (%)	Dutch companies (No)	Dutch companies (%)
Number of companies reporting extraordinary items	16	64	8	32	6	24	17	68
Reasons given for extraordinary items								
Alienation of a product and from a partially unused provision for restructuring measures			1	4				
Diminution in value of tangible fixed assets of participating interest	2	8			2	8		
Leeuwarden							1	4
Consolidation of acquired fixed assets whose valuation needed downward adjustments			1	4			1	4
The proceeds from disposition of shares			1	4			4	16
Losses/gains incurred up to subsidiaries disposal	9	63	2	8	1	4	4	16
Income or expenses not arising from ordinary activities			2	8				
A provision formed for the reorganization of a majority participating interest							5	20
Change to the national concept as regards the repossessing of radioactive fuel assemblies in the scheduled plant			1	4				

Table 11.9 (*continued*)

	British companies (No)	British companies (%)	German companies (No)	German companies (%)	French companies (No)	French companies (%)	Dutch companies (No)	Dutch companies (%)
Exceptional depreciation/ amortization on tangible assets			1	4	2	8		
Valuation changes for inventories of product			1	4				
Fine payable for exceeding the quota			1	4				
Risk associated with reorganization of the company's pension scheme			1	4				
Reviewing fixed assets and investments			1	4				
Gain/loss on sale of fixed assets	6	24	1	4	3	12	5	20
Results from acquisition or divestment of subsidiaries							2	8
Incidental nature							1	4
Restructuring of expenses							1	4
Cost associated with the increase of capital			1	4				
Extraordinary credit			1	4				
Extraordinary income/ expense from current operations			1	4				
Gain or loss on sale interest in subsidiaries			4	16	1	4	1	4
Provision written back and transferred charges sales repurchase commitments					2	8		
Abortive bid costs					1	4		
Reorganization cost					1	4		
Non-incurring items			2	8			1	4

INTEREST RATE SWAPS

Swaps are one of a number of capital market techniques that were developed in response to the need to manage an acceptable contingent risk caused by volatile interest and exchange rate. Since 1982 interest rate swaps have become popular financial tools and according to T. S. Arnold (1984) the volume of interest rate swaps have grown from $100 million in the beginning of the 1980s to $80 billion by the end of 1984.

However, before proceeding any further it is useful to define the swaps. According to Luke (1988) swaps are

> transactions where two unrelated borrowers independently borrow identical principal amounts from different lenders for the same period and with interest calculated on a different basis, and agree to make payments to each based on the interest cost of the other's borrowing.

An interest rate swap occurs where each party can access a particular market on comparatively better interest rate terms than others. However, T. S. Arnold (1984) believes that companies are involved in swaps as a result of the growing globalization of capital markets. They attempt to escape the boundaries of national markets to meet their requirements in raising debts or investing funds. Frederick and Militello (1984) listed four fundamental objectives of swaps financing:

1. they reduce financing costs;

2. reduce or eliminate funding uncertainty;

3. the creation of otherwise unavailable long-term forward foreign exchange cover;

4. the attainment of limited or inaccessible long-term funding in a particular currency.

In fact, swaps agreements are used to overcome problems associated with currency exposure, interest rate exposure, and restrictions imposed by the financial market. In the case where swaps are used to hedge against currency exposure, the swap agreement allows a party to lock into a desired rate of exchange. For instance, a British company exports its products mainly to the United States. The British company expects to receive $10 million in three years which will be converted into sterling. If the exchange rate is 1.75 today and expected to be lower in three years' time and the British company did nothing to hedge the exposure, it may face currency exchange loss when reporting its dollars. In this situation, the British company can enter a swap agreement locking into an exchange rate of 1.75 when it converts its dollars.

However, one may ask why a company bothers to get involved in a swap agreement since it can borrow funds on the terms it desires. Wishon and Chevalier (1985) give several reasons why this is not possible or less desirable. Any new borrowing might necessitate recognition by existing covenants on less favourable terms and it might contradict the contents of other agreements. The existing debt may carry a more favourable interest rate than is available on other new debts, or the cost of procuring a replacement debt for existing borrowing may be prohibitive. Wishon and Chevalier added that the separate swap approach may be the least cost alternative for a newly issued debt. One other possible reason for engaging in a swap agreement is that the involved party becomes able to predict the behaviour of the interest rate. In general, managements engage in a swap agreement to take advantage of least cost financing agreement and to control interest rate risks.

The rational for swaps can be illustrated by employing the following example: Two parties may sign a legal contract that governs the exchange of cash flows in the future. Intermediaries arrange swap transactions. They play two major roles, market makers and/or brokers. Market makers are less common and often enter interest rate swaps as an actual counterpart to the company or financial institution. Brokers do not enter swaps; therefore, the swap cannot be extended until the broker locates a counterpart desiring the exact swap specified by the customer. In this case, the swap is not legally connected with the assets or liabilities of either party, because no principal is exchanged. Hence, the credit risk of each counterpart is limited to the payments it will receive from its partner in the agreement. If one side defaults the other stops payments. Under these complex swap agreements companies often use interest rate swaps to transform floating rate debt costs on the commercial paper market or bank credit facilities into an attractive fixed rate or to unlock high-coupon, fixed rate debt. For example, suppose that borrower K can raise a floating debt at London Interbank Offered Rate (LIBOR) + 0.85%. Company K would like to lock into a fixed rate but can only raise a fixed rate at 12%. Company L can raise a fixed rate fund at 10% but wants a floating rate debt because its view is that the interest rate will fall. It can borrow variable rate money at LIBOR + 0.35%. Hence, the comparative advantages are shown below.

	Borrower K	Borrower L	Difference
Cost of fixed rate	12%	10%	2%
Cost of variable rate	LIBOR + 0.85%	LIBOR + 0.35%	0.5%

It should be noted that the difference between Borrower K and Borrower L before swapping is 2% and it is reduced to 0.5% after the swap. Thus, making a net saving is 1.5% (2% − 0.5%).

Suppose that Borrower K will issue £5 million variable rate debt at LIBOR + 0.85 and borrower L will issue £5 million fixed rate cost of 10%. Under the swap terms, Borrower K will receive LIBOR on the £5 million from the investment bank and pay 10.65%; Borrower L will pay interest at LIBOR and receive 10.5%.

The savings of each party involved are as follows:

	Borrower K
Payment on roll-over loan	LIBOR + 0.85%
Receipt from swap agreement	LIBOR
Payment through swap agreements	00.65%
Effective cost of borrowing (0.85% + 10.65%)	11.50%
Cost of raising own fixed rate debt	12.00%
Saving (12% − 11.5%)	00.50%

	Borrower L
Payment on fixed rate loan	10.00%
Receipt from swap agreement	10.50%
Payment through the swap agreement	LIBOR
Effective cost of borrowing [LIBOR − (10.5% − 10%)]	LIBOR − 0.50%
Cost of borrowing own roll-over	LIBOR + 0.35%
Saving (0.5% + 0.35%)	00.85%

The investment bank makes a return of 0.15% (10.65 − 10.5%) by receiving 10.65% from borrower K and paying 10.5% to borrower L.

As one can notice, interest rate swaps have arisen as a means whereby organizations can gain access to borrowing on more favourable terms than could be achieved with a direct loan. In addition, the counterparts are all better off since they ultimately obtained financing at lower rates. In this respect, Freyne (1985) contended that swaps, as a treasury tool for the management of currency exposure and interest rate risk and to arbitrage, will continue without rivals for the coming 10 years and he affirmed that swaps are here to stay. Interest rate swaps are often considered as off-balance sheet financing techniques. Swap agreements are generally not shown on the balance sheet. Wishon and Chevalier (1985) argued that interest rate swaps do not provide borrowed funds for support of the business. They modify the terms of existing obligations. However, modifying the terms of obligations plays a major role in financing business operations. Any saving in interest payments will be used to finance another company's activities. Nevertheless, a company might report the swap agreement on the balance sheet by recognizing gross assets and liabilities equal to the present value of the expected future receipts and payments relating to the agreement. Even so, this might not exist in practice and reporting gross swap receivables and payables on the balance sheet would be inconsistent with the agreement established for other formal agreements. It may also result in confusion about the legal offsetting amounts that may occur. In addition, in cases where these amounts are periodically adjusted during the term of the agreement to show changes in market interest rates, significant volatility would be involved. Interest rate swap transactions seek to transfer market risk. Their occurrence might not be reported at all, either in the accounts of the company involved in borrowing or in the accounts of the financial institution who brings the parties together and acts as an intermediary, possibly providing guarantees.

In general, anticipated future cash flows relating to a swap are not recorded until interest is accrued on the related debt obligations. Non-recognition of gains or losses inherent in a swap position tends to be offset by an unrecognized gain or loss on debt obligation that relates to the swaps. In all cases, T. S. Arnold (1984) argued that interest rate swaps are off-balance sheet items because companies mention a swap in footnotes to the financial statements if it is material in nature. Frederick and Militello (1984) demonstrated that most of the creative accounting being displayed in today's financial marketplace falls under the generic phrase of swap financing. The off-balance sheet finance problem comes to exist in the case of a swap defaults. Hence, the most debated issue for corporate borrowers using swaps is the accounting when an agreement is terminated. Some believe that any gain or loss on termination should be deferred and amortized as an interest adjustment over the remaining life of the underlying financial instrument. Others have argued that, because there are no remaining cash flows or risks associated with the agreement, any gains or losses should be recognized immediately in the income statement, similar to the extinguishment of debt. However, the choice gives birth to window dressing, and hiding information on the expected contingent liabilities associated with the default of the swaps results in off-balance sheet financing. However, Brindle (1986), in the *Survey of UK Published accounts* (1985–1986), says that he believes that the interest rate swaps agreements are not strictly off-balance sheet financing, but the disclosure of its existence may be vital to assess the company's obligations. In spite of this, Brindle dealt with the interest rate swaps under the off-balance sheet financing chapter in the survey. According to Samuels *et al.* (1989) the outstanding debt of the United States related to interest rate swaps grew from zero in 1982 to reach £400 billion at the end of 1987. They also reported that in 1987 it was estimated that off-balance sheet financing by the major UK banks related to interest swap amounted to £200 million. Only £20 million (10%) were disclosed as contingent liabilities. The difference was not being disclosed.

However, FASB has addressed similar issues to the termination of swaps in statement No. (80), and the analysis is compelling. If gains or losses on the future position are deferred, they become part of the carrying value of the hedged assets or liabilities. On the termination of the hedge, the cost of the carrying value of the hedged assets or liabilities is not adjusted. The board acknowledged that a cancelled future contract, if viewed by itself, embodies no more risk to the enterprise. But the board concluded that the gain or loss deferred before termination should continue to be deferred, pending disposition of the hedged item, because the enterprise has taken the position that future contracts cannot be viewed by themselves. Rather, it has been linked with assets/liabilities transactions, and the accounting treatment should continue to be consistent with that view. The ICAEW (1987) issued a technical release (TR 677) *Accounting for Complex Capital Issues*, and one of the examples of such a complex issue which the release discussed was interest rate swaps. The release recommends that:

There should be full disclosure of the arrangements in the notes to the financial statements, so that the commercial effect on the whole transaction, including any possible risk of exposure in the event of failure of the swap party, is clearly explained.

Actually, disclosing information on interest rate swaps agreements is important in assessing the company's financial position. Excluding this information from the balance sheet results in providing incomplete information to financial statements users and therefore inaccurate decisions may be taken.

PROJECT FINANCING ARRANGEMENTS

In addition to the product financing arrangements, a company may also be involved in a variety of long-term commitments typically associated with project financing arrangements. Hence, project financing arrangements arise when:

1. two or more entities form a new entity to construct an operating plant that will be used by those entities.

2. The new entity borrows funds from two or more original entities to construct the project and repay the debt from the proceeds received from the project. Payment of the debt is guaranteed by the entities that formed the new entity.

The advantage of such an arrangement is that the entities do not have to report the liability on their balance sheets. For example, suppose that both AB and CD put up £2 million and formed a separate company to build a chemical plant to be used by both companies, and the newly formed company has borrowed £10 million to construct the plant. In this case, neither AB nor CD reports the £10 million debt on their balance sheets. They only disclose the guarantee of payment of the debt of the new company in the case where the proceeds from the project are insufficient to cover the debt service requirements (this complies with the content of the FASB No. (5) *Accounting for Contingencies*).

In some cases, the project financing arrangements become more formalized through the use of take-or-pay contracts, through-put contracts, or investment in joint ventures, where less than a majority own entities involved in the project financing arrangements.

Under *take-or-pay contracts*, a purchaser of goods signs an agreement with a seller to pay a specific amount periodically in return for products or services. The purchaser must make specified minimum payments even if delivery of contracted products and services is not taken. In general, the take-or-pay contracts are associated with project financing arrangements. For instance, in the example above, BP and Shell signed an agreement that they would purchase products from this new plant and that they would make certain minimum payments, even if they did not take delivery of the goods.

Through-put arrangements are similar in concept to take-or-pay contracts except that a service instead of the product is provided by the asset under construction. For instance, suppose BP and Shell become involved in a project financing arrangement to build a pipeline (instead of a plant) to transport their various products. An arrangement is signed that requires BP and Shell to pay a specific amount in return for transportation of the product. In addition, these companies are obliged to provide specified minimum quantities to be transported in each period and are required to make cash payments even if they do not provide the minimum quantities to be transported. However, in practice inconsistent methods might be used to account for and disclose the unconditional obligations in take-or-pay or through-put contracts involved in a project's financing arrangements. In general companies try to develop these types of contracts to get their debts off the balance sheet.

A corporate joint venture is a separate, specific project organized for the benefit of several corporations. The term would be applied to a joint undertaking for a specific purpose, such as the development or sale of a tract of land, the construction of a bridge or dam, the purchase or resale of securities, or the exploration and drilling for oil and gas.

Under the joint venture arrangements (as in the case of forming a captive finance subsidiary as discussed below), consolidation of less than the majority of owned subsidiaries is prohibited, each particular investor in these entities must be accounted for on the cost or equity method of accounting depending upon the degree of influence which the parent has over its investment. By establishing the joint venture, the company will be involved in project financing without having to reflect these transactions on their balance sheets. The liability and related assets are not recorded in any of the investor's consolidated financial statements, nor are the related financing costs evident from this form of fragmentary reporting. The debt is usually guaranteed directly or indirectly by at least one of the participants, although at least one of the participants may be a passive investor or credit grantor whose purpose is to finance the project. The other participants' commitment to fund the project is by ensuring repayments of the project debt. Such commitments are usually in the form of take-or-pay or through-put contracts (see above).

Although the debt of the joint venture is in reality that of the sponsor (because of the conditional guarantee via the take-or-pay contract or a similar commitment), the arrangement structure utilizing current accounting rules precludes this obligation from being recorded by the sponsor. Hence, how can this be explained as far as the substance over form principle is concerned? In this respect, *APB Opinion* (18) *The Equity Method of Accounting for Investment in Common Stock* requires investors to account for investments in corporate joint ventures by the equity method in their consolidated financial statements (if the investment is material). Summarized information of the investment should be presented in the notes in separate statements. If the venture is unincorporated, in some cases the investor may account for his investment on a pro rata basis, since usually he has an undivided interest in each asset and is proportionately liable for his share of each liability. However, this accounting is mostly limited to the oil and gas industry and the real estate business. The substance of the transaction is that the contract obligation will commit the investors to transfer their obligations which are required to be recorded in the investors' accounts. Nevertheless, the investor may argue that such a commitment is an executory contract (a promise for a promise) and should not be recorded until at least one of the parties fulfils his commitment. The investor's position not to record the executory contract is fully backed by *APB statement* No. (4) *Generally Accepted Accounting Principles.* In fact, it is obvious that, under the present accounting rules, the joint venture events are not required to be recorded in the investor's books. At all events, the FASB in 1980, as part of its conceptual framework project, issued concepts statement No. (3), which defined the elements of financial statements of a business enterprise. A major change in emphasis by the FASB was the redefinition of a liability so as to include executory contracts. In connection with off-balance sheet financing, the FASB No. (47) *Disclosure of Long-term Obligations*, requires disclosure of unconditional purchase obligations such as take-or-pay or through-put contracts if they are not recorded in the financial statements. However, Brindle (1986) and (1987) reported several examples of financing through a company in which the investor has less than a majority owned interest under the off-balance sheet chapter of *UK Published Accounts* of (1985–1986) and (1986–1987).

CAPTIVE FINANCE COMPANIES

To serve as a vehicle for financing their operations, companies often establish a completely owned subsidiary. For instance, General Motors corporation has its General Motors Acceptance Corporation (GMAC). These companies are referred to as captive finance companies and usually receive transfers of certain amounts of receivables and debt at their inception. As a result of this, the captive finance company buys receivables from the major company and issues debts to fund the purchases. In this situation, the question to be raised is whether the captive finance company (GMAC) should be consolidated with the major company (GM) for financial reporting purposes?

In general, these companies are not consolidated on the basis that combining dissimilar entities (manufacturing GM, and financing GMAC) distorts the financial statement and they become misleading. On the other hand, others argue that the balance sheet of the company with a captive finance subsidiary that is not consolidated is not comparable to the balance sheet of a company that finances its own receivables.

In fact, creating a finance subsidiary relieves the major company's financial statements of the liability of financing its own receivables. By transferring receivables to the captive finance subsidiary, the major company's liquidity ratios are improved. In addition, this technique increases the borrowing ability of the major company. In this respect, Flowers (1986) demonstrated that it did not take companies long to realize the advantages they obtain by creating a finance subsidiary. He related the popularity of the captive finance subsidiary to the advantages it offers to the major company's treasurer. Flower quoted Louis E. Levy in management accounting as saying:

> the fact that an accounting decision to consolidate a finance subsidiary, or the decision whether or not to capitalize a lease, can affect the amount of credit available to a company defies logic.

The authority for eliminating finance company subsidiaries from the consolidation is para. (3) of *Accounting Research Bulletin* No. (51) (AICPA) and the company law and SSAP 14 *Group Accounts*. The rational for paragraph 3 of ARB 51 is that the operations of the finance company and non-finance company are dissimilar and that their combined financial statements are not meaningful. These subsidiaries are reported under the equity method. In addition, the 7th Directive contains an exception to its requirements to consolidate majority owned subsidiaries if doing so would obscure the true and fair view.

Thus, suppressing a huge amount of debts will result in overstated returns on assets of consolidated groups. However, FASB Statement No. (14) *Financial Reporting for Segments of A Business Enterprise* requires a business enterprise comprised of heterogeneous units to report the relevant financial information of each significant unit.

An AICPA (1978) report to the FASB questioned whether the consolidation of a finance subsidiary would result in improved comparability among the companies that finance receivables through subsidiaries and those that carry their own receivables. The report included another five issues concerning the accounting for captive finance:

1. Are users provided better information if financial subsidiaries are not consolidated?

2. Would a requirement that a finance subsidiary be consolidated allow for adequate disclosure of matters unique to these subsidiaries?

3. Should uniqueness of operations, including the different risk of financial activities, justify exclusion from consolidation?

4. Does the failure to include assets and liabilities that are owned and controlled by an entity from its consolidated balance sheet result in an incomplete presentation?

5. Would technical problems arise from consolidating an entity's balance sheet that otherwise is presented in unclassified fashion?

The FASB is currently examining the concept of the reporting entity as part of its reconsideration of consolidation procedures. The Accounting Standards Executive Committee of AICPA requires the FASB to consider the problem of non-consolidation of the finance subsidiary company. In the issued paper to the Standards Board, the accounting standard division concluded that the present practice should be changed. It concluded that *Accounting Research Bulletin* No. (51) should be interpreted to provide criteria to specify those finance subsidiaries that should be considered. However, it did not recommend amending the bulletin to eliminate the possibility of the exclusion of finance subsidiaries from the consolidation.

The ability to choose whether or not to consolidate finance subsidiaries has the potential to affect several balances on the group's balance sheet. Hence, the analyst who fails to recognize reporting choice while evaluating relative liquidity, solvency, or profitability ratios, is likely to be misled. In this respect, Copeland and Mckinnon (1987) conducted research designed to evaluate what they called *the financial distortion* argument to measure the comparability of the companies which use alternative reporting practices in the US general merchandise industry. They found that alternative accounting practices for finance subsidiaries were most likely to affect four common financial ratios: current ratio, return on assets, debt to equity ratio and receivable turnover. In the same manner, Benis (1979) examined the implications of the widespread practice, of the non-consolidated finance company subsidiary, on the balance sheet and on the resulting analysis of those balance sheets. He noted significant changes (generally adverse changes) in three ratios where the non-consolidated finance subsidiary is consolidated with its affiliates. The three ratios are: current ratio, debt equity and return on assets ratios. Likewise, Burnett *et al.* (1979) found diversities in the procedures used by companies in reporting the income of non-consolidated subsidiaries. They argued that the diversity of reporting practices make financial statements analysis and comparison between companies much more difficult.

OPTIONS

A company may be involved in the purchase or sale of options to allow it to transfer risk to another party or to issue options to purchase shares in the company itself. The company may face the risk of fluctuations in the interest rate, in foreign currency exchange rates and in the price of raw materials. Any company expected to make payments, or to receive money in the future, may be concerned that unfortunate movement may affect its profits. Thus the company looks for a speculator to take part of its risk and write an option. The company purchases the option for a premium, and this allows it to buy or to sell the items subject to the contract at a specific price during a specific period of time. However, the premium is recorded as an asset by the buyer, the writer of the option will treat the premium as liabilities. If the buyer decides to exercise the option, the gross amount that may have to be delivered does not need to be reported in the balance sheet.

According to Samuels *et al.* (1989) until the end of 1988, there was no standard on the treatment of options in the United Kingdom or the United States. After this date both the ICAEW and AICPA have issued papers in which the subject of options is discussed. The main problem in accounting for options concerns the treatment of realized and unrealized gains or losses arising from the change in the market values of the options (that is, should they be taken to the current profit and loss account?). One treatment, for instance, is to defer the gain and loss. Samuels, *et al.* illustrated that the recommended treatment in the United States, is to recognize such amounts in the current income statement for all except those options where they meet the criteria of hedged accounting. In this case assets and liabilities need to be identified as being hedged so that the appropriate time can be determined in which gains and losses are to be recognized. The following example amplifies this point.

Suppose a UK company borrowed $2 million in January 1992. The spot rate of exchange at this date was $1.6 = £1. The main problem facing the company is that if the dollar becomes stronger then it will have to pay more than £1,250,000 ($2 million/1.6). In order to avoid paying more, the company decided to buy a call option entitling it to buy $2 million with a 31 December expiration date at a strike price of $1.5 (the strike price is the price written into the contract at which the holder of the option can buy the dollar from the writer of the option). The price of the option is 1.5 pence per dollar (i.e. a total of £30,000). Suppose the company who bought the option closes its accounts at the end of June when the option price was 3 pence per dollar and the spot rate is 1.52 per pound. If the company follows the American approach in treating the option as a hedge on the loan, then at 1 January the company should debit cash and credit loan by £1,250,000. In addition, the company should debit the option held and credit cash by £30,000. On 30 June, the company should report a loss of [($2 million / $1.52) − £1,250,000] £65,789 and the loan should be credited by the same amount. The option loan should be increased to £60,000. Therefore the option loan should be debited by £30,000 and the foreign exchange loss should be credited by the same amount. The total effect is a foreign exchange loss of £35,789. If the gains or losses are deferred until the expired date of the option, then the reported losses and the loans will not appear in the financial statements.

The Results of the Analysis of the European Sample Surveyed

An attempt has been made to detect liabilities and commitments driven away from the balance sheet. The result is reported on Table 11.10.

Table 11.10 illustrates that different types of commitments and liabilities are driven away from the balance sheet. However, this was not consistent among the surveyed European companies.

Table 11.10 Examples of liabilities or financial obligations not included in the balance sheet

	British companies		German companies		French companies		Dutch companies	
	(No)	(%)	(No)	(%)	(No)	(%)	(No)	(%)
Discounted notes receivable	1	4	4	16	3	12		
Discounted bills	2	8	17	68	2	8	4	16
Capital commitment with respect of assets on order	3	12	3	12			8	32
Contingencies to the extent that on the basis of the available information the company is likely to be held liable					2	8		
Long-term rental commitments			9	36			9	36
Long-term obligations regarding lease	1	4	5	20	7	28	6	24
Short-term rental and lease commitment			1	4				
Abandonment costs	1	4						
Future well costs	1	4						
Several liabilities for debts arising out of the credit facilities provided by a number of banks			1	4				

Table 11.10 (*continued*)

	British companies (No)	(%)	German companies (No)	(%)	French companies (No)	(%)	Dutch companies (No)	(%)
Some of the consolidated companies of the group are also partners with several liabilities only part of their liabilities included in the consolidated balance sheet	1	4						
Guarantees given to banks on behalf of non-consolidated participating interest	20	80	18	72	5	20	9	36
Warrantee contracts			15	60			1	4
Mortgages to secure third parties liabilities	2	8	1	4				
Commitments to tender for shares in companies for which third parties hold put options			2	8				
Option fees			1	4				
Contingent obligation from issuance or transfer of notes			1	4				
Pledges for indebtedness			1	4				
Capital payments obligation towards group companies	2	4	6	24				
Collaterals			3	12			1	4
Liabilities arising from legal transactions	6	24			3	12	1	4
Provision for retirement benefits					5	20		
Commitment on sale or purchase contracts							1	4

REVIEW QUESTIONS

1. Define off-balance sheet financing and window dressing. Explain how they might mislead the users of the financial statements.

2. Off-balance sheet financing can be divided into two classes. Identify these classes and their implications for financial statements.

3. Non-subsidiary dependent companies represent an opportunity for the use of creative accounting. Explain how. What should be done to eliminate their use?

4. Two companies operate in the same business with the same stock. They are looking for various means to improve their earnings per share ratio. Discuss different approaches that can be employed to improve their earning per share ratio.

5. Show how acquisition accounting represents a challenge for the accounting profession.

6. Many approaches have been suggested as to how to account for foreign currency. The choice between these approaches gives rise to opportunities of creative accounting. Discuss.

7. Since it is difficult to identify what is meant by extraordinary items, accountants can find ways to abuse this concept. Show how accountants do this.

8. Define interest rate swaps and show how they may represent an opportunity for creative accounting.

9. When does a project financing arrangement arise? Discuss its advantage(s), if any. Show how the parties participating in the arrangement may gain from it.

10. Take-or-pay, joint ventures, throughput and captive finance companies all present opportunities for the use of creative accounting. Illustrate how they do so.

CHAPTER 12

Creative accounting: Summary and some Empirical Evidence on its Nature and Use

INTRODUCTION

The preceding chapters illustrated different aspects of creative accounting: its causes and effects, the attempts made to tackle it, and some examples of creative accounting that might be used. This chapter provides empirical evidence on the issue of creative accounting.

THE EMPIRICAL STUDY'S OBJECTIVES

From review, several issues remain unsolved. These are:

1. Whether the use of creative accounting is likely to be practised by all companies irrespective of their status, or whether quoted companies, for instance, are more likely to adopt creative accounting more than unquoted companies.

2. The link between the use of creative accounting and the industry in which a company operates.

3. The creative accounting techniques that are frequently used in practice.

4. The motives behind the use of creative accounting.

5. The consequences of the continued use of creative accounting.

6. The legitimacy or otherwise of the use of creative accounting.

7. The seriousness of the problem.

8. Whether creative accounting is a solvable problem.

9. The measure(s) to be taken to minimize the use of creative accounting.

The above mentioned issues, discussed in the literature, reveal a lack of extensive and formal empirical research. In this cahpter, an attempt has been made to remedy this by undertaking an empirical examination of these issues. The external auditors of companies might be expected to have a substantial knowledge and experience of the use of creative accounting and their views have therefore been sought to form the basis of empirical evidence. In the rest of this section we shall look at some of the research questions that need to be asked and some of the hypotheses that need to be tested.

Research Questions

Research question 1. Is the use of creative accounting explained by the industry in which the company operates?

One of the more compelling arguments against uniformity in accounting measurement method is that different industries have different requirements. Flexibility is therefore required to permit a 'fair' picture of the performance and financial position to be presented. Thus, preparers of accounts are offered substantial opportunities to be selective in the choice of measurement methods and this should only be regarded as creative accounting if the 'special industry needs' argument is being used as an excuse to justify more dubious reasons. In such a case, it would obviously be very difficult to distinguish between 'legitimate' choice and 'creative accounting' choice, and yet there are other situations where the use of creative accounting is more clear cut. It was therefore decided to test for an *industrial effect* on the use of creative accounting.

Research question 2. What techniques of creative accounting are most frequently used?

Technical Release 603 provides definitions for off-balance sheet financing and window dressing (see Chapter 4). In addition, Release and Exposure Draft 42 has listed many examples of creative accounting which fall within the definition of off-balance sheet financing and window dressing. Furthermore, the literature provides more examples of devices that might be employed by various companies for the purpose of creative accounting. However, in practice, it is difficult to prove that a company employed a specific accounting technique for the purpose of creative accounting (falling within the TR 603 definition) and, if this is obtainable, it is still difficult to provide accurate information on which technique(s) is more frequently used. Therefore, it was felt useful to attempt to ascertain the techniques of creative accounting that are most frequently employed by different companies.

Research question 3. What are the motives behind the use of creative accounting?

The literature demonstrates that creative accounting might be attributed to the following reasons (see the details in Chapter 4).

1. To reduce gearing ratios and to reduce limits on borrowing. According to the agency theory managers may try to minimize the monitoring cost (agency cost) by entering into contracts which restrict their borrowing and limit their gearing ratios. Therefore, management may involve the use of creative accounting to get around contract restrictions.

   Some have related the use of creative accounting to companies led by poor management. Poor management is difficult to detect in any objective way. There are indicators such as high staff turnover but deteriorating gearing ratios are perhaps acting as a surrogate for signals about poor management and therefore creative accounting might be used to distort the signal.

2. Pressure from big institutional investors. It could be argued that managers are forced by the users of the accounts in general, and the City in particular, to manipulate their accounts. They would justify the use of creative accounting on the grounds that financial analysts and other commentators have a fixation about a few key ratios and numbers in the accounts and they are too lazy to make a real effort to understand the business beyond these key ratios and numbers. They like to see steady progress in the company's net income, earnings per share, etc., and they react negatively if a company's results are different from that of the market's expectations.

3. Desire to control dividends. It might be argued that investors may well place a positive utility on dividends stability and pay a premium to the company that offers it. Stable dividends may convey the management's view that the future of the company is better than a reported drop in earnings may suggest. Thus, management may be able to affect the expectations of investors through the information content of the dividends. Therefore, it is expected that the company may use creative accounting to report a stable level of dividends.

4. Desire to reduce taxation. Taxes play a significant role in determining the retained earnings and therefore dividends to be paid. As the payment for taxes is reduced, the amount of payment available for stockholders is greater. Lower reported earnings reduce government pressure (tax) on the company. Since it is difficult to restrict the manager's choice between accounting procedures (monitoring cost is very high), the manager is expected to adopt procedures to reduce the reported income. Some argue that companies prefer not to report better returns. The more profit the company reports, the more tax it pays and the unions may put pressure on the company to increase their wages. On the other hand, controlling the levels of taxes may contribute to the stability of the company's dividends policy (discussed above). Therefore, one would expect companies to adopt schemes of creative accounting to reduce tax payments.

Research question 4. What measures ought to be taken to eliminate the use of creative accounting?

Technical Release 603 recommended that in order to give a true and fair view the economic substance of the transaction should be considered in determining its nature, rather than its legal form, and as a consequence, its accounting treatment (see the details in Chapter 4). It is suggested that the balance sheet of a company should be adjusted to reflect the substance of the transaction. However, the ASC has based its argument in ED 42 on the premise that a transaction's accounting treatment should fairly reflect its commercial effects. They go on to say that the 'commercial effect' does not imply that accounting measurement should necessarily portray economic values. By analyzing the commercial effect of a special purpose transaction, it is possible to ascertain the benefits and obligations that follow from it. By analyzing these benefits and obligations the substance of the transaction becomes clear. Consequently, rather than pursue the substance over the legal form argument, the Exposure Draft concentrates on identifying and dealing with the commercial effects of the transaction. The American experience, however, through the massive number of FASBs pronouncements issued, suggests that the only way to eliminate the use of creative accounting is to issue specific standards for particular devices of creative accounting (a proposal which is supported by Hopwood and Page, 1987; and Mitchell, 1988). The argument against this is that more and more detailed rules might lead simply to resourceful managers devising ever more ingenious schemes to get round them. Therefore, it is useful to examine the support for the above arguments.

Research Question 5. What are the perceived consequences of the continued use of creative accounting?

It is argued that the continued use of creative accounting puts in danger the purpose of preparing the accounts (Wild, 1987a). Some believe that the continued use of creative accounting represents a serious threat to the integrity of financial reporting (Samuels *et al.*, 1989). Others contend that the continued use of creative accounting is threatening the survival of the ASC (Hopwood and Page, 1987; Tweedie and Kellas, 1987). Therefore, it is useful to test the consequences of the continued use of creative accounting.

Hypotheses

General Hypothesis 1. Creative accounting is more likely to be practised by quoted companies than unquoted companies.

One possibility is that creative accounting is more likely to be employed by quoted companies rather than unquoted companies. Those who support this argue that quoted companies tailor their accounts to meet the demands of the stock market. The demands require that a company should maintain a steady growth in earnings, and it should consistently live up to market expectations. This argument implies that dividends and retained earnings have an impact on share prices because they communicate information to investors about the firm's profitability. When a firm's payment ratio (i.e. the percentage of earnings paid to shareholders in cash) is stable over time, and it changes its ratio, investors may believe that the firm's management is announcing a change in the expected future profitability of the firm. Accordingly, the price of the share may react to this change. Thus, the successful company is one that can keep the balance between signalling optimistic noises when the analysts' predictions are being made and matching these with the reported results. Thus, to the extent that the managers of quoted companies have incentives to boost their share price and improve stock market ratings, if they feel that creative accounting can help in this, then it might well be an attractive option.

Alternatively, those who believe that unquoted companies are the most likely to make use of creative accounting argue that it is difficult to fool the stock market. The market is efficient to the extent that it can detect any attempt towards the use of creative accounting. As unquoted companies are not subject to the scrutiny of the stock market, it might be thought to be easier for them to adopt schemes of creative accounting. The unquoted companies may employ creative accounting to provide themselves with access to lenders. They may also use creative accounting to minimize tax liabilities. The use of creative accounting may help unquoted companies if they are considering making the transition to a full stock exchange listing.

It is hypothesized that of these two alternatives, the use by quoted companies is the most likely and this is the reason for the general hypothesis 1.

General Hypothesis 2. The use of creative accounting is considered by external auditors to be a legitimate business tool.

The issuance of Technical Release 603 reflects concern that the use of creative accounting techniques has the potential to mislead users of financial statements. Some consider the use of creative accounting as an artificial one which ought to be banned.

It could be argued that certain liabilities which have been removed from, or even never shown upon the balance sheet, should appear on the face of financial statements despite their strict legal status. The Institute of Chartered Accountants in England and Wales (TR 603) believes that companies take advantage of the law and use the concept of a true and fair to hide the economic reality of their financial statements. Wild (1987a) shows that the use of creative accounting casts doubt on the purpose of preparing the accounts. Morgan (1989) demonstrates that the reason behind the use of creative accounting is to remove assets and the related liabilities from the company's balance sheet to improve the company's financial position. Hence, this is perceived as misleading and ought to be banned. However, the Law Society (*Accountancy*, 1988) disagreed with these proposals. The Society defended its proposal on the ground that it is essential to reduce to the minimum the element of subjectivity in the preparation of the accounts, and accordingly, to have as much objectivity as possible in relation to basic items included in the accounts. Accordingly, relying on the economic substance leaves the door open for many subjective judgments.

Therefore, it is useful to test whether or not creative accounting is considered to be a legitimate business tool.

General Hypothesis 3. The use of creative accounting is perceived by external auditors to be a serious problem.

The FASB manager responsible for a project on off-balance sheet financing is quoted by Wild (1987a) as saying that the project is one of the largest and most complex that the board ever addressed. The chairman of the working party set up by the ICAEW (1987) to look into the creative accounting problem, described the problem as 'potentially a very serious problem'. Creative accounting is seen as a bad thing since it distorts a company's results and its financial position, and it might lead to an inefficient allocation of resources in the economy. Thus, creative accounting can cause a serious problem which should be monitored.

General Hypothesis 4. Creative accounting is perceived by external auditors to be a problem that can never be completely solved.

It is argued that at the time a new accounting standard is issued, companies will find ways to minimize its impact. There seems to be a suggestion here that flexibility = creative accounting. The extreme examples presumably could be eliminated. The fine distinction between 'a legitimate' choice of accounting measurement method and a 'creative accounting' choice is where the difficulty lies. Without doubt, companies do need flexibility in accounting measurements. It is unlikely that a specific and tight definition of a true and fair view will be seen in the foreseeable future. Hence, it will be impossible for the external auditor to stop the use of creative accounting. In this respect, Kanter (1984) illustrates that when environment and structures are hospitable to innovation, people's natural inventiveness and power skills can make almost any thing happen. Likewise, Davis (1989) illustrates that, regardless of how many rules and regulation the profession implements, there will always be those who find a way to beat the system. Thus it is difficult to eliminate the use of creative accounting.

METHODOLOGY AND RESULTS

Although much has been written on the topic of creative accounting, little empirical evidence exists regarding its use in practice. This chapter represents an attempt to remedy this by undertaking an empirical examination which focuses attention on issues as to whether the use of creative accounting is likely to be practised by all companies irrespective of their status, or whether quoted companies are more likely to adopt creative accounting; it investigates the link between the use of creative accounting and the industry in which a company operates; it examines the techniques of creative accounting most frequently used in practice; it looks at the motive(s) behind the use of creative accounting; it examines the legitimacy or otherwise of the use of creative accounting; it assesses the consequence of the continued use of creative accounting; and looks at the measures to be taken to minimize its use.

Because it is acknowledged that creative accounting is a topic of much concern it would be unproductive to ask companies about their creative accounting practices. However, it is clearly important in any examination of creative accounting to obtain information about the extent to which it is used by companies. If the reporting companies themselves are ruled out then some other source of information must be found. One group who ought to be able to provide reliable information and authoritative opinions on the use of creative accounting are the external auditors. It is also clear that they might also be rather cautious in disclosing information about their clients and, even if they are willing to, would certainly prefer not to identify themselves or their clients. It was therefore felt that a postal questionnaire, which guaranteed the anonymity of both the respondents and their clients, would be a possible way of obtaining information from auditors about the various types of creative accounting they had encountered.

Five of the top eight firms of accountants agreed to take part. Five copies of the questionnaire were sent to the technical partners of each of these firms for distribution amongst their senior auditing colleagues/partners. An additional firm outside the top eight was also contacted and also issued with five copies of the questionnaire. It has to be acknowledged, however, that leaving the responsibility of distributing this questionnaire to the technical partners resulted in some loss of control over the sample frame, yet this was seen as the only way in which the anonymity of the respondents could be assured.

A further opportunity that presented itself was in January 1989 when the ICAEW advertised a course entitled *Off-Balance Sheet Financing: Where Are We in the Debate?* A letter was sent to the director of the course to enquire as to the possibility of distributing the questionnaire to the participants during the course of the seminar. As the people attending this course were likely to have some knowledge of, or interest in, creative accounting it was felt that they might make a suitable group to which a questionnaire of this nature sensibly might be issued. The director granted his permission after consultation with the ICAEW.

The questionnaire had originally been designed for completion by auditors. Since the course participants were drawn from a range of backgrounds, the questionnaire was amended slightly to take this into consideration. The course participants were expected to number forty, according to the ICAEW.

Out of the 30 questionnaires sent to the technical partners of the six firms of accountants, 20 were returned completed (a response rate of 67%). In addition, the local office of two major firms agreed to discuss the questionnaire and take part in the survey by submitting completed questionnaires. This resulted in a total sample size of 22 (an analysis of the responses from this group is reported in Naser and Pendlebury (1992a)).

The OBSF course that took place in London in May was attended by 35 people; 18 completed the questionnaire that day and 2 returned it by post, giving a response rate of 57.1%.

An important point to be mentioned, however, is that the use of approximate frequencies in the questionnaire (i.e. 1–3 times, more than 3 times, etc.) sacrificed accuracy. However, these frequencies had been used to make it easier for respondents when answering the questionnaire, in the hope that this would increase the response rate.

Respondents' Employment Details

As mentioned earlier, the questionnaire originally was designed for completion by auditors. After the decision was taken to enlarge the sample by distributing the questionnaire to the off-balance sheet finance course participants, it was anticipated that the course participants might well be drawn from a range of different backgrounds. The questionnaire was therefore amended slightly to take this into consideration and in practice it was necessary to obtain information concerning the respondents' position. This was done by including a question which asked respondents to provide information of their previous and current position. To obtain reliable and useful information on the issue of creative accounting, it was important to identify individuals who had auditing experience with different companies. Thus, the questionnaire included a question on the respondents' auditing experience. The result of these questions are reported in Tables 12.1 and 12.2.

Table 12.1 shows that, as far as OBSF course respondents current position is concerned, 90% of them are employed as external auditors. There are therefore many similarities with the auditing sample. This suggests that the two separate samples in fact provide a good basis for useful comparison.

Table 12.1. The respondents' employment details.

	External auditor		Financial accountant		Financial analyst	
	(No)	(%)	(No)	(%)	(No)	(%)
OBSF course sample						
Previous position	13	65.0	6	30.0	1	5.0
Current position	18	90.0	1	5.0	1	5.0

Table 12.2. The analysis of the respondents' auditing experience.

	Less than 1 year		1-3 years		4-6 years		More than 6 years	
	(No)	(%)	(No)	(%)	(No)	(%)	(No)	(%)
Auditing experience:								
Auditing sample	–	–	–	–	7	31.8	15	68.2
OBSF course sample	–	–	–	–	7	35.0	13	65.0

Respondents' Auditing Experience

Again the similarities between the two samples is evident from Table 12.2, with 68.2% of the auditing sample and 65% of the OBSF course sample having had more than 6 years auditing experience.

Status of the Audited Companies

The general hypothesis 1 stated that creative accounting is more likely to be practised by quoted companies than unquoted companies. The questionnaire included a question on the number of detected examples of creative accounting in companies that have different status. The results are reported in Table 12.3.

Table 12.3 excludes from the analysis those respondents with no experience of auditing that type of company. The remaining columns first show the number of respondents with experience and second show the approximate frequency with which they stated that they had come across the use of creative accounting for that type of company. In an attempt to obtain precise information on the link between the size of the unquoted companies and the use of creative accounting, the distributed questionnaire to the OBSF course participants categorized the unquoted companies into small, medium and large. This resulted in different categories in each sample. Hence, one may argue that

Table 12.3. An analysis of the use of creative accounting by status of the company.

	No auditing experience of this type of company	With auditing experience of this type of company	Frequency with which examples of creative accounting encountered					
			Never		1–5 times		More than 5 Times	
	(No)	(No)	(No)	(%)	(No)	(%)	(No)	(%)
Auditing sample								
Quoted companies	7	15	1	7	11	73	3	20
Unquoted public companies	4	18	6	33	9	50	3	17
Private companies	2	20	4	20	9	45	7	35
OBSF course sample								
Quoted companies	–	20	–	–	15	75	5	25
Small sized unquoted companies	14	6	–	–	5	83	1	17
Medium sized unquoted companies	1	19	–	–	17	89	2	11
Large sized unquoted companies	3	17	–	–	16	94	1	6

this possibly made it difficult to compare the two samples. Yet, the main point of this question was to ask whether the use of creative accounting is more likely to be practised by quoted companies than unquoted companies.

Table 12.3 illustrates that 15 out of 22 (68.1%) of the auditing sample respondents have had experience of auditing quoted companies. Of these 15, 1 (7%) had never encountered any example of creative accounting, 11 (73%) had found between 1–5 examples and 3 (20%) had come across more than 5 examples. The table also shows that 18 out of 22 (81.8%) have had experience of auditing unquoted public companies. 6 of these 18 (33%) had never encountered the use of creative accounting, 9 (50%) had detected between 1–5 examples and 3 (17%) had found more than 5 examples. From Table 12.3, it can be seen that 20 out of 22 (89.9%) have had experience of auditing unquoted private companies. Of these 20, 4 (20%) had never encountered examples of creative accounting, 9 (45%) had detected 1–5 examples, and 7 (35%) had found more than 5 examples.

As far as the OBSF course respondents' experience with companies of different status is concerned, Table 12.3 reported that 20 (100%) of them have had experience of auditing quoted companies. Of these 20, 15 (75%) had encountered 1–5 examples of creative accounting, and 5 (25%) had come across more than 5 examples. However, 6 out of 20 (30%) have had auditing experience with small sized unquoted companies. Of these 6, 5 (83%) had detected 1–5 examples of creative accounting and 1 (17%) had found more than 5 examples. The table reveals that 19 (95%) have had experience of auditing medium sized companies. Of these 19, 17 (89%) had encountered 1–5 examples of creative accounting and 2 (11%) detected more than 5 examples. From the table, it can be noted that 17 out of 20 (85%) have had auditing experience with large sized unquoted companies. Of these 17, 16 (94%) had found 1–5 examples of creative accounting and 1 (6%) had come across more than 5 examples.

The point of interest is that unquoted private companies appear to be the most frequently involved in the use of creative accounting (the auditing sample). The next most frequently involved in the use of creative accounting are the quoted companies. The table illustrates, however, that unquoted public companies are the least frequently involved in the use of creative accounting. Likewise, the OBSF course respondents reported that all of the companies whose accounts they have had experience of auditing were involved in the use of creative accounting.

The auditing sample appears to point to creative accounting being most frequently encountered in unquoted companies. Whereas the OBSF course sample points to quoted companies being the more frequent users of creative accounting.

The above outcomes may offer weak support for the argument provided in Hypothesis 1, in which it was stated that creative accounting is more likely to be practised by quoted companies than unquoted companies. The results thus confirm that creative accounting is being employed by companies operating under different status.

This particular question was used as a double-check on the responses to Question 4, which concerns the examples of off-balance sheet financing and window dressing detected by the respondents. If a respondent declared that he/she had no auditing experience of any of the categories identified in the questionnaire companies, then such respondents would not be expected to answer Question 4. Hence, those who provided a negative answer to Question 2 and answered Question 4 would have been excluded from the analysis. A careful check of each questionnaire revealed that it was not necessary to exclude any of the respondents.

Industrial Classification of the Audited Companies

It could be argued that creative accounting is associated with the particular industry in which the business operates. The questionnaire therefore includes several different kinds of industries in order to examine to what extent this argument is valid (Research Question 1). The responses are reported in Table 12.4.

Table 12.4 excludes from the analysis those respondents who did not answer

Table 12.4. The analysis of the use of creative accounting in different industries.

Industry classification	No answer/no auditing experience (No)	With auditing experience of this type of industry (No)	Never (No)	Never (%)	1–5 times (No)	1–5 times (%)	More than 5 times (No)	More than 5 times (%)
Auditing Sample								
Oil and gas	20	2	2	100				
Retail distribution	10	12	4	33	5	42	3	25
Manufacturing	4	18	7	39	9	50	2	11
Hotel and leisure	10	12	7	59	4	33	1	8
Services	1	21	7	34	11	52	3	14
Banking and financial institutions	13	11	1	9	10	9	1	9
OBSF Course Sample								
Oil and gas	9	11			10	90	1	10
Retail disribution	11	9			8	89	1	11
Manufacturing	14	6			4	67	2	33
Hotel and leisure	12	8	1	13	4	50	3	37
Services	7	13			12	92	1	8
Banking and financial institutions	5	15			13	87	2	13

the question and those respondents who had no experience of auditing that type of industry. The table shows that only 2 out of 22 (9%) of the auditing sample respondents had had auditing experience within the oil and gas industry and neither of these had ever encountered the use of creative accounting. The table indicates that 12 out of 22 (54.5%) of the respondents had auditing experience with the retail distribution industry. Of these 12, 4 (33%) had never encountered the use of creative accounting, 5 (42%) had found between 1–5 examples of creative accounting and 3 (25%) had come across more than 5 examples.

The table also demonstrates that 18 out of 22 (82%) of the respondents have auditing experience with the manufacturing industry. Of the 18, 7 (39%) had never encountered any example of creative accounting, 9 (50%) had detected

1–5 examples and 2 (11%) had found more than 5 examples. Table 12.4 reflects that 12 out 22 (54.4%) of the respondents had auditing experience with companies operating in the hotel and leisure industry. Of the 12, 7 (59%) had never come across examples of creative accounting, 4 (33%) had found 1–5 examples and 1 (8%) had detected more than 5 examples. On the other hand, the table shows that 21 (95.5%) of the respondents had auditing experience with companies related to the services industry. Of the 21, only 7 (33%) had never noted examples of creative accounting, 11 (52%) had found 1–5 examples and 3 (13%) had encountered more than 5 examples. Only 9 out of 22 (41%) of the respondents had had auditing experience with banks and financial institutions. Of the 9, 1 (11%) had never come across examples of creative accounting, and 8 (89%) had encountered 1–5 examples.

Five respondents added to the list of industries provided in the questionnaire. These included pension companies, professional institutions, road building, shipping, consulting engineers, property development of houses and buildings, coal and car parks.

Contrary to the auditing sample, the OBSF course sample showed that 11 out of 20 (55%) of the respondents had had auditing experience with companies operating in the oil and gas industry. Of the 11, 10 (90%) had noticed 1–5 examples of creative accounting and 1 (10%) had found more than 5 examples. 9 out of 20 (45%) of the course participants have had experience with companies in the retail distribution industry. Of these 9, 8 (89%) had detected 1–5 examples of creative accounting and 1 (11%) had found more than 5 examples. Only 6 out of 20 (30%) of the participants showed experience with companies in the manufacturing industry. Of the 6, 4 (67%) had found 1–5 examples of creative accounting and 2 (33%) had come across more than 5 examples. 8 out of 20 (40%) had had auditing experience with the hotel and leisure industry. Of the 8, 1 (13%) had never found examples of creative accounting, 4 (50%) had detected 1–5 examples and 3 (37%) had found more than 5 examples. The table demonstrates that 13 (65%) of the respondents had auditing experience with companies operating in the services industry. Of the 13, 12 (92%) had found 1–5 examples of creative accounting, 1 (8%) had encountered more than 5 examples. 15 out of 20 (75%) of the respondents showed auditing experience with the banking and financial institution industry. Of the 15, 13 (87%) had noticed between 1–5 examples of creative accounting, 2 (13%) had encountered more than 5 examples.

It can be noted that, from the auditing sample, the banking and financial institution industry is the most frequently involved in the use of creative accounting. The next most frequently involved in the use of creative accounting is the retail distribution and services industry. The OBSF course sample demonstrated that all companies from different industries show some involvement in the use of creative accounting. Indeed, the results illustrate that creative accounting is likely to be used by companies operating in any industry.

Examples of Creative Accounting

a) Off-Balance Sheet Financing

To throw some light on specific issues, such as Research Question 2, the respondents were asked to provide information on the examples of creative accounting (i.e. off-balance sheet financing and window dressing) they had encountered in practice (Research Question 2). The examples that were included in the questionnaire were those that were the ones most frequently encountered during the literature survey which have been discussed in earlier chapters. The results are provided in Tables 12.5 and 12.6.

From Table 12.5, leasing appears to be the most frequently encountered example of off-balance sheet financing for both sample groups, with 18.2% of

Table 12.5. Some examples of methods of off-balance sheet financing and the frequency encountered.

	Never		1–3 times		3–7 times		More than 7 times	
	(No)	(%)	(No)	(%)	(No)	(%)	(No)	(%)
Auditing sample:								
Operating or finance lease	9	40.9	5	22.7	4	18.2	4	18.2
Non-consolidated subsidiary	11	50.0	19	40.9	2	9.1		
Schemes to remove debt from balance sheet	15	68.2	6	27.3	1	4.5		
Interest rate swaps	20	90.9	2	9.1				
The formation of joint ventures to finance a major project	10	45.5	9	40.9	2	9.1	1	4.5
Transfer of debt with recourse to an unrelated third party	16	72.7	2	9.1	3	13.6	1	4.5
OBSF course sample:								
Operating or finance lease	3	15.0	6	30.0	9	45.0	2	10.0
Non-consolidated subsidiary	2	10.0	12	60.0	3	15.0	3	15.0
Schemes to remove debt from balance sheet	7	35.0	12	60.0			1	5.0
Interest rate swaps	7	35.0	7	35.0			6	30.0
The formation of joint ventures to finance a major project	8	40.0	8	40.0	2	10.0	2	10.0
Transfer of debt with recourse to an unrelated third party	13	65.0	7	35.0				

the auditing sample reporting its use had been met more than 7 times and 45% of the OBSF sample stating that they had come across its use between 3 and 7 times, and 10% more than 7 times. For the auditing sample the use of joint venture schemes appeared to be the next most frequently encountered type. Whereas, for the OBSF sample, the second most frequently encountered scheme was the use of non-consolidated subsidiaries. The two samples also revealed other differences in the ranking of possible examples of off-balance sheet financing. Thus, for example the method that the auditing sample encountered least frequently was the use of interest rate swaps, but for the OBSF sample this method was encountered relatively frequently and the transfer of debt with recourse to an unrelated third party occupied the 'least frequent' position. In addition to the examples of off-balance sheet financing provided in the questionnaire, respondents were also given the opportunity to write in other examples they had come across. One of the respondents added 'manipulation of stock' to the list and stated that this had been met between 1 and 3 times. It is interesting to note that all of the listed examples of off-balance sheet financing were used (in one way or another) by many companies but to varying degrees.

As noted above, the examples of operating or finance lease reported by both samples are relatively high. This might suggest that the effectiveness of SSAP 21 needs to be given careful consideration. However, since the questionnaire did not specify the period in which the respondents detected the use of creative accounting, then it is possible that most of the reported examples occurred before SSAP 21 became effective. However, if many of these examples occurred after SSAP 21 became effective, then the objective of the SSAP of restricting one of the more obvious methods of off-balance sheet financing might not have been entirely met. Post SSAP 21, creative accounting presumably takes the form of either a greater use of operating leases, or a choice of leasing arrangements which fall just outside the definition of a finance lease (see the discussion provided in Chapter 4). It was reported above that the use of interest rate swaps was rarely encountered by the auditing sample, but was discovered relatively frequently by the OBSF course sample. This might reflect the fact that the OBSF course participants have more experience with banking and financial institutions where schemes of interest rate swaps might perhaps be more likely to occur. A point of interest is that the respondents of both samples reported many examples of companies making use of non consolidated subsidiaries. The overriding requirement in section 230 (5) and 228 of the *Companies Act* 1985 is that a company's or group's financial statements are required to give a true and fair view.

It is hoped that the replaced definition recently provided by ED 50 and CA 89 will limit the number of off-balance sheet financing schemes used in this area. In all events, the low number of the other example of off-balance sheet financing reported by both samples does not necessarily imply that the companies did not employ them for the purpose of creative accounting. It might be difficult to detect these examples because they are not used as openly as the more frequently reported examples.

Alternatively, it might be that they were employed quite properly, i.e. not for creative accounting, or that at least the auditors gave the company the benefit of the doubt on this point. Furthermore, it might be that they were used but that they were relatively unimportant and therefore were not detected. Indeed, the outcomes may answer Research Question 2 – What technique of creative accounting are frequently most used? It should be noted that different schemes are used frequently.

b) Window Dressing

As was the case with the examples of off-balance sheet financing, the questionnaire included a list of window dressing examples. Table 12.6 discloses that, for the auditing sample, switching from one accounting policy to another appeared to be the most frequently encountered, with 22.7% of the respondents claiming to have encountered this scheme between 3–7 times and 9.1% more than 7 times. The next most frequently encountered was the revaluation of fixed assets. The least frequently encountered was the repurchase of a company's own shares.

Similarly, switching from one accounting policy to another was probably the most frequently detected by the OBSF course sample with 55% of respondents claiming to have come across this scheme between 3–7 times and 5% more than 7 times. Yet, revaluation of fixed assets and abuse of acquisition accounting were only marginally less frequent. It is interesting to note that these 2 examples attracted a much larger 'never' response from the auditing sample than from the OBSF sample. The least frequently encountered example was the overnight sale and repurchase of assets.

The results show that flexibility in the choice of accounting measurement methods which can, of course, be a perfectly legitimate practice if the true intention is to reflect a true and fair view, is perceived by auditors to be the most frequent example of the use of creative accounting.

Both sample groups provided much evidence for the revaluation of fixed assets representing an opportunity for creative accounting. Such opportunities are not restricted to the balance sheet since the revaluation will affect the depreciation charges and therefore the profit and loss account. Another potential area of creativity is the treatment of the accumulated depreciation (see the discussion in Chapter 7).

The abuse of acquisition accounting also offers many opportunities for creative accounting. Goodwill is an obvious example. Another is the distinction

Table 12.6. Some examples of methods of window dressing and the frequency encountered.

	Never		1–3 times		3–7 times		More than 7 times	
	(No)	(%)	(No)	(%)	(No)	(%)	(No)	(%)
Auditing sample								
Sale and repurchase of inventory	18	81.8	3	13.6	1	4.5		
Abuse of acquisition accounting	15	68.2	5	22.7	1	4.5	1	4.5
Overnight sale and repurchase of assets	17	77.3	2	9.1	3	13.6		
Revaluation of fixed assets	10	45.4	8	36.4	3	13.6	1	4.5
Repurchase of company's own shares	19	86.4	2	9.1	1	4.5		
Switching from one accounting policy to another	5	22.7	10	45.5	5	22.7	2	9.1
OBSF course sample								
Sale and repurchase of inventory	15	75.0	4	20.0	1	5.0		
Abuse of acquisition accounting	2	10.0	7	35.0	8	40.0	3	15.0
Overnight sale and repurchase of assets	19	95.0	1	5.0				
Revaluation of fixed assets	2	10.0	9	45.0	6	30.0	3	15.0
Repurchase of company's own shares	16	80.0	4	20.0				
Switching from one accounting policy to another			8	40.0	11	55.0	1	5.0

between merger accounting and acquisition accounting. Under merger accounting no goodwill is created and therefore the need for write off does not arise, which either protects reserves or avoids an annual deduction for amortization in the profit and loss account. Under merger accounting, the distributable reserves are immediately enlarged, which may be useful for a company which is short of retained earnings out of which to pay dividends (for more details see the discussion in Chapter 11).

As in the case of the off-balance sheet financing examples, all of the listed examples of window dressing are reported to be used in practice to varying degrees. Three of the respondents added to the list further examples, such as back to back loans, removal of client's balances on a temporary basis, and extraordinary items. 77.3% of the respondents indicated that they had encountered at least 2 of the listed examples of window dressing, with only 9.1% of the respondents having encountered none of the examples.

The Senior Auditors' Ability to Detect the Use of Creative Accounting

In an attempt to analyze the number of examples of creative accounting encountered by the senior auditors, Table 12.7 has been prepared. Although the questionnaire did not specify the period of time over which the respondents detected the use of creative accounting, the high number of reported cases might suggest that off-balance sheet financing schemes have occurred quite frequently in recent years because it is unlikely that the respondents would go very far back in time when remembering the examples they reported.

Table 12.7 demonstrates that (given the assumption in the footnote to the table) 186 cases of window dressing were detected by the auditing sample respondents and 391 by the OBSF course participants. The table shows a widespread use of window dressing and it is clear that the incidence of window dressing is greater than that of off-balance sheet financing. This might point to the fact that these two types occupy quite different places in the range of creative accounting practices. In other words, creative accounting can range from genuine attempts to present a true and fair view (where most of the examples of window dressing are located) to the more dubious practices of off-balance sheet financing. The external auditor might find it easier to detect

Table 12.7. A comparison between the reported cases of creative accounting (off-balance sheet financing and window dressing) by auditors from both samples with 4–6 years experience and over 6 years experience.

	Number of cases of OBSF reported (x)	Number of cases of window dressing reported (x)
Auditing sample		
4–6 years experience (N=7)	34	42
Average per respondent	5	6
More than 6 years experience (N=15)	136	144
Average per respondent	6	7
OBSF course sample		
4–6 years experience (N=7)	79	190
Average per respondent	11	12
More than 6 years experience (N=13)	86	201
Average per respondent	15	16

companies employing schemes of window dressing while this might not be the case when dealing with off-balance sheet financing schemes. Hence, the auditor requires a great deal of experience to be able to detect companies attempting to adopt off-balance sheet financing. This phenomenon can be recognized by connecting the respondent's audit experience with the average number of examples of creative accounting (off-balance sheet financing and window dressing) detected per respondent. Those who have been in the profession for 4–6 years, (auditing sample) reported an average of 5 cases of off-balance sheet financing and 6 cases of window dressing, whilst those who have had more than 6 years of service, encountered an average of 6 cases of off-balance sheet financing and 7 cases of window dressing. The participants of the OBSF course, with 4–6 years of experience, detected an average of 11 cases of off-balance sheet financing and 13 cases of window dressing, whilst those who have served in the profession for more than 6 years, detected an average of 14 cases of off-balance sheet financing and 16 cases of window dressing. Table 12.7 summarizes the frequency of occurrence of off-balance sheet financing and window dressing and also provides an analysis of how this is distributed between auditors with more than 6 years experience and those with between 4 and 6 years experience.

The above information may lead to the conclusion that the respondents require less effort to detect the use of window dressing than to detect off-balance sheet financing schemes (the reported cases of window dressing are far more than those of off-balance sheet financing). In addition, the OBSF course participants reported more examples than those of the auditing sample respondents. This might be explained on the grounds that all of the course participants were interested in attending the course and one should expect them to be well prepared for such a subject.

Reasons Behind the Use of Creative Accounting

It is important to know the main reasons that might lie behind the use of creative accounting devices. The questionnaire contained 5 reasons (which had been taken from the literature) and the respondents were asked to state the extent to which they agreed or disagreed with them (Research Question 3). The results are reported in Table 12.8.

From Table 12.8 it can be seen that the auditing sample considered that the desire to meet limits on borrowing and gearing ratios was the reason with which they were most in agreement, with over 90% either agreeing or agreeing strongly.

The 'desire to control dividends' and 'pressure from big institutional investors' resulted in the least amount of agreement but these reasons did result

Table 12.8. The frequency of the reasons given by respondents for the use of creative accounting.

Reasons behind the use of creative accounting	Strongly agree (No)	(%)	Agree (No)	(%)	No view (No)	(%)	Disagree (No)	(%)	Strongly disagree (No)	(%)
Auditing Sample										
To meet limits on borrowing and gearing ratios	6	27.3	14	63.6	1	4.5	1	4.5		
Desire to reduce taxation	4	18.2	10	45.5	3	13.6	3	13.6	2	9.1
Desire to control dividends	2	9.1	3	13.6	14	63.6	3	13.6		
The pressure from big institutional investors	3	13.6	2	9.1	12	54.5	5	22.7		
OBSF course sample										
To meet limits on borrowing and gearing ratios	17	85.0	3	15.0						
Desire to reduce taxation			8	40.0	3	15.0	9	45.0		
Desire to control dividends					10	50.0	10	50.0		
The pressure from big institutional investors	2	10.0	2	10.0	7	35.0	9	45.0		

in a large proportion of 'no view' responses, which unfortunately leaves the picture far from clear. The reason that attracted most agreement from the OBSF course respondents was the desire to meet limits on borrowing and gearing ratios. All of the respondents indicated that they agreed or strongly agreed. Other reasons attracted little support and, although the 'no view' response clouded the issue, as before the position is slightly less equivocal with the balance of opinion being disagreement. The results might be attributed to the agency theory. The agency theory suggests that, in order to minimize agency costs, managers are willing to enter into contracts which limit their borrowing levels or limit their gearing ratios. Therefore, it is predictable that these two would be seen as frequent reason for using creative accounting.

The Legitimacy and Strength of the Creative Accounting Problem

There are differences in opinion surrounding the legitimacy or otherwise of the use of creative accounting. Some believe that the use of creative accounting is legitimate but not ethical, others argue that it is illegitimate and should be banned (General Hypothesis 2). Opinion also differs about the seriousness of the problem (General Hypothesis 3) and whether it can ever be completely eliminated (General Hypothesis 4). Hence, the respondents were asked for their views on these issues. The results are shown in Table 12.9.

Table 12.9 indicates that 45.5% of the auditing sample respondents agreed or strongly agreed that creative accounting is a legitimate business tool. If these respondents accept that the purpose of creative accounting is to mislead, then it is difficult to explain these responses. A clear majority of the OBSF course sample disagree with the statement that creative accounting is a legitimate business tool and this suggests that Hypothesis 2 should be rejected. The position is less clear for the auditing sample with 10 respondents reporting some degree of disagreement and 2 being undecided.

The respondents were also asked if they considered the use of creative

Table 12.9. The analysis of opinion about the legitimacy or otherwise of the use of creative accounting.

The use of creative accounting is considered to be	Strongly agree		Agree		No view		Disagree		Strongly disagree	
	(No)	(%)	(No)	(%)	(No)	(%)	(No)	(%)	(No)	(%)
Auditing Sample										
A legitimate business tool	2	9.1	8	36.4	2	9.1	9	40.9	1	4.5
A serious problem	1	4.5	11	50.0	5	22.8	5	22.7		
A problem that never can be completely solved	8	36.4	13	59.1	1	4.5				
OBSF course sample										
A legitimate business tool			5	25.0			14	70.0	1	5.0
A serious problem			15	75.0			5	25.0		
A problem that can never be completely solved	7	35.0	12	60.0			1	5.0		

accounting as a serious problem. Table 12.9 shows that 55% of the auditing sample respondents agreed or strongly agreed that the use of creative accounting is a serious problem, whereas 75% of the OBSF course participants agreed with this proposal. This supports the contents of General Hypothesis 3 that the use of creative accounting is perceived to be a serious problem.

The respondents were also asked if they thought that it would be possible to eliminate the creative accounting problem. Table 12.9 demonstrates that 95.5% of the auditing sample respondents agreed that the creative accounting problem can never be completely solved. Likewise, 95% of the OBSF course participants believed that it is difficult to put an end to the use of creative accounting. This strongly supports the contents of General Hypothesis 4 that creative accounting perceived by external auditors can be a problem that can never be completely solved.

Even though the auditing sample respondents were confused as to whether or not the use of creative accounting is legitimate, they were very confident that the creative accounting problem will continue. However, they demonstrated that creative accounting is a serious problem but had some reservations. The OBSF course participants were confident that creative accounting is not a legitimate business tool and they strongly supported the contentions that creative accounting is both a serious problem and one that is difficult to eliminate.

Table 12.10. The consequences foreseen by the respondents of the continued use of creative accounting.

The consequence if creative accounting is continued to be used	Strongly agree		Agree		No view		Disagree		Strongly disagree	
	(No)	(%)	(No)	(%)	(No)	(%)	(No)	(%)	(No)	(%)
Auditing sample										
Reluctant to use statutory accounts for decision-making	1	4.5	12	54.5	4	18.2	5	22.7		
Serious threat to the integrity of financial reporting	1	4.5	15	68.2	1	4.5	5	22.7		
OBSF course sample										
Reluctant to use statutory accounts for decision-making			14	70.0	1	5.0	5	25.0		
Serious threat to the integrity of financial reporting	3	15.0	11	55.0			6	30.0		

The Consequences of the Continued Use of Creative Accounting

The respondents were asked about the main consequences they can foresee from the continued use of creative accounting (Research Question 4). The possible consequences that were included in the questionnaire were summarized versions of the ones that appear to occur most frequently in the review of the literature. The responses are reported in Table 12.10.

Table 12.10 reveals that 59% of the auditing sample respondents and 70% of the OBSF course participants agreed or strongly agreed that the continued use of creative accounting will put the usefulness of the statutory accounts for decision-making purposes in jeopardy. Table 12.10 also shows that 72.7% of the auditing sample respondents and 70% of the OBSF course participants agreed or strongly agreed that the continued use of creative accounting represents a serious threat to the integrity of financial reporting. 65% of the OBSF course respondents disagreed that the continued use of creative accounting represents a serious threat to the survival of the ASC. Only 9.1% of the auditing sample respondents disagreed but the picture here is much less clear, because of 36.4% of the respondents recorded 'no view' (see the discussion about who should enforce accounting regulations in section 2.4 of Chapter 2).

It can be noted that the majority of the respondents agreed that the continued use of creative accounting may distort the purpose of the accounts. In addition, the use of creative accounting will threaten the integrity of financial reporting. However, the respondents were not sure whether the use of creative accounting puts the survival of the ASC in danger. However, the Dearing proposals to some extent anticipated the end of the ASC in its present form.

What Should be Done to Eliminate the Use of Creative Accounting

Given that Table 12.9 indicates that the majority of respondents believe that creative accounting 'can never be completely solved', it might be somewhat irrelevant to report their views on the steps needed to eliminate the use of creative accounting. However, if there is also a belief, as shown in the response reported in Table 12.10, that creative accounting threatens the integrity of financial reporting, then there is presumably also a belief that steps should be taken to try to eliminate the use of creative accounting (Research Question 5). The responses to the question asking what should be done to eliminate the use of creative accounting need therefore to be reconsidered in this context and are reported in Table 12.11.

Table 12.11 reveals more differences than had been found previously between the two samples in their response to the question 'What should be done to

Table 12.11. An analysis of respondent's opinions on what should be done to eliminate the use of creative accounting.

To eliminate creative accounting it is necessary to have	Strongly agree		Agree		No view		Disagree		Strongly disagree	
	(No)	(%)	(No)	(%)	(No)	(%)	(No)	(%)	(No)	(%)
Auditing sample										
More detailed accounting legislation	3	13.6	9	40.9	2	9.1	6	27.3	2	9.1
Stricter standards	3	13.6	14	63.6	4	18.2	1	4.5		
More standards aimed at specific problem case	6	27.3	13	59.1	3	13.6				
Greater accounting disclosure	4	18.2	11	50.0	2	9.1	5	22.7		
Greater reliance on the concept of substance over form	9	40.9	8	36.4	2	9.1	2	9.1	1	4.5
OBSF course sample										
More detailed accounting legislation	5	25.0	12	60.0	1	5.0	2	10.0		
Stricter standards			13	65.0	1	5.0	6	30.0		
More standards aimed at specific problem case	4	20.0	13	65.0	1	5.0	2	10.0		
Greater accounting disclosure			13	65.0	2	10.0	5	25.0		
Greater reliance on the concept of substance over form	2	10.0	13	65.0			5	25.0		

eliminate the use of creative accounting?' The solution that attracted the most agreement from the auditing sample was that there should be more standards aimed at specific problem cases. None of the respondents registered disagreement with this solution. Whereas, for the OBSF course respondents the solution that captured the greatest degree of agreement was the use of more detailed accounting legislation. However, it is important to point out that the support for the use of more detailed accounting legislation was only marginally better than the proposal 'more standards aimed at specific problem cases'. On the other hand, the more detailed accounting legislation solution received the lowest level of agreement from amongst the auditing sample, with only 54.5% of the respondents agreeing. Thus, respondents from both samples agreed on the importance of the use of 'more standards aimed at specific problem cases' to minimize the use of creative accounting.

A further example of differences between the two samples can be seen from the response to the suggested solution of 'stricter standards'. Only 5% of the auditing sample disagreed with this solution, but 30% of the OBSF course sample disagreed. The results reported in Table 12.11 also show considerable support for greater reliance on the concept of substance over form. This is true for both sample groups. What is interesting about Table 12.11 is that the respondents show support for all of the solutions identified in the question. This suggests that the auditors feel that the correct approach is not to think of substance over form and detailed presentation as being mutually exclusive, but rather that they should be used collectively to combat creative accounting.

SUMMARY AND CONCLUSIONS

In this chapter, an attempt has been made to carry out an empirical investigation into some of the issues raised about the incidence of creative accounting. These include the reasons for its use and the consequences of its continued use. For this purpose, external auditors were contacted and invited to complete the questionnaire. The analysis of the questionnaire findings reveals that the use of creative accounting is likely to be practised by companies operating under different status and in different industries.

Although the questionnaire did not specify the period of time within which the respondents encountered the use of creative accounting, the respondents disclosed that they had detected many cases of companies adopting creative accounting schemes.

The analysis also demonstrates that the driving forces behind the use of creative accounting are the attempts by companies to improve their gearing ratios and to meet the limits on borrowing. In fact, the respondents disclose that creative accounting is perceived to be an illegitimate business tool which represents a problem that can never be completely eliminated.

The consequences of the continued use of creative accounting, according to the respondents, are that it will lead to a reluctance to use statutory accounts for making decisions, and it will put at risk the integrity of financial reporting. The respondents stressed that the reliance on the concept of substance over form and the issuance of specific standards aimed at specific accounting problem areas, are requirements in the move towards eliminating the use of creative accounting.

The widespread use of creative accounting reported by the respondents offers a potential challenge to the efficient market hypothesis. One consequence of market efficiency, it is argued, is that the market cannot be fooled by cosmetic accounting procedures used by companies to improve their financial results. However, companies would not adopt schemes of creative accounting to the extent reported by external auditors unless they felt that they could benefit. In other words they must believe that they can fool the market.

The market theory argument and the agency theory explanation offer an interesting and persuasive alternative to regulation. However, the consequences of market failure are such that few governments and professional bodies of accountants have been willing to let market forces prevail. Regulation is therefore a reality. One extreme solution might be to make creative accounting illegal. The problem with this is that it would lead to great uncertainty about the boundary between creativity and legitimacy. This might result in stifling innovation and development and force accounting practices into a very narrow range of techniques that are generally agreed to be legal.

An alternative might be to place a greater responsibility on external auditors to draw attention to creative accounting devices and to state that accounts containing creative accounting devices do not give a true and fair view. It has to be remembered that the questionnaire responses reflect that external auditors detected a widespread use of creative accounting. As Naser and Pendlebury (1992a) point out: 'The crucial question that then needed asking is "what did they do about it?" Did they ask the companies involved to give explanations and assurances that it would not happen again? Did they qualify the accounts? Did they turn a blind eye? Unfortunately such a question was ruled out for inclusion in the questionnaire because it was felt that it would jeopardize the response rate. However, the question does need answering.'

Alternatively, it might just have to be accepted that creative accounting is a fact of life. If accounting numbers are to have an important role in monitoring the actions of agents (managers), then managers must be expected to use creative accounting techniques to maximize their personal welfare. Perhaps the role of regulation is simply to ensure that creative accounting is kept within tolerable limits.

Bibliography

Abdel-Khalik, R. (1981), 'The economic effects on lessees of FASB Statement No. (13)', *Accounting for Leases*, Stanford, CT: FASB.

Accountancy (1986), 'Off-balance sheet finance: The beginning of the end', January, p. 3.

Accountancy (1988), 'Restructuring radical but non statutory', December, p. 5.

Accounting Research Bulletin (1961), *Restatement and Revision of Accounting Research Bulletins*, Final Edition, No. 43, New York: AICPA, p. 11.

Adams, R. (1988), 'Continuing conflict, and how to resolve it', *Accountancy*, July, pp. 21–2.

AICPA (1959), 'Committee on Accounting Procedures, Consolidated Financial Statements', *Accounting Research Bulletin No. 51*, New York: AICPA.

AICPA (1978), *Issue Paper: Reporting Finance Subsidiaries in Consolidating Financial Statements* New York: AICPA.

Akerlof, G.A. (1970), 'The markets for "lemons": Qualitative uncertainty and the market mechanism', *Quarterly Journal of Economics*, **84**, pp. 488–500.

Alchain, A. A. and Kessel, R (1962), 'Competition, monopoly and the pursuit of money', in *Aspects of Labour Economics*, Princeton, NJ: Princeton University Press, pp. 157–75.

Aldwinkle, R. (1987), 'Off-balance sheet finance the legal view', *Accountancy*, June, pp. 19–20.

Allinghan, M. (1976), 'Fairness and utility', *Economie Applique*, **9**, pp. 257–66.

APB Opinion No. (4) (1964), *Accounting For Investment Credit*, March, New York: AICPA.

APB Opinion No. (5) (1964), *Reporting of Leases in Financial Statements of Lessee*, September, New York: AICPA.

APB Opinion No. (6) (1965), *Status of Accounting Research Bulletins*, October, New York: AICPA.

APB Opinion No. (7) (1966), *Accounting For Leases in Financial Statements of Lessors*, May, New York: AICPA.

APB Opinion No. (9) (1966), *Reporting the Results of Operations*, December, New York: AICPA.

APB Opinion No. (10) (1966), *Omnibus Opinion – 1966*, December, New York: AICPA.

APB Opinion No. (16) (1970), *Business Combination*, August, New York: AICPA.

APB Opinion No. (17) (1970), *Intangible Assets (Amended)*, August, New York: AICPA.

APB Opinion No. (18) (1971), *The Equity Method of Accounting for Investment in Common Stock*, New York: AICPA.

APB Opinion No. (21) (1971), *Interest on Receivables and Payables (Amended)*, August, New York: AICPA.

APB Opinion No. (29) (1973), *Accounting for Non Monetary Transactions (Amended)*, May, New York: AICPA.

APB Opinion No. (30) (1973), *Reporting Results of Operations*, June, New York: AICPA.

APB Opinion No. (31) (1973), *Disclosure of Lease Commitments By Lessees*, June, New York: AICPA.

Archibald, G. C. and Donaldson, D. (1979), 'Notes on economic equality', *Journal of Public Economics*, October, pp. 205–14.

Argenti, J. (1976), *Corporate Collapse: The Cause and Symptoms*, New York: McGraw Hill.

Arnold, J. A. (1984), 'Capital market efficiency and capital reporting', in B. Carsberg and S. Dev (eds), *External Financial Reporting*, Englewood Cliffs, NJ: Prentice Hall.

Arnold, J. A., Hope, T. and Southworth, A. (1985), *Financial Accounting*, Hemel Hempstead: Prentice Hall.

Arnold, T. S. (1984), 'How to do interest rate swaps', *Harvard Business Review*, September–October, pp. 96–101.

Arrow, K. J. (1963), *Social Choice and Individual Values*, 2nd edn, New Haven, CT: Yale University Press.

Ashton, R. (1976), 'Cash flow accounting: a review and critique', *Journal of Business Finance and Accounting*, Winter, pp. 63–81.

Bacharach, M. (1976), *Economics and the Theory of Games*, London: Macmillan.

Ball, R. and Foster, G. (1982), 'Corporate financial reporting: A methodological review of empirical research', *Journal of Accounting Research Supplement*, pp. 161–234.

Ball, R., Walker, R. and Whittered, G. (1979), 'Audit qualification and share prices', *Abacus*, **15**, pp. 23–4.

Bamber, L. (1986), 'The information content of annual earnings releases: A trading volume approach', *Journal of Accounting Research*, Spring, pp. 40–56.

Baumol, W. J. (1980), 'Theory of equity in pricing for resource conservation', *Journal of Environmental Economics and Management*, December, pp. 308–20.

Baumol, W. J. (1982), 'Applied fairness theory and rationing policy', *American Economic Review*, September, pp. 639–51.

Beaver, W. (1968), 'The information content of annual earnings announcements', *Supplement to Journal of Accounting Research*, pp. 67–92.

Beaver, W. (1981), *Financial Reporting: An accounting revolution*, Englewood Cliffs, NJ: Prentice Hall.

Benis, M. (1979), 'The nonconsolidated finance company subsidiary', *The Accounting Review*, October, pp. 808–14.

Benston, G. J. (1969), 'The value of SEC's accounting disclosure requirements', *The Accounting Review*, July, pp. 515–38.

Benston, G. J. (1973), 'Required disclosure and the stock market: An evaluation of the securities Exchange Act of 1934', *American Economic Review*, pp. 132–55.

Benston, G. J. (1976), *Corporate Financial Disclosure in the UK and the USA*, Saxon House.

Benston, G. J. (1979), 'Required periodic disclosure under the Securities Acts and proposed Federal Securities Code', *University of Miami Law Review*, September, pp. 1471–84.

Benston, G. J. (1982a), 'Accounting for corporate accountability', in H. G. Maune (ed.), *Corporate Governance: Past and present*, New York: KCG Publications, pp. 70–123.

Benston, G. J. (1982b), 'Accounting and corporate accountability', *Accounting, Organization, and Society*, **7**, pp. 87–105.

Benston, G. J. (1983), 'An analysis of the role of accounting standards for enhancing corporate general and social responsibility', *Journal of Accounting and Business Finance*, pp. 5–17.

Bernstein, L. A. (1970), 'Reporting the results of operations' assessment of APB Opinion No.9, *Journal of Accounting*, July, pp. 57–61.

Blaug, M. (1980), *The Methodology of Economics*, Cambridge: Cambridge University Press.

Boersema, J. and Helden, H. (1986), 'The case against interest capitalization', *CA Magazine*, October, pp. 62–7.

Brandt R. and Green, P. F. (1982), 'Leasing and Hire Purchase', in L. C. L. Skerrat and D. J. Tonkin (eds.), *Financial Reporting 1982–1983*, London: ICAEW, pp. 122–9.

Brief, R. (1965), 'Nineteenth century accounting error', *Journal of Accounting Research*, **3**, pp. 12–31.

Brief, R. (1966), 'The origin and evolution of nineteenth century asset accounting', *Business History Review*, **40**, pp. 1–22.

Brief, R. (1967), 'A late century contribution to the theory of depreciation', *Journal of Accounting Research*, **5**, Spring, pp. 27–38.

Brief, R. (1970), 'Depreciation theory in historical perspective', *Accountant*, **163**, 26 November, pp. 737–9.

Brindle, I. (1986), 'Off-balance sheet financing', in L. C. L. Skerrat and D. J. Tonkin (eds), *Financial Reporting 1985–1986*, London: ICAEW, pp. 73–91.

Brindle, I. (1987), 'Off-balance sheet financing', in D. J. Tonkin and L. C. L. Skerrat (eds), *Financial Reporting 1986–1987*, London: ICAEW, pp. 49–62.

Bromwich, M. (1981), 'The setting of accounting standards: The contribution of research', In M. Bromwich and A. G. Hopwood (eds), *Essay in British Accounting Research*, London: Pitman.

Bromwich, M. (1985), *The Economics of Accounting Standard Setting*, Hemel Hempstead, Prentice Hall.

Brown, D. J. (1983), 'Depreciation of fixed assets', in L. C. L. Skerrat and D. J. Tonkin (eds), *Financial Reporting 1982–1983*, London: ICAEW, pp. 60–6.

Bryant, R. (1989), 'The value of separable intangibles', *Accountancy*, March, pp. 106–10.

Burnett, T., King, T. and Lemboke, V. (1979), 'Equity method reporting for major finance company subsidiaries', *The Accounting Review*, October, pp. 815–23.

Burton, J. (1967), 'Continuous contemporary accounting: Additivity and action', *The Accounting Review*, October, pp. 751–7.

Burton, J. (1970), 'Second thoughts on continuous contemporary accounting', *Abacus*, September, pp. 39–55.

Burton, J. (1974a), 'Forecasts: a changing view from the securities and exchange commission', in *ABP No.18, The Equity Method of Accounting for Investment in Common Stock*, New York: AICPA, 1971. Reprinted in Prakash and Rappaport (eds), *Public Reporting of Corporate Financial Forecasts*, New York: Commerce Clearing House, pp. 81–91.

Burton, J. (1974b), 'Third Thoughts', *Abacus*, December, pp. 129–37.

Carr, J. (1985), 'Why accounting for lease is inconsistent', *Accountancy*, July, pp. 119–20.

Carty, J.P. (1984), 'Fixed Assets', in D. J. Tonkin and L. C. L. Skerrat (eds), *Financial Reporting 1983–1984*, London: ICAEW, pp. 49–63.

Cartlett, G. R. and Olsen, N. O. (1968), *Accounting for Goodwill, Accounting Research Study No. 10*, New York: AICPA, pp. 17–18.

Chaney, P. K. (1985), 'Defeasance: Financial tool or window dressing?', *Management Accounting*, November, pp. 52–5.

Chatfield, M. (1977), *A History of Accounting Thought*, San Diego, CA: Dryden Press.

Chow, C. W. (1983a), 'The impact of accounting regulation on bond holders' and shareholders' wealth: The case of the Securities Acts'. *The Accounting Review*, July, pp. 485–520.

Chow, C. W. (1983b), 'Empirical studies of the economic effects of accounting regulation: Findings, problems, and prospects', *Journal of Accounting Literature*, Spring, pp. 73–109.

Christenson, C. (1983), 'The methodology of positive accounting', *The Accounting Review*, January, pp. 1–22.

Collins, D. (1975), 'SEC product line reporting and market efficiency', *Journal of Financial Economics*, June, pp. 125–64.

Collins, M., Rozef, M. and Dhaliwal, D. (1980), 'The economic determinants of the market reaction to proposed mandatory accounting changes in the oil and gas industry', *Journal of Accounting and Economics*, **2**, pp. 29–62.

Collins, M., Rozef, M. and Dhaliwal, D. (1981), 'The economies determinations of the market reaction to proposed mandatory accounting changes in the oil and gas industry: A cross sectional analysis', *Journal of Accounting and Economics*, **3**, March, pp. 37–71.

Committee on Land Development Companies (1973), *Accounting for Retail Land Sales*, New York: AICPA, pp. 7–8.

Cook, A. (1989), 'Off-balance sheet finance: Where are we in the debate?', *Course at London Press Centre*, May.

Coopers & Lybrand Deloitte (1989), 'Brand and other intangibles', *Auditing and Accounting Newsletter*, Special edition, January.

Copeland, R. M. and Mckinnon, S. (1987), 'Financial distortion and consolidation of captive finance in general merchandise industry', *Journal of Business Finance and Accounting*, Spring, pp. 77–97.

Couchman, C. B. (1928) 'Limitation of the present balance sheet', *Journal of Accountancy*, October, pp. 253–69.

Councell, G. (1984), 'Woolworths – asset valuation–split depreciation: Not playing the game', *Accountancy*, October, pp. 10–11.

Crawford, V. (1977), 'A game of fair division', *Review of Economic Studies*, June, pp. 235–47.

Crawford, V. (1979), 'A procedure for generating Pareto-efficient egalitarian-equivalent allocations', *Econometrica*, January, pp. 49–60.

Crawford, V. (1980), 'A self-administered solution of the bargaining problem', *Review of Economic Studies*, pp. 385–92.

Davis, J. R. (1989), 'Financial statements: Ambiguity, ethics, and the bottom line', *Business Horizon*, May/June, pp. 65–70.

Demski, J. S. (1973), 'The general impossibility of normative accounting standards', *The Accounting Review*, October, pp. 718–28.

Demski, J. S. (1974), 'Choice among financial reporting alternatives', *Accounting Review*, **49**, April, pp. 221–32.

Derwent, R. A. (1991), 'Discounting', in D. J. Tonkin and L. C. L. Skerrat (eds), *Financial Reporting 1990–1991*, London: ICAEW, pp. 29–54.

Dieter, R. (1979), 'Is lessee accounting working?', *The CPA Journal*, August, pp. 13–19.

Dieter, R. and Watt, A. (1980), 'Get off the balance sheet', *Financial Executive*, January, pp. 42–49.

Dillon, G. J. (1977), 'The role of accounting in the stock market crash of 1929', *PhD Dissertation*, University of Michigan.

Dixon, R. L. (1953), 'Creap', *Journal of Accounting*, July, pp. 48–55.

Dubis, B. and Neimark, D. M. (1982), 'Disclosure regulation and public policy: A sociohistoric reappraisal', *Journal of Accounting and Public Policy*, pp. 33–57.

Dukes, R., Dyckman, T. and Elliot, J. (1980), 'Accounting for research and development costs: The impact on research and development expenditures', *Journal of Accounting Research Supplement*, pp. 1–26.

E40 (1991), *Financial Instruments*, September, IASCO.

Eckel, L. G. (1976), 'Arbitrary and incorrigible allocation', *Accounting Review*, October, pp. 764–77.

ED 27 (1980), *Accounting for Foreign Currency Translations*, ASC.

ED 29 (1981), *Accounting for Lease and Hire Purchase Contracts*, ASC.

ED 37 (1985), *Accounting for Depreciation*, May, ASC.

ED 42 (1988), 'Special purpose transactions', *Certified Accountant*, May, pp. 21–5.

ED 47 (1990), *Accounting for Goodwill*, February, ASC.

ED 48 (1990), *Accounting for Acquisition and Merger*, February, ASC.

ED 49 (1990), *Reflecting the Substance of Transactions in Assets and Liabilities*, May, ASC.

ED 50 (1990), *Consolidated Accounts*, June, ASC.

ED 51 (1990), *Accounting for Fixed Assets and Revaluations*, May, ASC.

ED 52 (1990), *Accounting for Intangible Fixed Assets*, May, ASC.

Edey, H. C. (1963), 'Accounting principles and business reality', *Accountancy*, November, pp. 998–1002, 1083–88.

Edey, H. C. (1984), 'Revalued assets try again, Deleittes?', *Accountancy*, p. 18.

Edwards, J. R. (1976), 'The accounting profession and disclosure in published accounts 1925–1935', *Accounting and Business Research*, **6**, pp. 289–303.

Edwards, J. R. (1989), 'Industrial cost accounting developments in Britain to 1830: A review article', *Accounting and Business Research*, **19**, pp. 305–17.

Egginton, D. (1984), 'Fixed assets: Costs, lives and depreciation', *Accountancy*, November, pp. 138–45.

Egginton, D. (1987), 'The long and short of assets lives', *The Accountant Magazine*, March, pp. 26–7.

Far, A. F. (1933), 'Give the stockholder the truth: How American finance can restore confidence', *Scriber's Magazine*, **93**, 228–34.

FASB, Accounting Research Bulletin No. 51 (1959), *Consolidated Financial Statements*, August, Stanford, CT: FASB.

FASB, Statement No. (3) (1974), *Reporting Accounting Changes in Interim Financial Statements*, December, Stanford, CT: FASB.

FASB, Statement No. (5) (1975b), *Accounting for Contingencies*, March, Stanford, CT: FASB.

FASB, Statement No. (8) (1975c), *Accounting for Translation of Foreign Currency Transaction and Foreign Financial Statements*, October, Stanford, CT: FASB.

FASB, Statement No. (12) (1975d), *Accounting for Certain Marketable Securities*, December, Stanford, CT: FASB.

FASB, Statement No. (13) (1976a), *Accounting for Leases*, November, Stanford, CT: FASB.

FASB, Statement No. 14 (1976b), *Financial Reporting for Segments of A Business Enterprise*, SFAS No. 14, Stanford, CT: FASB.

FASB, Interpretation No. 19, (1976c) *Lessee Guarantee of the Residual Value of Leased Property*, Stanford, CT: FASB.

FASB, Discussion Memorandum (1976d), *Accounting for Business Combinations and Purchase Intangibles*, Stanford, CT: FASB, p. 48.

FASB, Statement No. (19) (1977), *Financial Accounting and Reporting by Oil and Gas Producing Company*, October, Stanford, CT: FASB.

FASB, Statement No. (24) (1978), *Reporting Segmental Information in Financial Statements That Are Presented in Another Enterprise's Finanacial Report*, December, Stanford, CT: FASB.

FASB, Statement No. (29) (1979a), *Determining Contingent Rentals*, June, Stanford, CT: FASB.

FASB, Statement No. (34) (1979b), *Capitalization of Interest Costs*, Stanford, CT: FASB, Paragraph 7.

FASB Statement of Financial Accounting Concepts No. 3 (1980), *Elements of Financial Statements of Business Enterprises*, Stanford, CT: FASB, Paras 43–49.

FASB, Statement No. (47) (1981a), *Disclosure of Long Term Obligations*, March, Stanford, CT: FASB.

FASB, Statement No. (48) (1981b), *Revenue Recognition When Right of Return Exists*, March, Stanford, CT: FASB.

FASB, Statement No. (49) (1981c), *Accounting For Product Financing Arrangements*, June, Stanford, CT: FASB.

FASB, Statement No. (52) (1981d), *Foreign Currency Translation*, December, Stanford, CT: FASB.

FASB, Statement No. (68) (1982a), *Research and Development Arrangement*, October,

Stanford, CT: FASB.

FASB, Statement No. (69) (1982b), *Disclosure About Oil and Gas Producing Activities*, November, Stanford, CT: FASB.

FASB, Statement No. (76) (1983a), *Extinguishment of Debt*, November, Stanford, CT: FASB, p. 5.

FASB, Statement No. (77) (1983b), *Reporting by Transferor of Receivables with Recourse*, December, Stanford, CT: FASB.

FASB, Statement No. (80) (1984a), *Accounting For Future Contracts*, August, Stanford, CT: FASB.

FASB, Technical Bulletin No. 84–4 (1984b), *In-Substance Defeasance of Debt*, October, Stanford, CT: FASB.

FASB, Statement No. (95) (1987), *Statement of Cash Flow*, Stanford, CT: FASB.

FASB, Technical Bulletin No. 85–2 (1985), *Accounting For Collateralized Mortgage Obligations (CMOs)*, March, Stanford, CT: FASB.

Fitzpatrick, L. (1939), 'The story of bookkeeping, accounting and auditing', *Accounting Digest*, **4**, March, p. 217.

Flowers, R. E. (1986), 'Accounting for certain off-balance sheet financing', *The CPA Journal*, February, pp. 36–42.

Flynn, J. T. (1934), *Security Speculation: Its Economic Effects*, New York: Harcourt.

Foster, G. (1980), 'Accounting policy decision and capital market research', *Journal of Accounting and Economics*, **2**, pp. 29–62.

Foster, G. (1986), *Financial Statement Analysis*, 2nd edn, Englewood Cliffs, NJ: Prentice Hall.

FRED 1 (1991), *The Structure of Financial Statements: Reporting of Financial Performance*, December, ASB.

Frederick, C. and Militello, J. R. (1984), 'Swap Financing: A new approach to international transactions', *Financial Executive*, October, pp. 34–39.

Fremgen, J. M. and Liao, S. S. (1981), *The Allocation of Corporate Indirect Costs*, 6th edn, Englewood Cliffs, NJ: Prentice-Hall.

Freyne, A. (1985), 'Swaps: A new instrument for treasurers', *Accountancy*, October, pp. 163–6.

Friedman, D. (1980), 'Many, few, one: Social harmony and the shrunken choice set', *American Economic Review*, March, pp. 225–32.

Friedman, M. (1953), 'The methodology of positive economics' in *Essays in Positive Economics*, Chicago: University of Chicago Press, pp. 3–43.

Gagon, J. M. (1967), 'Purchase versus pooling of interest: The search for predictor', in *Empirical Research in Accounting: Selected Studies 1967*, Supplement to Volume 5 of *Journal of Accounting Research*, pp. 187–204.

Gerboth, D. L. (1972), 'Mudding through with the ABP', *Journal of Accountancy*, May, p. 45.

Gerboth, D. L. (1973), 'Research, intuition and politics in accounting inquiry', *The Accounting Review*, July, pp. 475–82.

Gibbons, C. and Freedman, J. (1991), 'ED 49: The importance of being legal', *Accountancy*, March, p. 29.

Glautier, M. W. E. and Underdown, B. (1976), *Accounting Theory and Practice*, London:

Pitman.

Glosten, L. R. and Milgrom, P. R. (1985), 'Bid, ask, and transaction prices in specialist market with heterogeneously informed traders', *Journal of Financial Economics*, March, pp. 71–100.

Gonedes, N. J. and Dopuch, N. (1974), 'Capital market equilibrium, information production and selective accounting techniques: Theoretical framework and review of empirical work', *Journal of Accounting Research, Supplement*, **12**, pp. 48–169.

Goodfellow, J. M. (1988), 'Now you see them, now you don't', *CA Magazine* (Canadian), December, pp. 16–23.

Grace, E. (1988), 'Clearly spelling out the true and fair view', *Accountancy Age*, 30 June, p. 18.

Gray, R., Owen, D. and Maunders, K. (1987), *Corporate Social Reporting*, Englewood Cliffs, NJ: Prentice Hall.

Gray, S. (1988), 'Accounting for acquisition and mergers: A unified approach', *The Accountant Magazine*, July, pp. 20–23.

Griffiths, I. (1986), *Creative Accounting*, London: Unwin.

Griffiths, I. (1987), 'Merger accounting: Is flexibility distorting the market?', *The Accountant Magazine*, September, pp. 17–20.

Grinyer, J. R. (1987), 'Revaluation of fixed assets in accrual accounting', *Accounting and Business Research*, Winter, pp. 17–24.

Grossman, S. J. (1977), 'The existence of future markets, noisy, rational expectations and information externalities', *Review of Economic Studies*, **44**, pp. 431–49.

Grossman, S. J. and Hart, O. D. (1980) 'Disclosure laws and takeover bids', *Journal of Finance*, May, pp. 323–34.

Harvey, D. (1992), 'First time for cash flow', *Certified Accountant*, January/February, pp. 18–19.

Harvey, M. and Keer, F. (1983), *Financial Accounting Theory and Standards*, Hemel Hempstead: Prentice Hall.

Hayek, F. A. (1952), *The Counter Revolution of Science*, New York: Free Press.

Healy, P. (1985), 'The impact of bonus schemes on the selection of accounting principles', *Journal of Accounting and Economics*, **7**, April, pp. 85–107.

Hendriksen, E. S. (1970), *Accounting Theory*, rev. edn, Homewood, IL: Richard D. Irwin.

Hendriksen, E. S. (1982), *Accounting Theory*, 4th edn, Homewood, IL: Richard D. Irwin.

Hills, J. (1984), 'Deep discounted bonds – or how to get an interest-free loan', *Fiscal Studies*, August, pp. 62–7.

Hodgson, E. (1986), 'Extraordinary items', in L. C. L. Skerrat and D. J. Tonkin (eds), *Financial Reporting 1985–1986*, London: ICAEW, pp. 27–52.

Hodgson, E. (1988), 'Extraordinary items', in L. C. L. Skerrat and D. J. Tonkin (eds), *Financial Reporting 1987–1988*, London: ICAEW, pp. 3–16.

Holgate, P. (1984), 'Much comment, little consensus', *Accountancy Age*, 30 September.

Hopwood, A. and Page, M. (1985), 'Accounting and the economics future', *Accountancy*, pp. 82–3.

Hopwood, A. and Page, M. (1987), 'The future of the accounting standards,

Accountancy, September, pp. 114–16.

Horngren, C. T. (1972), 'Accounting principles: Private or public sector', *Journal of Accountancy*, May, pp. 37–41.

Horngren, C. T. (1973), 'The marketing of the accounting standards', *Journal of Accountancy*, October, pp. 61–6.

Horwitz, B. and Kolodny, R. (1980), 'The economic effects of inventory uniformity in the financial reporting of R & D expenditures', *Journal of Accounting Research Supplement*, pp. 38–74.

Horwitz, B. and Kolodny, R. (1982/1983), 'Who is short sighted', *Journal of Accounting and Business Research*, pp. 79–82.

Howe, R. E. and Roemer, J. E. (1981), 'Rawlsian justice as the core of game', *American Economic Review*, December, pp. 880–95.

Hutson, T. (1988), 'A tool for growing business', *The Accountant*, February, No. 5810, pp. 13–20.

IAS (1) (1975), *Disclosure of Accounting Policy*, January, IASC.

IAS (5) (1976), *Information to be Disclosed in Financial Statements*, October, IASC.

IAS (16) (1982), *Property, Plant and Equipment*, March, IASC, pp. 248–55.

IAS (23) (1983), *Capitalising of Borrowing Costs*, March, IASC.

IASC (1989), 'Framework for the preparation and presentation of financial statements', *Accountancy*, September, pp. 141–8.

Ijiri, Y. (1983), 'On the accountability-based conceptual framework of accounting', *Journal of Accounting and Business Policy*, pp. 75–81.

Ijiri, Y. (1978), 'Cash flow accounting and its structure', *Journal of Accounting, Auditing and Finance*, May, pp. 331–48.

Ijiri, Y. (1980), 'Recovery rate and cash flow accounting', *Financial Executives*, March, pp. 54–60.

Jensen, M. C. (1976), 'Reflection on the state of accounting research and the regulation of accounting', *Stanford Lectures in Accounting 1976*, Stanford School of Business, Stanford University.

Jensen, M. C. and Meckling, W. H. (1976), 'Theory of the firm: Managerial behaviour, agency costs and ownership structure', *Journal of Financial Economics*, October.

Jensen, M. C. and Meckling, W. H. (1978), 'Can the corporation survive?', *Financial Analysts Journal* **34**, January–February, pp. 31–7.

Jensen, M. C. and Smith, C. W. (1985), 'Stockholder, manager, and creditors interests: Applications of agency theory', in E. L. Ealtman and M. G. Subrahamanyam (eds), *Recent Advances in Corporate Finance*, Homewood, IL; Dow-Jones Irwin, pp. 93–131.

Jones, G. (1989), 'Is leasing still valid?', *The Accountant*, March, pp. 12–14.

Kalt, J. P. and Zapan, M. A. (1984), 'Capture and ideology in economic theory of politics', *The American Economic Review*, June, pp. 729–300.

Kanter, R. S. (1984), *The Change Masters*, London: Unwin.

Kieso, D. E. and Weygandt, J. J. (1980), *Intermediate Accounting*, 3rd edn, New York: John Wiley and Sons.

Kieso, D. E. and Weygandt, J. J. (1985), *Intermediate Accounting*, 5th edn, New York: John Wiley and Sons.

Kohler, E. L. (1926), 'Tendencies in balance sheet construction', *The Accounting Review*, pp. 1–11.

Lawson, G. H. (1970), 'Comments' *Accountancy Age*, 24 July, pp. 1–2 and 6 November, pp. 10–11.

Lawson, G. H. (1971), 'Cash flow accounting', *The Accountant*, 28 October, pp. 386–89.

Lawson, G. H. (1976),'Rationale of cash flow accounting', *The Investment Analyst*, December, pp. 5–12.

Lee, T. A. (1972), 'The relevance of accounting information including cash flows', *The Accountant Magazine*, January, pp. 30–4.

Lee, T. A. (1980), 'Reporting cash flows and net realizable values', *Discussion Paper 5*, University of Edinburgh.

Lee, T. A. (1981), 'Cash flow accounting and corporate financial reporting', in M. Bromwich and A. Hopwood (eds), *Essays in British Accounting Research*, London: Pitman, pp. 63–78.

Lee, T. A. (1982), 'Cash flow accounting and the allocation problem', *Journal of Business Finance and Accounting*, Autumn, pp. 341–52.

Lee, T. A. (1992), 'Making cash flow statement useful', *Accountancy,* April, p. 35.

Leftwich, R. (1978), 'Accounting information in private market: Evidence from private lending agreements', *The Accounting Review*, **53**.

Leftwich, R. (1980), 'Market failure fallacies and accounting information', *Journal of Accounting and Economics*, December, pp. 193–211.

Leftwich, R. (1981), 'Evidence of the impact of mandatory changes in accounting principles on corporate loan agreements', *Journal of Accounting and Economics*, March, pp. 3–36.

Leftwich, R. (1983), 'Accounting information in private markets: Evidence from private lending agreements', *The Accounting Review*, **58**, January, pp. 23–42.

Letchet, N. H. and Norton, J. C. (1987), 'The oil and gas industry: Recognition of current market conditions', in D. J. Tonkin and L. C. L. Skerrat (eds), *Financial Reporting 1986–1987*, London: ICAEW, pp. 63–78.

Lev, B. (1988), 'Towards a theory of equitable and efficient accounting policy', *Accounting Review*, January, pp. 1–22.

Lev, B. and Ohlson, J. (1982), 'Market-based empirical research in accounting: A review interpretation and extension', *Journal of Accounting Research Supplement*, pp. 249–322.

Lev, B. and Penman, S. H. (1987), 'Voluntary forecast disclosure, non-disclosure, and stock prices', *Unpublished working paper*, March, University of California-Berkeley.

Litherland, D. A. (1951), 'Fixed assets replacement a half century ago', *Accounting Review*, October, p. 475.

Littleton, A. C. (1933), *Accounting Evolution to 1900*, New York: American Institution Publishing Company, reprinted by Russel and Russel.

Lowe, E. L. Puxty, A. G. and Laughlin, R. C. (1983), 'Simple theory for complex process: Accounting policy and the market in myopia', *Journal of Accounting and Public Policy*, pp. 19–42.

Luke, J. (1988), 'Interest rate swaps', *Public Finance and Accountancy*, 27 May, pp. 163–6.

Macdonald, N. C. L. (1987), 'Depreciation and revaluation of fixed assets', in D. J. Tonkin and L. C. L. Skerrat, (eds), *Financial Reporting 1986–1987*, London: ICAEW, pp. 3–28.

May, G. O. (1936), *Twenty Five Years of Accounting Responsibility, 1931–1936*, New York: American Institute Publishing Company, vol. 2, p. 341.

May, R. J. and Sundem, G. L. (1976), 'Research of accounting policy: An overview', *The Accounting Review*, October, pp. 747–63.

McNicholas, M. and Manegold, J. G. (1983), 'The effect of information environment on the relationship between financial disclosure and security price variability', *Journal of Accounting and Economics*, April, pp. 49–74.

Mead Committee (1978), *Structure and Reform of Direct Taxation*, London: George Allen and Unwin.

Mellows, J. S. and Hudson, K. B. (1988), 'Property companies', in L. C. L. Skerrat and D. J. Tonkin (eds), *Financial Reporting 1987–1988*, London: ICAEW, pp. 95–108.

Meyers, S. L. (1976), 'A proposal for coping with the allocation problem', *Journal of Accountancy*, April, pp. 52–6.

Milne, G. (1989), 'Majec numbers in a melting pot', *Accountancy Age*, 26 January, p. 18.

Mitchell, G. (1988), 'Crossing the standards barrier', *Accountancy Age*, 14 July, p. 14.

Morgan, N. (1989), 'Off-balance sheet finance: where are we in the debate?', Course at London Press Centre, 8 May.

Morse, D. (1981), 'Price and trading volume reaction surrounding earnings announcements: A closer examination', *Journal of Accounting Research*, Autumn, pp. 374–83.

Morse, D. and Ushmar, N. (1983), 'The effect of information announcement on the market microstructure', *The Accounting Review*, April, pp. 247–58.

Morse, D. and Buckman A. (1981), 'Toward a financial accounting: Welfare and public information', *Journal of Accounting Research*, Autumn, pp. 399–433.

Morse, D. and Richardson, G. (1983), 'The LIFO/FIFO decision', *Journal of Accounting Research*, Spring, **21**, pp. 106–27.

Mueller, D. C. (1979), *Public Choice*, Cambridge: Cambridge University Press.

Naser K. and Pendlebury M. (1992a), 'A note on the use of creative accounting', *British Accounting Review*, July, **24**, pp. 111–18.

Naser K. and Pendlebury M. (1992b) 'Creative touch', *Certified Accountant*, November, pp. 36–8.

Nobes, C. W. and Akrikam, P. R. (1977), 'Inflation accounting: Problems of depreciation under CCA system', *Accountancy*, February, pp. 40–5.

Norton, G. P. (1976), '*Textile Manufacturing' Bookkeeping for the Counting House, Mill and Warehouse*, London: Simpkin, 1889, reprinted by New York: Arno Press.

Ohlson, J. (1979), 'On financial disclosure and behaviour security prices', *Journal of Accounting and Economics*, December, pp. 212–32.

Owens, P. (1984), 'Why SSAP 21 isn't the answer', *Accountancy*, January, pp. 49–51.

Paterson, R. (1984), 'Reserve accounting', *The Accountant Magazine*, June, pp. 234–5, 238.

Paterson, R. (1986), 'Foreign currency translation', in L. C. L. Skerrat and D. J. Tonkin (eds), *Financial Reporting 1985–1986*, London: ICAEW, pp. 53–72.

Paterson, R. (1988), 'Fair value accounting following an acquisition', in L. C. L. Skerrat and D. J. Tonkin (eds), *Financial Reporting 1987–1988*, London: ICAEW, pp. 43–65.

Paterson, R. (1990), 'Reserve accounting', in D. J. Tonkin and L. C. L. Skerrat (eds),

Financial Reporting 1989–1990, London: ICAEW, pp. 97–113.

Patient, M. (1984), 'Depreciation on revalued fixed assets', *Accountancy*, June, p. 15.

Paton, W. A. and Littleton, A. C. (1940), 'An introduction to corporate accounting standards', *American Accounting Association Monograph* No.3.

Peasnell, K. V. (1989), 'The challenge of off-balance sheet financing to accountants', *Lecture* The University College of Wales Aberystwyth, 6 November.

Peasnell. K. V. and Yaasnah, R. A. (1988), 'Off-balance sheet financing', *Certified Research Report 10*, The Chartered Association of Certified Accountants.

Peltzman, S. (1976), 'Toward a more general theory of regulation', *Journal of Law and Economics,* August, **19**, pp. 211–40.

Percy, J. P. and Green, P. F. (1982), in D. J. Tonkin and L. C. L. Skerrat (eds), *Survey of Published Accounts 1981–1982*, London: ICAEW.

Philip, T. (1984), 'Capitalization of interest cost', *Accountancy*, June, pp. 128–31.

Philips, S. M. and Zecher, J. R. (1981), 'The SEC and the public interest', Cambridge, MA: MIT Press, pp. 42–50.

Pimm, D. (1991a), 'Disclosing the undisclosed risk', *Accountancy*, April, p. 34.

Pimm, D. A. (1991b), 'Off-balance sheet financing', in D. J. Tonkin and L. C. L. Skerrat (eds), *Financial Reporting 1990–1991*, ICAEW., pp. 135–61.

Pollard, S. (1965), *The Genesis of Modern Management: A study of industrial revolution in Great Britain*, London: Edward Arnold.

Popper, K. R. (1959), *The Logic of Scientific Discovery*, New York: Basic Books.

Popper, K. R. (1972), *Objective Knowledge*, Oxford: Oxford University Press.

Popper, K. R. (1980), *The Logic of Scientific Discovery*. London: Hutchinson.

Rickwood, C. (1983), 'Capitalized interest', *The Accountant*, 29 September, pp. 11–15.

Ripley, W. Z. (1926), 'Ripley gives his remedier for evaluating big business evils', May–October, New York: Clark Boardman.

Roberts, C. (1990), 'Foreign currency disclosure', in L. C. L. Skerrat and D. J. Tonkin (eds), *Financial Reporting 1989–1990*, pp. 133–58.

Ronen, J. (1979), 'The dual role of accounting: A financial economic perspective', in J. L. Bicksler (ed.), *Handbook of Financial Economics*, Amsterdam: North Holland.

Ronen, J. and Schiff, M. (1978), 'The setting of accounting standards: Private or public?', *Journal of Accountancy*, March, pp. 66–71.

Ross, S. (1979), 'Disclosure regulation in financial markets: Implications of modern finance theory and signaling theory', in F. R. Edwards (ed.), *Issues in Financial Regulation*, New York: McGraw-Hill, pp. 177–202.

Rutherford, B. A. (1982), 'The interpretation of cash flow reporting and other allocation problem', *ABACUS*, June, pp. 40–9.

Rutteman, P. J. and Daley, M. C. (1985), 'Leasing and hire purchase', in D. J. Tonkin and L. C. L. Skerrat (eds), *Financial Reporting 1984–1985*, London: ICAEW, pp. 180–200.

S20 (1974), *Valuations of Property Company Assets and Their Disclosure in Directors' Reports or Accounts of Companies*. February, London: ICAEW.

Samuels, J. (1981), 'Commentatory on papers by Professor Lawson and Lee', in M. Bromwich and A. Hopwood (eds), *Essays in British Accounting Research*, London: Pitman, pp. 101–3.

Samuels, J., Rickwood, C. and Piper, A. (1989), *Advanced Financial Accounting*, 2nd edn, London: McGraw-Hill.

Schaefer, S. M. (1985), 'Less is more: The attraction of zero coupon bond financing', *The Treasures*, October, pp. 21–6.

Schwert, G. W. (1977), 'Public regulation of national securities exchanges: A test of the capture hypothesis', *The Bell Journal of Economics*, Spring, pp. 128–50.

Scott, R. A. and Scott, R. K. (1979), 'Instalment accounting: Is it inconsistent?', *Journal of Accountancy*, November, pp. 52–8.

Sen, A. K. (1970), *Collective Choice and Social Welfare*, San Francisco, CA: Holden-Day.

Shark, J. K. and Shamis, G. S. (1979), 'Reporting foreign currency adjustments: A disclosure perspective', *The Journal of Accountancy*, April, pp. 59–65.

Skinner, R. C. (1987), 'Allocation and the validity of the incremental principle', *Accounting and Business Research*, **18** no. 69, Winter, pp. 75–8.

Smith, T. (1992), *Accounting for Growth*, London: Century Business.

Solomons, D. (1978), 'The politicizition of accounting', *Journal of Accountancy*, November, pp. 65–72.

Sprouse, R. T. (1983), 'Standard setting: The American experience', in M. Bromwich and A. G. Hopwood (eds), *Accounting Standards Setting: An international perspective*, London: Pitman.

SSAP 1 (1971, Revised), *Accounting for Associated Companies*, ASC.

SSAP 2 (1971), *Disclosure of Accounting Policies*, November, ASC.

SSAP 4 (1974), *Accounting For Government Grant*, ASC, issued April 1974; revised July 1990.

SSAP 6 (1974), *Extraordinary Items and Prior Years Adjustment*, ASC, issued April 1974; revised August 1986.

SSAP 9 (1975), *Stock and Work in Progress*, ASC, issued May 1975; Part 6 added August 1980; revised September 1988.

SSAP 12 (1977), *Accounting for Depreciation*, ASC issued December 1977; amended November 1981; revised January 1987.

SSAP 13 (1977), *Accounting for Research and Development*, December, ASC.

SSAP 14 (1978), *Group Accounts*, September, ASC.

SSAP 17 (1980), *Accounting for Post Balance Sheet Events*, August, ASC.

SSAP 19 (1981), *Accounting for Investment Properties*, November, ASC.

SSAP 20 (1983), *Foreign Currency Translation*, April, ASC.

SSAP 21 (1984), *Accounting for Lease and Hire Purchase Contracts*, August, ASC.

SSAP 22 (1984), *Accounting for Goodwill*, ASC, issued December 1984; revised July 1989.

SSAP 23 (1985), *Accounting for Acquisition and Merger*, April, ASC.

Staubus, G. J. (1961), *A Theory of Accounting for Investors*, University of California Press, pp. 397–412.

Sterling, R. R. (1979), *Towards A Science of Accounting*, Houston, TX: Scholars Book Co.

Stevens, R. and Waterhouse, P. (1986), 'Accounting for lease', *Certified Accountant (UK)*, December, pp. 14–18.

Stewart, J. E. and Neuhausen, B. S. (1986), 'Financial instruments and transactions: The

CPA's new challenge', *Journal of Accountancy*, August, pp. 102–12.

Svensson, L. (1980), 'Some views on a fair wage structure', *Ekonomiska Samfunddets Tidskrift*, **33**, pp. 155–66.

Swanney, W. D. R. (1983), 'Property companies', in L. C. L. Skerrat and D .J. Tonkin (eds), *Financial Reporting 1982–1983*, London: ICAEW, pp. 248–52.

Sykes, A. (1976), 'The lease-buy decision: A survey of current practice in 202 companies', *Management Survey Report No. 29*, British Institute of Management.

Taylor, P. and Turley, S. (1985a), 'The prospects for SSAP 21: What preparers think', *The Accountant Magazine*, April, pp. 183–5.

Taylor, P. and Turley, S. (1985b), 'The view of management in accounting for leases', *Accounting and Business Research*, Winter, pp. 47–51.

Taylor, P. and Turley, S. (1986), *Modern Development in Accounting and Finance: The regulation of accounting*, Oxford: Basil Blackwell.

Thomas, A. L. (1975), 'Accounting and the allocation fallacy', *Financial Analysts Journal*, September, pp. 37–41, 68.

Thomas, A. L. (1975), 'The FASB and the allocation fallacy', *The Journal of Accounting*, November, pp. 65–8.

Thomas, A. L. (1969), 'The allocation problem in financial accounting theory', *Studies in Accounting Research No. 3*, Sarasota, FL: American Accounting Association.

Thomas, A. L. (1974), 'The allocation problem: Part two', *Studies in Accounting Research No. 9*, Sarasota, FL: American Accounting Association.

Thomas, A. L. (1980), *A Behaviour Analysis of Joint Cost Allocation and Transfer Pricing*, Champaign, IL: Stipes.

Tinker, A. M., Merino, B. D. and Neimark, M. D. (1982), 'The normative origins of positive accounting theories: Ideology and accounting thought', *Accounting, Organisation and Society* **7**, No. 2, pp. 167–200.

Tonkin, D. J. (1987), 'Examples from the survey tables', in D. J. Tonkin and L. C. L. Skerrat (eds), *Financial Reporting 1986–1987*, London: ICAEW, pp. 119–48.

Tonkin, D. J. (1991), 'Survey tables and examples', in L. C. L. Skerrat and D. J. Tonkin (eds), *Financial Reporting 1990–1991*, London: ICAEW, pp. 165–268.

Tonkin, D. J. and Robertson, W. R. (1991). 'Brands and other intangible fixed assets', in D. J. Tonkin and L. C. L. Skerrat (eds), *Financial Reporting 1990–1991*, London: ICAEW, pp. 3–28.

Tonkin, D. J. and Watson, L. I. (1986) 'Survey table', in L. C. L. Skerrat, and D. J. Tonkin (eds), *Financial Reporting 1985–1986*, London: ICAEW, pp. 143–59.

Tonkin, D. J. and Watson, L. I. (1987), 'Survey tables', in D. J. Tonkin and L. C. L. Skerrat (eds), *Financial Reporting 1986–1987*, London: ICAEW, pp. 153–70.

Tonkin, D. J. and Watson, L. I. (1988), 'Survey tables and examples', in L. C. L. Skerrat and D. J. Tonkin (eds), *Financial Reporting 1987–1988*, London: ICAEW, pp. 163–218.

Tonkin, D. J. and Watson, L. I. (1990), 'Survey tables and examples', in L. C. L. Skerrat and D. J. Tonkin (eds), *Financial Reporting 1989–1990*, London: ICAEW, pp. 193–241.

TR 603 (1986), *Off-Balance Sheet Financing and Window Dressing*, London: ICAEW.

TR 677 (1987), *Accounting For Complex Capital Issues*, London: ICAEW.

Tweedie, D. and Kellas, J. (1987), 'Off-balance sheet financing', *Accountancy*, April, pp. 91–5.

Venkatesh, P. and Chiang (1986), 'Information asymmetry and the dealer's bid-ask spread: A case study of earnings and dividend announcements', *Journal of Finance*, December, pp. 1089–102.

Walter, W. H. (1986), 'Factoring', *The CPA Journal*, June, pp. 66–72.

Walton, P. and Wyman, H. (1988), 'The concept of regulation', *Accountancy*, August, p. 70.

Watts, R. (1973), 'The information content of dividends', *Journal of Business*, pp. 191–211.

Watts, R. (1977), 'Corporate financial statements: A product of the market and political process', *Australian Journal of Management*, April, pp. 53–75.

Watts, R. (1980), 'Can optimal accounting information be determined by regulation?', in J. W. Buckley and J. F. Weston (eds), *Regulation and the Accounting Profession*, (Belmont, CA: Wadsworth), pp. 153–62.

Watts, R. (1981), 'Planning the next decade', in Sir R. Leach and E. Stamp (eds), *British Accounting Standards: The first 10 years*, Cambridge: Woodhead Faulkner.

Watts, R. and Zimmerman, J. (1978), 'Towards a positive theory of the determination of accounting standards', *The Accounting Review*, January, pp. 112–34.

Watts, R. and Zimmerman, J. (1979), 'The demand for and supply of accounting theories: The market for excuses', *The Accounting Review*, pp. 273–305.

Watts, R. and Zimmerman, J. (1986), *Positive Accounting Theory*, Englewood Cliffs, NJ: Prentice-Hall.

Weetman, P. (1988a), 'Off-balance sheet finance: The quest for an accounting solution', *The Investment Analyst*, July, pp. 4–10.

Weman, P. (1988b), 'Off-balance sheet finance: The ASC' answer', *The Accountant Magazine*, May, pp. 24–5.

Westwick, C. (1986), 'Problems in merger and acquisition accounting', *Accountancy*, April, pp. 164–8.

Whiteley, C. (1990), 'Off balance sheet finance: Practical guide', *Accountancy*, July, p. 28.

Whittington, G. (1987), 'Positive accounting: A review article', *Accounting and Business Research*, **12**, No. 68, Autumn, pp. 327–76.

Wild, K. (1987a) 'Off-balance sheet finance: Why all the fuss', *Accountancy*, June, pp. 20–1.

Wild, K. (1987b), 'Merger accounting and goodwill', in D. J. Tonkin and L. C. L. Skerrat (eds), *Financial Reporting 1986–1987*, London: ICAEW, pp. 29–48.

Wilkins, R. M. (1987), 'Takeovers', in L. C. L. Skerrat and D. J. Tonkin (eds), *Financial Reporting 1986–1987*, London: ICAEW, pp. 117–41

Wilson, R. (1975), 'Informational economies of scale', *Bell Journal of Economics*, Spring, pp. 184–95.

Winjum, J. O. (1972), *The Role of Accounting in Economics Development of England 1500–1750*, Urbana, IL: Centre of International Education and Research.

Wishon, K. and Chevalier, L. S. (1985), 'Interest rate swaps: Your rate or mine', *Journal of Accountancy*, September, pp. 63–84.

Worth, B. L. and Derwent, R. (1990), 'Complex capital issues', in D. J. Tonkin and L. C. L. Skerrat (eds), *Financial Reporting 1989–1990*, pp. 69–84.

Zimijewski, M. and Hagerman, R. (1981), 'An income strategy approach to the positive theory of accounting standard setting/choice', *Journal of Accounting and Economics*, **3**, August, pp. 129–49.

Zimmerman, J. L. (1979), 'The cost and benefits of allocation', *Accounting Review*, July, pp. 504–21.

Zimmerman, J. L. (1980), 'Positive research in accounting', in R. D. Nair and T. H. Williams (eds), *Perspectives on Research*, (Graduate School of Business, University of Wisconsin, pp. 107–28.

Zimmerman, J. L. (1983), 'Taxes and firm size', *Journal of Accounting and Economics*, **5**, August, pp. 119–49.

Appendix

A list of the surveyed British, German, Dutch and French Companies.

BRITISH COMPANIES

1. Hillsdown Holdings Plc.		1989
2. TECO Plc.		1989
3. Grand Metropolitan		1989
4. British Gas		1989
5. The Electricity Council		1988/1989
6. Ford Motor Company Ltd.		1989
7. ASDA		1989
8. Great Universal Stores Plc.		1989
9. B.A.T. Industries		1989
10. British Aerospace		1989
11. BICC Group		1989
12. BP		1989
13. Berisford International Plc.		1989
14. Bass Plc.		1989
15. Shell UK Ltd.		1989
16. Unilever		1989
17. BTR		1989
18. Gallaber Ltd.		1989
19. Ladbroke Group Plc.		1989
20. Tarmac		1989
21. British Railways Board		1988/1989
22. Boots Company Plc.		1989
23. Guiness Plc.		1989
24. Dalgety Plc.		1989
25. Thorn EMI		1990

GERMAN COMPANIES

1. Bertelsmann	1988/1989
2. BMW	1989
3. Mannesmann	1989
4. Robert Bosch GMBH	1989
5. Asko Deutsche Kaufhaus Aktiengesellschaft	1989
6. Daimler-Benz	1989
7. Bayer	1989
8. Henkel	1989
9. Lufthansa	1989
10. Quelle	1989
11. Deutsche Bundespost	1989
12. Deutsche BP Aktiengesellschaft	1989
13. Degussa	1989
14. Continental Aktiengesellschaft	1989
15. Fried. Krupp GMBH	1989
16. Hoechst	1989
17. Hoechst AG	1989
18. Klockner & CO Aktiengesellschaft	1989
19. Klockner- Werke Aktiengesellschaft and affiliated companies	1989
20. Otto Versand Hamburg	1989
21. MAN Aktiengesellschaft- Munich	1989
22. OPEL	1989
23. Salzgitter AG	1989
24. BASF	1989
25. VEBA	1989

DUTCH COMPANIES

1. Gist-Brocades	1990
2. Wolters Kluwer	1989
3. Vendex International N.V.	1990/1991
4. Wesanen	1989
5. Friesland Dairy Food Products	1990
6. DAF	1989
7. Coberco	1990
8. Nedlloyd	1990
9. Hagemeyer	1990

10. Koninklijke Ahold nv	1990
11. Saralee/ D.E	1990/1991
12. Buhrmann–Tetterode nv (BT)	1991
13. Internatio–Muller nv	1989
14. Elsevier	1989
15. Royal Dutch Papermills	1989
16. Otra	1989
17. Oce–van der Grinten N.V.	1989
18. Hollandsche Beton Groep N.V.	1989
19. Philips	1989
20. VRG–Groep N.V.	1989
21. Verenigd Bezit VNU	1989
22. Stork	1989
23. Gasunie	1989
24. Koninklijke Borsumij Wehry N.V.	1989
25. Van Leer	1989

FRENCH COMPANIES

1. Groupe Schneider	1989
2. Valeo	1990
3. French Railways (SNCF)	1990
4. Europe Casino	1990
5. LVMH Moet Hennessy. Louis Vuitton	1989
6. Loreal	1990
7. Rhone–Poulenc	1989
8. Societe Auxillaire D'enterprises (SAE)	1989
9. Electricite de France (EDF)	1990
10. HAVES	1990
11. Aerospatiale	1990
12. French BP	1990
13. Imetal	1989

14. Matra 1989
15. Hachette 1989
16. Compagine Generale D'electricite 1989
17. Promodes 1989
18. Michelin 1990
19. Saint-Gobain 1989
20. Dumez 1989
21. Compagine Generale Des Eaux 1989
22. elf aquitaine 1989
23. Chargeurs 1989
24. Carrefour 1989
25. Compagnie Francaise de l'Afrique
    Occidentale (CFAO) 1989

Author index

Subject index